Iron: Workers 1989   16 1:00

SINGLES MINISTRY HANDBOOK

SINGLES MINISTRY HANDBOOK

Douglas L. Fagerstrom,
Editor

VICTOR BOOKS®

A DIVISION OF SCRIPTURE PRESS PUBLICATIONS INC.
USA CANADA ENGLAND

TABLE OF CONTENTS

FOREWORD

This book is not the last word on how to minister to single adults. Nor is it the first. However, it is the most comprehensive resource for single adult ministry. It reveals the experiences in the trenches of dedicated leaders in churches large and small across America who have given many hours a week loving and caring for single adults.

It is also the long-standing dream of some of us who have been around long enough to have asked the question: "What's a single adult, and what's a single adult ministry?"

This book attempts to address some of the many "who, why, how, and what" questions being asked regarding single adult ministries.

Its authors are and have been on the front line of this emerging ministry that began in the early '70s. They are pioneers in the true sense of the word, and they are still learning. They care deeply about the ministry and those who share it with them.

This is not an answer book. It is merely a guide book. Use it with wisdom and prayer! It should motivate you and expand your vision. It will provide the first step in many areas of single adult ministry.

We dedicate it to the millions of single adults in our society without whom this ministry would not exist.

Jim Smoke
Tempe, Arizona
1988

PREFACE

In our mind's eye we can see the Lord Jesus walking past the gate of the sheepfold in pursuit of the one lost sheep. That one is alone and afraid. That one is in danger and pain. That one is lost. The shepherd's role is to find the sheep, nurture the sheep, bind up its wounds, and bring it back inside the gate to protect and help it to grow.

The shepherd does not leave the sheep alone. The shepherd does not leave the sheep in want. The shepherd does not condemn the sheep as wayward, but "restores his soul" and places him back with the rest of the sheep.

Single adults are without question the fastest growing subculture of our world. Second to that is the senior adult phenomenon, and many seniors are also single.

The church of Jesus Christ has not kept up with the singles boom. The percentage of singles in the church is not close to the percentage in society. The church must catch up if we are to reach this large and wonderful mission field that God has placed before us.

We must learn about and love single adults.

We must discover and understand their needs.

We must remove the myths and overcome our fears.

We must reach out with hearts of compassion and acts of mercy.

We must share the Gospel of Jesus Christ with a generation that is in pursuit of love, peace, and intimacy.

It is from the church (God's people) that single adults can discover from God's Word who they are, what their gifts are, receive love and encouragement, and find help in their time of need. It is here that ministry begins and lives are changed.

A Ministry to Adults

Singles are adults. One half of America's adults are single. Yet, we tend to treat the single adult as a single adolescent. Interchangeably this book uses the term "adult single" and "single adult." The key word in under-standing needs and ministry of the "single adult" is the word "adult." Singles see themselves as adult first and single second. Even single adult parents see being a parent and living as an adult ahead of their singleness. Ministries will do well to do the same. Singles want to be accepted as what they are, adult men and women with adult problems and adult situations. They learn as adults learn. They cry and laugh like adults. They lead like adults. They are adults.

New Beginning

This book is a starter manual for single adult ministry. For the ministry just beginning, it is a comprehensive resource for discovering who singles are, what needs they have, and how to start a ministry with singles. For the established ministry, it provides the foundation and outline for begin-ning new programs and gaining a fuller understanding of what must be done in ministry.

A Comprehensive Guide

It would be impossible to provide the last or inclusive word on the multi-plicity of singles ministry needs in one volume. Many books have been written on each subject, that is here covered in one or two brief chapters (see the Bibliography). However, the purpose here is to provide an over-view of each of the needs, major concerns, and areas of singles ministry that are most significant. This book will be a guide and road map to establish direction, clarity, purpose, and design in singles ministry.

Deep Conviction

Each of the authors in this book has a deep love and compassion for single adults. They have served well in the trenches. They have agonized, wept, shared, and grown with singles from coast to coast. They speak to us from their hearts, experience, and biblical conviction of God's call to ministry with adult singles. You will learn from them. Listen closely to the voice of God's shepherds who know well the Good Shepherd.

Dedication

This book is dedicated to Jesus Christ, the Good Shepherd, who binds up the wounds of every single adult and brings the lost into His forever family. And with deepest gratitude this book is given with love for my wife Donna and daughter Darci who have loved singles with me for the last eight years of ministry. And humble appreciation and God's richest bless-ing is extended to the authors of this book, my dear friends in life and ministry, who I know dedicate this book to singles leaders and all singles everywhere.

Doug Fagerstrom

NEED FOR A SINGLES MINISTRY

▪ ▪ ▪ ▪ ▪ ▪ ▪ ▪ ▪ ▪ ▪ ▪ ▪ ▪ ▪

1. WHY HAVE A SINGLES MINISTRY?

"The church of Jesus Christ has answers singles are searching for. Help is available if they are made to feel welcome into the fellowship of believers, and taught the Word of God and the love of Jesus Christ."

Greg Pearson

The culture we live in today is vastly different from the culture 20 years ago. In order to maintain our effectiveness, we, the body of Christ, need to continually reassess our focus and make appropriate changes. We first need to identify the areas of greatest need in the communities we serve. We then must take inventory of the resources available to us to meet the needs we have identified. Finally, we must set goals and develop programs to minister to the people we have identified as having the needs we can meet.

One of the areas where our culture has changed is our move away from the nuclear family. Where once each person's primary social group was his family, now we find our society much more fragmented, breaking down into groups and subgroups with special interests and special needs. People are now finding their identities through their involvement with these specialized groups, subscribing to the actions and moral values of the groups. The effect of all this has been for people to move away from the family, family values, and away from the people and places where our inherent needs for intimacy and a spiritual connection can be met.

The evidence for this is easy to identify particularly in our growing single community. According to The American Statistics Index (1986) over one third of the population in the United States over the age of 18 is single. That percentage is growing year after year. Singles are searching for identity, intimacy, and meaning in their lives. These are needs that can be met by sharing the love of God, the meaning of life through His Son, and fellowship with others in the body of Christ.

Singles Have Many Needs
Singles in general have many things in common. Loneliness is one. The need to connect with another human being on a casual level and on an intimate level are basic needs all humans have. As children grow through childhood and then adolescence, a major growth task is to develop the

socializing skills necessary to connect with others in these ways. Many singles struggle in these areas. Some, because they didn't (for whatever reasons) develop the appropriate skills as they grew up, and others, because of painful relationships in the past, are unsure of the skills they have.

Another need that is common to all humans is the need for a relationship with God. Singles spend a great deal of time attempting to satisfy this need, which is often misidentified. This is the need that is experienced as a "void" or "something missing" in a person's life. This is that intangible something that gives satisfaction with life and real meaning to the human existence.

Depression is also common among singles as are other psychological difficulties. After struggling to have intimacy or spiritual needs met and not being successful, psychological problems can be the result. Singles often turn to alcohol or other mood-altering drugs to avoid the pain of unfulfilled needs for intimacy and a spiritual connection. Alcohol and drugs can ease the pain but certainly lead to problems that are devastating to the lives of those who become involved and devastating for those who care about the person using them.

Singles who have never been married have many unique needs. They certainly struggle with the needs mentioned, but are also often under pressure from family members and from society as a whole to find a mate. These outside pressures can lead to questions about sexual identity and other psychological difficulties. Another need for these individuals is for recognition as complete human beings. In our culture there seems to be some unspoken rule that unless a person is or has been married, they are not capable of participating in the mainstream of social interaction.

Those in the singles community who have suffered the pain of divorce have other specific needs. Often after a divorce, all areas of an individual's life are in shambles. God seems to be far away, the feeling of rejection can be emotionally devastating, financial responsibilities are overwhelming, children can become a burden, and there are often other intense emotions to deal with, such as guilt, shame, anger, or even rage. The future can often look bleak to a single who has been through a divorce.

For those who have lost a spouse due to death the needs also are great. The sense of loss and emptiness can and often does lead to depression. These individuals compound the problem by isolating themselves from even those who care about them. With these people too, there can be financial problems or children to deal with, and they can feel abandoned by God. Certainly this group needs support and guidance through the grief process.

The Church Can Be the Place for Meeting Singles' Needs

Singles in all of these situations can most assuredly be considered a field ripe for harvest (see John 4:35-36). The singles population, possibly more than any other, is searching for answers to their questions and something to fulfill their lives. The church of Jesus Christ has answers singles are searching for. Help is available if they are made to feel welcome into the fellowship of believers, and taught the Word of God and the love of Jesus Christ. Through the Word of God, we can offer hope where hopelessness has been, the hope for eternal life, and hope for an abundant life filled with joy as a member of His kingdom.

When singles are welcomed and encouraged to become involved in fellowship with others, it offers them an opportunity to interact with others in a nonjudgmental and accepting environment. This type of environment meets many of the needs singles have and offers them an opportunity for growth that is unavailable anywhere else.

The alternatives available for singles are very limited and, in most cases, reinforce or compound the problems rather than help solve them. For example, there are the bars and singles clubs where materialistic and immoral values are encouraged. There are also health clubs, spas, sports clubs, and special interest social organizations, none of which have the ability to provide the kind of nurturing needed to help people reach their potential, much less God's design.

The resources needed to establish a ministry for singles are minimal. A place is needed where singles can feel welcomed and gather freely. Also needed is an atmosphere of acceptance and genuine caring. It is important to accept singles where they are, not to judge them, but to love them and allow them to express themselves in whatever way they are able. In this setting singles can grow and become what Christ wants them to be.

There are several specific needs that can be addressed that will bring about positive change in the lives of single adults. These are the growth factors that can be incorporated into the programs we design to meet the needs we identify. Some of these factors are as follows.

The need for hope. Many singles, after struggling with life's problems, come to a point where a happy and meaningful life seems unattainable. Often due to the experiences of life, individuals become unable to see their situations and possible solutions clearly. They become hopeless, for all practical purposes, unable to help themselves and unable to ask for help. Hope comes by hearing the Good News of eternal life and the joy of an abundant life through Jesus Christ.

The need for understanding. A very basic need for all humans is the need to be understood. Understanding is one of the first steps in making a connection with another individual. When one person listens to another to the degree that he or she hears and understands what is said, the implied message is that this person cares enough about the other to take the time to listen.

To feel understood is to feel valued and can be the first step in rebuilding a shattered self-esteem. The painful experiences of life often reduce one's feelings of self-worth to a very low point. Low self-worth leads to feeling unlovable or unlikable. When this occurs the act of someone reaching out and caring enough to listen can begin reversing this process.

The need for commonality. Singles who are in or have gone through painful situations tend to blame themselves for whatever situation they are in. This blaming can lead to feelings of guilt, shame, isolation, and the sense that no one else has ever been where they are or done the terrible things they have done to get there. In an honest and loving fellowship of caring people, it takes little time to understand, through the sharing of others, that no individual is alone in his or her condition. Others have had or are involved in similar circumstances.

The need for information. There is a need for information about coping with life's difficulties. There are many pertinent issues facing singles, especially the need for understanding about values and principles to live by. Some of the struggles are around spirituality, social skills, dating, sexuality, financial principles, and many other subjects pertaining to everyday life.

The need for personal feedback. Individuals without the benefit of significant caring others in their lives can go through life not knowing or being able to identify their own behaviors that keep them from socializing in an appropriate way. In a loving and caring environment, feedback can be given and received that will help these individuals know themselves and make changes that will facilitate more appropriate and more fulfilling interaction with others.

The need for role models. Many have never seen what it's like to live a healthy, well-balanced life, where Christ's love flows and where joy is present. It is often this kind of role modeling that gives an individual the permission and motivation to pursue the same kind of life.

The need for interpersonal learning. Singles in many situations choose to isolate themselves from others. This can be the result of many attempts at socializing and being unsuccessful. A place to learn about social and interpersonal skills and an environment where these skills can be practiced can turn these individuals toward more satisfying lives.

The need for belonging. Everyone needs to feel a sense of belonging to a primary social group. An individual's identity is often shaped by the primary social group he belongs to. The values and actions of the group as a whole become the identity and actions of the individual. Belonging to a fellowship of Christian singles can be a way of comfortably taking on solid spiritual values and being open to God's will.

These are a few, but certainly not all, of the factors a church that chooses to open its doors to minister to singles can provide. The payback can far outweigh the investment. The result for choosing to minister to singles can be felt in many areas of the church's fellowship. As single adults learn and grow, they become concerned with the functioning of the mainstream of the church, becoming responsible leaders committed to serving God and the needs of the church.

A singles ministry can be a very effective method of reaching out into the community and providing community service. Church growth can be

16

facilitated by a singles ministry. All areas of the church can benefit from reaching out and touching the lives of singles in the communities we serve.

Greg Pearson
Chemical Dependency Counselor at St. Mary's Hospital
Minneapolis, Minnesota

Greg wrote this chapter when he was actively involved as a single adult in the singles ministry at Wooddale Church, Eden Prairie, Minnesota. Greg experienced God's personal inner healing from the pain of divorce and substance abuse.

2. THE CHURCH'S HISTORY OF MARRIAGE, DIVORCE, REMARRIAGE, AND SINGLENESS

"In the 1500s, one third of the marriages lasted less than 15 years. At the close of the Reformation, 10 percent of the European population was unmarried."

Harold Ivan Smith

Singleness as a conspicuous subculture required a long pilgrimage through history and tradition, a journey that is still "in progress." Only through an examination of that process can we understand how single adults have grown to 36 percent of the population in contemporary American society.

In the Early Church
The attitudes of the early church were shaped by its conviction that the second coming of Jesus was imminent. Paul said, "Because of the present crisis" (1 Cor. 7:26), everyone should remain in the state in which he [she] is called, whether married or single. However, Paul left no doubt that he preferred singleness.

But when Paul died and when those who had been taught by Paul and the other apostles died, the church began interpreting what they had taught. Some of the early church fathers allowed *syneiasaktism* or spiritual marriages between men and unmarried or widowed women. They shared homes, even their beds, in chastity.

As early as A.D. 100, divorce had sparked debate among the church fathers, perhaps in response to the licentious culture the church battled. In A.D. 140, Hermas concluded that apostasy, covetousness, adultery, and idolatry constituted valid grounds for divorce; Jerome agreed. However, Origen and later Chrysostom argued for adultery as the only grounds. The Romans historically permitted divorce and remarriage as long as there was mutual agreement.

By A.D. 311, in response to the number of superfluous divorces, Emperor Constantine decreed more limited grounds that were stricter on women than on men.

After the Council of Neocaesarea in A.D. 314, the church chose to show its opposition to remarriage by forbidding priests to attend (and thereby bless) second ceremonies. The remarried could only receive Communion after they had done "appropriate" penance. The church argued that remarriage clouded the children's economic inheritance and also kept properties from passing into the hands of the church for its disposal.

Tertullian raised the argument that if nuptial ties existed beyond divorce—as many leaders insisted to support their doctrine of indissolubility—surely the ties survived the death of a mate as well.

In A.D. 306, the Council of Elvira ruled that a woman who divorced her mate—even on the grounds of adultery—was to be excommunicated and could not receive Communion until her husband died. If she had no "valid" grounds, as defined by the church, she was forever denied Communion.

In 314, the Council of Arles advised husbands of adulterous wives not to remarry but stopped short of forbidding remarriage.

However, because of the extensive missionary evangelism, the Goths, Franks, Saxons—all of whom had long traditions permitting divorce and remarriage—came into the church. The church leaders were reluctant to alienate the delicate faith and political allegiances. So the Council of Arles implied that a bishop could grant permission to remarry. Eventually, the wealthy and powerful found annulment a way to avoid the stigma of remarriage and to eliminate barriers to remarriage.

As early as Pope Siricus, in 385, attempts had been made to require the celibacy of priests. Again, the motives were questionable: the church could confiscate the property of new priests and inherit that of dying priests.

Monasticism offered an alternative. Anthony gave up his worldly goods and took up the ascetic life in 270. Some people left weeping families to follow him and others into the solitude of the desert. Pachomius founded the first Christian monastery in 315. Some monks so despised women that they fled from them as swiftly as they would from the devil.

From Charlemagne to Pre-Reformation

By 1142, Gratian's *Decretum* had codified all previous interpretations of divorce so as to undergird the church's stance on indissolubility. Once intercourse had occurred, nothing could sever the bonds. The *Decretum* eliminated divorce on all grounds, but it opened the door to increased use of annulments which enriched the coffers of the Medieval church. Nothing produced more revenue or caused more scandal. If one could convince the church there had been lawful impediments, a *divortium vinculo matriomonii* could be obtained *for a fee*.

By the Medieval period, the monasteries had been reformed and more men chose to abandon the cares of this life. Therefore, there was a significant increase in the number of single women.

In 1191, Pope Clement III established a new tradition by not requiring repentant divorcées to return to their first mates. Instead, the pope ordered them to initiate sexual relations with the second mate "contritely and with sadness and reluctance."

Divorces became battles between the papacy and leaders. Innocent III battled with Philip Augustus over a petition for a divorce.

Other popes were known to grant dispensations in exchange for "economic considerations." Thus, canon law was not always followed or uniformly interpreted.

Single women during the Medieval period were recognized under law with rights to sue or to be sued. They could own lands and make wills. However, they had little power to defend their land. One woman pleaded, "Give me a strong man to be my husband, for I am sore pressed to defend my land."

But few women who owned land remained single. Heavy fines were imposed on serfs who did not marry since they challenged the system. By law, the children of a serf were the lord's and he always needed more workers to farm the land and to defend it.

Fathers who had too many daughters, faced with having to supply dowries competitive with other fathers, often had to place one or more daughters in a convent to reduce their financial load and to increase opportunities for other daughters.

Few men in western Europe married before their mid-20s, the average age being between 25 and 35. Since the law of primogeniture awarded everything to the oldest son, many younger sons were forced to either work for their older brothers, remain unmarried, or become clerics.

The intricate maze of ecclesiastical interference in marriage and family life, the mockery of a no-divorce stance which fostered incredible adultery and lewdness, and the sexual excesses of single priests and their concubines and offspring did not go unchallenged.

A young monk named Martin Luther prepared to speak out.

The Reformation

Because of the involvement with politically/economically advantageous marriages, the church had created an incredible maze of regulations on marriage, divorce, and singleness. Canon lawyers schemed to find loopholes for individuals willing to pay for such dispensations.

The family had three functions: to pass on life, to pass on name, and to pass on property. Parents chose spouses with an eye on marriages that could strengthen their own influence in European circles. Since so much emphasis was placed on the oldest son, many younger sons could not live in adulthood as they had been accustomed. Some married later or more humbly.

Convents filled with wealthy widows offered refuge and safety for mothers, sisters, and daughters. Convents were often used for confinement until a woman would agree to a divorce. Remarriage was a political or economic necessity for many.

Single women were still at the mercy of their parents in arranging marriages. However, rampant adultery offered romantic "love" to those forced into marriage. Fathers desirous of protecting virginity betrothed their daughters as early as three; some daughters were nominated in wills to marry a particular man. Yet, one third of the marriages lasted less than 15 years. Constant warfare, disease, and childbirth caused premature death and subsequent remarriage.

On October 31, 1517 a single adult, Martin Luther, tacked 95 theses to a church door and launched a social and religious revolution. Luther believed that the church's burdensome regulations mandated singleness for too many and thus fostered widespread immorality.

Luther attacked enforced celibacy. "It is certainly a fact," he declared, "that he who refuses to marry must fall into immorality." Those who had the gift of celibacy, Luther concluded, were "rare, not one in a thousand," and were "a special miracle of God." Moreover, Luther insisted that Scripture forbade only marriage to one's sister or mother. He wanted early marriage; men should be married by age 20, and women between 15 and 18. Luther saw this as a means to reduce temptation, corruption, and illegitimate births.

Luther also attacked "lazy, greedy rascals" who only wanted to marry wives who were "rich, beautiful, pious, and kind." Luther himself, at age 42, married an ex-nun, Catherine Von Bora. By doing this he challenged papal authority.

Luther insisted that adulterers be executed before they could debauch other women. He would not agree to automatic divorce because of adultery. At this time in Italy, male adulterers were fined while women could be killed. In England, women adulterers could have their ears and noses cut off and be denied burial in consecrated burial grounds.

The English church was rocked by the schism which developed over the marital career of Henry VIII (six wives) which, while challenging the pope, made mockery of canon law on divorce and remarriage for everyone else.

Among many who became "Protestants," adultery became an ipso facto cause for divorce. However, it became necessary to reinterpret "unbeliever." A person who deserted his wife could be said to have done an unchristian act and, therefore, came to be regarded as an unbeliever.

According to the reformers, other unchristian acts included refusing to have sex (after two or three warnings), preventing the spouse from living a godly life, and refusing to be reconciled after a separation. Bickering or marital tension were grounds for a separation from "bed and board" but not a divorce. Eventually, Luther slightly modified Paul's words to suggest, "It is better to *re*marry than to burn." (See 1 Cor. 7:8-9.)

The Catholics convened the Council of Trent to counter the Protestant trends, and reformed certain Catholic teachings, though maintaining that adultery was still only a grounds for separation. Anyone who suggested that marriage was superior to virginity or who dissolved a marriage for other than adultery was declared anathema.

Because of the shortage of unmarried heirs (but not necessarily males), dowries increased. Since the status of the male determined the status of the couple, women were encouraged to "marry up."

Widows fell prey to opportunists. "I wish you good speed with the widow" became a common expression among single men. Many women started putting their money or lands in trust for their children before they remarried. But many widowers preferred younger women who could give them children.

A parallel development was the publication of Thomas Cogan's medical treatise *The Haven of Health*, which praised sexual relations as "healthy" and condemned celibacy as harmful to the body. Marriage "quickeneth the minde, stirreth up the witte, reviveth the senses, driveth away sadnesse, madnesse, anger, melancholy, and fury." Thus, the Protestants could argue that medical opinion supported their theology.

The other major influence on singleness was John Calvin, a lifelong bachelor. Calvin, in his *Institutes of Christian Religion,* argued powerfully that marriage had two functions: procreation and as a remedy for sin and temptation. Yet, he had difficulty—as did Luther—in accepting the sensual pleasure of intercourse in marriage. Calvin noted that since marriage was ordained by God, he denounced any who jested about marriage. Such humor and skepticism came "directly from Satan's workshop." Any attack on marriage was an attack on God. For the majority of people, he taught, God not only permits but positively *commanded* marriage; any who resisted matrimony fought against God. Only those who had been "singled out by divine appointment" should remain unmarried.

For single adults in Geneva, the punishment for fornication was a fine plus six days on bread and water. Calvin proposed capital punishment for adulterers. He urged only a six-week engagement. He proposed four grounds for divorce: adultery, physical incapacity of the spouse for sex, desertion, and extreme religious incompatability—the latter necessary because of partners who became Protestants while the mate remained Catholic.

At age 30, Calvin married a widow to avoid the celibacy he criticized as "a yoke imposed on priests shut up in a furnace of lust with perpetual fire." He eventually complimented her after her death, "She never interfered with my work."

Slowly, the ideas of the reformers spread across Europe, motivating a generation to look for adventure in a new world. At the close of the Reformation, 10 percent of the European population was unmarried.

Colonization of the New World

There were two ways to gain status as a citizen of the new world: immigration or birth. Those who settled in the new world chose both. Through big families, the wilderness could be tamed, land cleared, the Indians scattered, and the blessings of God experienced.

Initially, a high death rate had to be overcome. Many did not survive the voyage to America. Colonists argued "it was a man's duty to marry; it was a woman's reason for existence . . . to continue the species and to be a helpmate to the man." So, they quickly remarried.

Thus, the first recorded marriage in the colonies was between Edward Winslow (a widower of seven weeks) and Susanna White (a widow of five weeks) on May 12, 1621.

Since marriage was considered beneficial to the person, society, and the church, any deviation from that was suspect. William Byrd II of Virginia remarked, "An old maid or old bachelor are as scarce among us and reckoned as ominous as a blazing star." Byrd insisted that his 19-year-old daughter was "the most antique virgin" he knew.

William Penn, founder of the Pennsylvania colony, urged his colonists to become a nursery of people. He introduced a bill into the colonial assembly requiring young men to marry. However, the bill did not pass since there were so few women to marry.

In New England, bachelors were assigned residences with "good families" by the court. In Connecticut, bachelors were fined. In other colonies, bachelors were closely watched by constables. Some only assigned land to married men. Maryland taxed bachelors and wine.

In most colonies, the scarcity of women naturally encouraged the marriage of any available unmarried maiden or widow. Some families "imported" female relatives from Europe to "the land of opportunity."

In some areas, because of the shortage of white women, males lived with Indian women, an arrangement that was troublesome for both the Europeans and the Indians.

The British had earlier learned from their attempts to colonize the West Indies that a lack of women caused a colony to be unstable, perhaps even to flounder. Soon entrepreneurs enticed women with the offers of marriage, money, and independence. Poor single women in England could exchange a few years of indentured servanthood for the promise of a "better life" *and* marriage in the new world.

In 1619, the Virginia Company voted to send shiploads of unmarried women to America. Sir Edwin Sandys implemented that order and brought 90 women. He carefully guarded their purity since this was perceived as an economic arrangement. Husbands-to-be paid 120 pounds of tobacco for a wife-to-be.

Clearly, single women had a special economic status under the law. They were under the protection of their fathers until they married, possessing all rights as men except that of voting. A woman, by marrying, turned over all her rights to her husband.

Maryland passed a law requiring that a widow/heiress marry within seven years or lose her inheritance. The phrase, "With all my worldly goods I thee endow," produced some concern for brides' fathers who were alarmed at potential opportunists. Soon "marriage settlements" were drawn up between wealthy families. The bride's family agreed to give a particular amount of money, goods, even slaves as a "marriage portion"; the groom's family supplied property.

Because of the high death rate, particularly in childbirth, quick second marriages were common. Because of the practice of primogeniture, there were few opportunities for younger sons other than the military or perhaps marriage to a wealthy widow, which made fathers suspicious.

Simply, the imperative to procreate dominated the social and religious thinking of the colonists.

Thus we have our history. Out of it comes many of today's values, morals, and beliefs. Some are caught in the tradition; others rebel, fighting tradition. Regardless of our history, we must answer today's questions from the Bible with a clear understanding of today's singles phenomenon.

Harold Ivan Smith
Executive Director of Tear-Catchers
Kansas City, Missouri

Dr. Smith completed his doctoral thesis on the "History of Single Adults in American Culture." Harold has authored several books and produced an award-winning film series, *One Is a Whole Number.*

3. TODAY'S SINGLE ADULT PHENOMENON: THE REALITIES AND MYTHS

*"Singles are the biggest purchasers of sports cars, condo-
miniums, and fashions; the greatest frequenters of restaurants (often 8-10 times a week), and are the target of most
major movies, television advertisements, and health clubs.
Singles go where singles are, singles are spending more
money, and singles are setting the trends."*

Carolyn Koons

Growing up in America meant that your dreams would come true, and
you would be right in step, walking the aisle to wedlock, eventually owning
your own home, raising 2.5 children, owning at least one R.V., a speed
boat, or a small vacation cabin, and living happily ever after. The dream
was a Noah's ark (two by two), "traditionally marrying" culture. However,
in the last three decades, marital patterns have changed, creating a new
singles subculture. Along with such major societal changes came new
attitudes, stereotypes, myths, and often, misunderstandings.

The Value System: Singles in a Couples World
Everywhere we look we see a couples world, and there is pressure to
keep it that way. At the same time, our society is changing, and at times
there is a contradiction of values. On one hand, we regard highly the
values of individualism, being unique in thoughts and actions, and being
competitive. On the other hand, we promote conformity, group consen-
sus, and community. For some, marriage is instrumental in fulfilling the
socialization process, drawing us closer to the norm or community. Cargan
and Melko, in their book *Singles: Myths and Realities,* conclude, "Thus the
state of marriage is thought of as the natural order of things, and those
who do not conform threaten this order; the result is that there is little
room in the system for the unaccompanied person." Thus the pressures
and stereotypes begin.

As marriage is viewed as a positive, "right" choice, singleness becomes
negative and a "wrong" choice, or a failure to achieve a state that is
positive. Many singles feel pressure from society, parents, and their own
internal pressure valve to fit in and become a part of the societal norm.
This begins the eternal search to find "the magic one-and-only." "Waiting

on God for the perfect person" and the attitude that "marriage is God's perfect will" is often proclaimed from the pulpits today, laying on tremendous guilt while impacting the self-esteem of thousands of single Christian men and women. This reality requires that we take a fresh look at singles in a couples world.

Historical Attitudes on Singleness Since 1900
Single adults have been around since the beginning of mankind, but they usually comprised only 2-3 percent of the adult population until the drastic rise in number in the last 20 years. Since the early 1900s, society's awareness of singles has increased, and its attitudes have changed. From 1900 through the 1920s, single women, no matter what their age, were labeled "old maids," a term rarely heard today. During the '30s and '40s, the Depression years, single women were noticed and called "spinsters." Society tried to attack the "problem" of female singleness (seldom were single men focused on) by writing major articles addressing the issue: "Does It Hurt to Be an Old Maid?" "Alarming Increase of Old Maids and Bachelors in New England," "Family Parasites: The Economic Value of the Unmarried Sister," "The Sorrowful Maiden and the Jovial Bachelor," and "There Is No Place in Heaven for Old Maids."

The 1950s and '60s saw a turn as divorce increased in the American culture. Articles took more of a questioning/coaching approach: "How to Be Marriageable: Results of a Marriage Readiness Course," "A Spinster's Lot Can Be a Happy One," "When Being Single Stops Being Fun," "How to Be Human Though Single," "Study Disputes Image of the Happy Bachelor." Lists such as "129 Ways to Get a Husband," "Six Ways of Being an Old Maid," and "Six Ways to Meet a Man" were published.

The open, and oft-referred to "new morality" of the 1970s unfortunately labeled singles as "Swinging Singles," which helped widen the growing barrier between married and single adult groups. Articles began to reflect a more aggressive singles lifestyle: "What Women Should Know about Single Men," *Bazaar*'s "A to Z List on Where to Find a Man," "Humanizing the Meat Market," "Celebrate Singleness: Marriage May Be Second Best," "Movin' On—Alone," and *Newsweek*'s issue, "49 Million Singles Can't All Be Right."

The 1980s carry even a different image of singles. Some refer to them as the "growing" singles, hardworkers, physically active and healthy, affluent and introspective. The categories will still continue to change. However, it appears that singleness is here to stay. Never again will America be a 97-percent-married and 3-percent-single adult population.

Myths and Stereotypes
Every subculture in society carries a list of fallacious statements and beliefs. Singles are not the only group identified by such beliefs. Some myths seem to be perpetuated longer and harder than others. Again, singles are

no exception. Society's attitude toward singles clusters around several specific notions, ideas, or myths about the nature of single people and the character of their lives. These traditional beliefs tend to promote an essentially negative or unfair image of the single life. But, as with all stereotypes or myths, there is an element of truth concealed somewhere within. Individuals and singles themselves must remember not to categorize, label, and stereotype singles. They are unique and different, as are all men and women. They need the freedom to shape their own self-images without being hampered by myths.

The following are some of the more common stereotypes associated with the singles' lifestyle.

Myth: All Singles Are Lonely

Because marriage has been considered the norm, and culture has often romanticized marriage as a blissful, all-consuming relationship, the period of singleness was thought of as just a passing phase to be resolved by the ultimate state of marriage. And with all of the negative aspects of singleness continually pinpointed (singles are second best, unfulfilled, maladjusted, irresponsible, and immature at best), it seems obvious that all singles must be lonely.

Studies were made comparing married and single adults. The problem of loneliness did not seem to be the issue of having someone with whom to do things. People often associate loneliness with being alone and don't know how to handle just being solitary and discovering their unique selves. However, the determining factor was whether or not they had someone (a special friend or friends) with whom to share their problems—a kind of kindred spirit. The significant find was that singles, especially never marrieds, were the least likely to associate being alone with unhappiness, discrediting the myth that "all singles" are lonely.

On the other hand, those recently divorced associated being alone with loneliness, and felt they had lost someone with whom to share. Overall, loneliness to married people was associated more with the quality and communication level of their marriage. Pairing did not necessarily eliminate loneliness. Married people seem to have fewer close personal friends, and turn to their spouses or children to have their social and emotional needs met. At times this can place undue pressure on this exclusive relationship.

Myth: Singleness Is Filled with a Glamorous Lifestyle

Myths are interesting because one often contradicts another, such as, "All singles are lonely." The reality is that singleness, just like marriage, is and should be a day-to-day growth process, filled with ups and downs, challenges, tough times, and good times. Singles should be encouraged and supported in their lives whether their singleness is seasonal or for the rest of their lives.

Myth: All Singles, Especially Women, Want to Get Married

Historically, it has been assumed that women are more dependent than men, and need the security that a mate could provide. It was an economical, sociological, and psychological necessity that women marry. Some have preached that individuals are only "half" persons, intended to spend their lives finding the other half in order to become one, or more precisely, whole. God never created "half" people. Our responsibility is our relationship with God, to mature in His grace and wisdom. Whole, giving, growing people need to be brought together in marriages, not people seeking their missing part.

There is a decided imbalance in the sex ratio of the adult population. Statistics point out that there are approximately 12 million more single women than single men. Add to this a large number of married people who will end up being divorced or widowed, and there is a sizeable population who will be single. As times change, men and women are finding more options, more freedom, and more career opportunities, with less pressure to get married. There may currently be more freedom to be single than at any other time in history.

Myth: Overall, Single Men Are Irresponsible

Society has a tendency to label anyone who does not conform to its expectations or standards as irresponsible. A few studies have attempted to indicate that the 39-year-old single male is one of the most irresponsible segments of society (highest crime rate, arrest rate, drug rate, entrance into mental institutions). But the 1980s provide a whole new perspective on male singleness. Young, educated, single men are running major companies. Singleness offers men a time of freedom for education and career as never before. Men, though often "taken-care-of" by Mom, aren't necessarily looking for just another person to take care of them. With the home conveniences available, and men learning cooking and living skills as young "bachelors," they are more apt to take their time to wait for just the right woman to spend their lives with.

Myth: Single Men and Women Are Sexually Frustrated

The "Swinging Singles" image and singles bars have promoted a stereotype that reflects on most singles. Currently there is more openness for people to discuss sexual matters. There is the reality that some singles are sexually active and/or living together. This is an area that must be addressed in the church. Preliminary studies are indicating that Christian singles, though not as high as the national average, are sexually more active than had been assumed. Still, regardless of reputation, the swinging single appears to be in the minority.

A national questionnaire was given to both married and single adults, dealing with problem areas and frustrations of singles. The results indicated that marrieds perceived that the number one problem singles face was related to sexual frustrations and expressions. Given the same question-naire, singles ranked sexual frustration fifth place on their priorities, with the biggest frustration having to do with "being left out" or "not included in especially couples or family events." The second frustration was that of finances and being the sole breadwinner. Third, finding meaningful, re-warding friendships was a struggle. Single parenting responsibilities ranked fourth in their struggles. Sexuality and intimacy are two areas that must be addressed with singles. It also needs to be noted that marriage does not preclude sexual frustration.

The Singles Industry

U.S. News and World Report states: "Millions of unmarried Americans are creating a new lifestyle that is affecting every part of the country." "What this means is that for some time to come, all of us are going to be living in a world comprised to a far greater extent of people living alone and liking it," says Joseph Peritz, a pollster and market analyst in New York City. He observes, "This is a trend with enormous implications for business, gov-ernment, and everyone else in our society."

Single people comprise the largest concentrated pool of sales prospects in the country today. It is, therefore, not surprising that a singles industry has emerged, to the tune of over $40 billion a year. And it is an industry that is making money and growing. Singles apartments, bars, dating ser-vices, magazines, and vacations are just a few of the options available. Singles are the biggest purchasers of sports cars, condominiums, and fashions; the greatest frequenters of restaurants (often 8-10 times a week), and are the target of most major movies, television advertise-ments, and health clubs. Singles go where singles are, singles are spend-ing more money, and singles are setting the trends.

The Church's Response

In order for the church to minister to singles and be a viable church in the '80s and '90s, it must redefine its mission and ministry. There needs to be a rethinking of biblical and theological roots for developing a perspective on singleness. The church also needs to expand its term "family," moving from a traditional family definition to one that includes singles, widows, single-parent families, extended families, expanded families, step families, and blended families. We must become the family we are, the family of God!

And, in order to minister to today's singles, the church must also think in new patterns of ministry. The traditional patterns of church ministries, specialized ministries, traditional time slots and church buildings, glamour programs, multi-staffs, and traditional family ministry programs must be reevaluated in the decades to come.

Most of all, myths and stereotypes must be erased throughout each of the segments of the church and society, in order to become community, a

29

place where one can find help, strength, healing, help, and wholeness.

Carolyn Koons
Executive Director for the Institute for Outreach Ministries
Azusa Pacific University, Azusa, California

Carolyn is an author plus a conference, workshop, and retreat speaker for singles ministry. Her development and research on the "singles phenomenon" has been an excellent resource to single adult leadership.

4. ESTABLISHING A BIBLICAL BASIS FOR THE SINGLE ADULT MINISTRY

"It is equally true that the Scripture is to be taught and utilized with care and compassion. The church exists to build up and not tear down, to welcome and not to exclude."

Bill Flanagan

A careful examination of Scripture reveals a deep concern for the "widows and fatherless" (children who have been orphaned or who are with just one parent), individuals who, in their singleness, are struggling or even conniving toward becoming married. The Apostle Paul teaches that in whatever state we are to be content (see Phil. 4:11). As he writes to the Corinthian Christians in his first letter we gain a glimpse of his convictions about singleness. Chapter 7 is an important one for careful study by singles leaders.

Biblical Principles for Ministry

There are no more specific biblical principles for a single adult ministry than there are for many other significant ministries in the church. Therefore, it is important to look at an overview of the directives the Scriptures give to us for ministry in general. All Christians have a mandate from Scripture for ministry. That mandate would always preclude the fact that the Bible is not only our focus, but our final authority for all that we believe and do.

One of the most powerful and succinct passages teaching biblical ministry principles is the concluding verses of Peter's Pentecost sermon (Acts 7:41-47). The emerging Christian community was challenged by Peter in this passage to grow in four different dimensions. Each of these areas of focus has particular application for single adult ministry.

Grow in numbers (Acts 2:41). We read at the beginning and the end of this passage that the Lord added daily to the size of the community new lives that were touched and changed by the Gospel. The fact that people were being "added" clearly teaches that they already had something going. Therefore, single adults don't need to build a church of their own but, rather, become integrated into the church as it exists, making it even more whole, complete, and balanced.

This verse teaches that 3,000 people were drawn to Jesus Christ and added to the body in one day. That means evangelism was a significant part of the ministry. This raises the question of our vision as well as our preparation to handle growth and integrate new people meaningfully into a congregation. Our ministries must be geared to grow, and the best way to grow in numbers is to keep focused on individuals. We are called to be shepherds, not ranchers. A shepherd knows his flock by name, while a rancher only knows how many head there are in his herd.

Grow up (Acts 2:42). We are called by God to grow in our personal and corporate spiritual life. The early church did this in four basic ways as taught in the text.

    a. Teaching of the Apostles
    b. Fellowshipping together
    c. Breaking of bread
    d. Praying for one another

We are called to grow up as a whole ministry to whole persons, never to isolate or compartmentalize human beings by marital status or in any other way. A single adult ministry, as any ministry in the church, needs to be a part of the total Christian life. Therefore, it is appropriate that our groups reflect the social, relational, sexual, recreational, intellectual, and spiritual dimensions of who we are as children of God. Single adult ministries that are biblically focused should not be narrowly tuned to spiritual development, but open to the totality of the human experience.

Grow out (Acts 2:43-45). The early church had a mission. It did not exist for itself alone, but reached out into the world with the message of Christ and with works of compassion and love.

Single adults are a mission field, but it can be equally true that single adults have a mission. They exhibit a special awareness and sensitivity that the church vitally needs to hear to accomplish its evangelistic task with tact, wisdom, and compassion. A single adult ministry, therefore, should never exist to meet only its own needs. It must exist to serve the larger community, seeing it as a mission field with deep spiritual and human needs.

There is always a beautiful tension and balance between our Lord's command to both "come" as well as "go." Come and get your needs met. Come and meet new friends. Come to events that offer stimulating opportunities for personal growth. But at the same time, "Go." Go into the world to work and play, to be disciples of Christ. If all we are saying is, "Come," sooner or later we will stagnate and die.

Grow together (Acts 2:46-47). The early church was a family, a community of togetherness, support, and encouragement. Few saw themselves as "Lone Ranger Christians." Faith to them was always personal, but never private. They were a people in process, growing together.

An important goal or measuring stick one can apply to any ministry is the exclamation of outsiders echoing an expression heard in the early church, "See how they love each other."

Growing together in the biblical sense means that single people be

32

integrated into the whole life of the congregation, not as a satellite appendage or "little leper colony." A church or ministry that is pleasing to God and that is focused biblically is one that grows in each of these four ways. The whole church includes those who are young and old, black and white, handicapped and healthy, male and female, educated and ignorant, rich and poor, married and single, focusing its energies together to bring praise and glory to Jesus Christ.

Practical Guidelines for Using Scripture in Your Single Adult Ministry

A singles ministry that keeps itself biblically focused will probably have several ways of utilizing the Word of God in its regular program.

Single adult class. Any singles ministry that involves a considerable number of people will center in a class, usually on Sunday morning, taught by a pastor or trained layperson. This class will focus on the Scriptures and will interpret biblical materials in the context of the issues of daily living that apply particularly to single adults. Usually these classes are ongoing in nature and are not focused on single adult issues as a steady diet. Most singles get bored with this and want to move on to other more important biblical studies.

Small group studies. Singles ministries that are growing in their Christian discipleship will employ small group experiences. The covenantal groups exist not just to study the Bible, but also for fellowship, personal sharing, and prayer. Many singles groups have small group ministries that utilize *open* groups where people can come and rotate in and out on a regular basis. These groups are particularly helpful for new people. Also, covenant groups that are *closed* after they are formed may be a crucial part of a ministry to develop trust, intimacy, healing, and spiritual growth.

Over the years, single adults have been turned off by churches that look down their noses and metaphorically hit singles over the head with their large 90-pound black Bibles. It is an axiomatic biblical principle that we accept people where they are, not where we think they ought to be. All of us need to be wary of using Scripture to judge, justify, or prove our point of view. While the Bible "is useful for teaching, rebuking, correcting, and training in righteousness, so that the man of God may be thoroughly equipped for every good work" (2 Tim. 3:16), it is equally true that the Scripture is to be taught and used with care and compassion. The church exists to build up and not tear down, to welcome and not to exclude.

We need to continually struggle to build a strong, biblical base and rationale for some of the difficult issues of our time. Single adults struggle with the issues of divorce, relationships, sex, and remarriage as much as anyone. They do not want to be confronted with pat answers but to struggle with God's will for their lives within the healthy tension that often exists between grace and the Law.

Bill Flanagan
Minister with Single Adults
St. Andrews Presbyterian Church, Newport Beach, California

Bill has been a singles pastor since 1971. As a pioneer in single adult ministry, Bill has developed a solid biblical base for ministry. He also serves as an adjunct professor at the Fuller Theological Seminary.

5. PHILOSOPHY AND STRATEGY FOR SINGLES MINISTRY

"I have seen far too many ministries 'crash and burn' due to their neglect in establishing an appropriate foundation—or philosophy of ministry, or strategy—for their ambitious programs."

Terry Hershey

Victor Frankl is right. If you know the "why," you can handle the "what." That truth applies to everything we do, including our ministries.

When churches tell me that they would like to begin a "ministry with single adults," and they need "some advice" on what to do first, my "advice" is nothing more than a question: "Why?" Unfortunately, most have not stopped to find an answer for that question. Consequently, ministries are seen as nothing more than "creative programming," which, if implemented properly will create a "successful" group. Emphasis is placed on immediate returns, numbers, and the pragmatic "cost-effectiveness" of the programming (which includes the potential numbers added to our church rolls, the money added to the church coffers, or the "warm bodies" added to the church volunteer force).

My concern is not to discourage goal-setting or "bigness" or creativity in programming, but I do want to raise a caution flag. I have seen far too many ministries "crash and burn" due to their neglect in establishing an appropriate foundation—or philosophy of ministry, or strategy—for their ambitious programs. We can always use more "zeal" in dreaming big for ministry with single adults. There is more to ministry than the program.

Real People

Single adults are real people with real needs. They live in a pressure-cooker world and are crying to belong and be known. Their cry may not be obvious or even audible, but that is the nature of this ministry. We must begin with the idea that we are on a journey to get to know people, to uncover unrealized potential, to provide the freedom to ask, question, and talk, and to give permission to find fulfillment in involvement and leadership. The potential of a ministry with single adults is limitless. But, we must do our homework. Let us not continue to rush headlong into our "dreams" for success without taking a good, hard look at the reasons why. The warning for us to heed is noted in the Gospel of Luke: "Suppose one of you wants to build a tower. Will he not first sit down and estimate the cost to see if he has enough money to complete it?" (14:28)

So an effective strategy—or philosophy of ministry, or answering the question why—begins with effective homework. What are the obstacles that prevent us from effective ministry? Are there any unseen barriers? Must we remove any internal stereotypes or myths about single adults or ministry with them?

To answer those questions and to build an effective philosophy of ministry, I believe that there are three issues for us to examine and incorporate into our dreams and plans and strategies.

Single Adults Should "Own" the Ministry

Whatever else may be said, this principle is vital. If our approach to ministry does not include an understanding that the people own what is going on, we are setting ourselves up for frustration and resentment.

The question is predictable: "We'd like to start a ministry for single adults; what can we do for them?" This "us and them" dichotomy is subtle and pervasive, and effects the entire ministry. You can hear it in our language. "My single adults." "My group." "My ministry." The assumption is loud and clear: We believe that single adults are ultimately irresponsible. And consequently, we talk to them that way. "Single adults just don't seem to care! They come late or they come on the wrong day! They are just not committed!" Our focus on the symptoms—the "irresponsibility" and noncommitment—only perpetuates the cycle. We feel more resentful of the very people to whom we have been called to minister. While waiting for these "irresponsible people" to "grow up" and "take responsibility," we feel it is our job to entertain them—to keep them busy and occupy their time. It is no wonder that most programming ideas are entertainment-oriented. They are based on a philosophy of ministry that assumes that single adults are irresponsible. How do we break this cycle?

First of all, we are not doing ministry with children or teenagers. These are adults. And they must be treated as adults. Second, the Bible is very clear that no one person—or even one special group of people—owns the ministry. We all own the body and, consequently, what goes on in the body. What does all this mean? Simply this: that we must never assume that the single adults with whom we minister will take responsibility; we must give it to them.

That approach represents a radical change for most of us. We have been so inculcated with the philosophy that says the "leader" does it all that we may not even be aware of those areas where we are encouraging "irresponsibility." Let me give you some examples. We "rescue" people. ("If you can't do it, don't worry, Terry will do it.") We don't trust people will do "as good a job" as we could. We are protective of "our" programs. We involve others by inducing guilt. Ask yourself: What are some ways that I can begin to "give away" responsibility? To "give away" ownership? To give people permission to be different? To train singles for ministry?

And at the same time, what are some ways that you could begin to be sensitive to the ways in which you encourage irresponsibility, and at the same time communicate with your behavior that you are the "only leader" and, therefore, the only one who can meet needs and make decisions?

Single Adult Ministry Is the Job of the Congregation

We are tempted to believe that the "problem" of single adult ministry can be solved simply by instituting a program. It is our hope that a central program can provide the necessary entertainment to "keep them busy" (as one pastor put it so matter-of-factly).

While there is nothing wrong with starting programs for single adults in the church, it is important to note that the success of such programs is built on the foundation of a congregation that is "welcoming" to single persons. Invariably, of course, many will respond to that statement by lamenting that their church "is not accepting of single adults, so now what?"

When I am asked to help a church "begin a ministry" with single adults, there is some preliminary groundwork that needs to be done. We begin by asking the staff and key lay leadership of the church this question: "What one-word description comes to your mind when you hear the phrase 'single adult'?" The question catches many off guard, and the responses are often predictable: "hurting, unwanted, lonely, noncommitted, 'losers,' uninvolved." Granted, those words may be true as "perceptions," but the fact remains that no blue-ribbon program in the world will succeed when built on the foundation of such negative stereotypes about single people.

The principle is this: Effective ministry begins with education, not programming. If you want to see change in your church, you must educate for change. We must begin by taking an honest look at the stereotypes and misconceptions that limit our congregation's effectiveness.

What are the prevalent stereotypes in your congregation? And what can we do about changing them? We can begin by examining our own motives and stereotypes. What is it that I believe about single persons, and how does it affect the way in which I approach ministry? (For example: Do I create an "us and them" barrier? Do I opt for "entertainment" programming because I perceive single persons as "irresponsible" and, therefore, incapable of entertaining themselves? Do I see single persons as essentially "incomplete" and subconsciously create a program for "dating and mating" purposes?)

It is also important that we take every opportunity to create dialogue in the other areas of our congregation. Has there ever been a sermon preached at your church on a "theology of singleness"? Have any of the single persons been given the opportunity to share their story with the congregation? Has the church board ever conducted a dialogue on the subject of single adults? Here's an idea that may help. Ask the church board for 15 minutes at the next board meeting. Invite three single adults from your congregation to attend. Their purpose? Each will take 5 minutes to tell the board what it is like to be a single person in your church. You are not asking for money or resources. You are simply beginning the process of dialogue. Why? Because if you want to see change, you must educate for change.

Ironically, some congregations are far more successful than they think. When one pastor approached me for advice in beginning a ministry in his church for single adults, I asked him the following questions: How many single adults are on the church board? How many single adults serve on key directional church task forces? How many serve as Sunday School teachers? How many sing in the choir, or are involved in other lay leadership positions? In other words, what is the general attitude of the congregation? Sadly, he didn't know the answers to the questions I had asked.

It has been said that "not all churches are called to have a single adult program, but all churches are called to minister with single adults." I agree. And it fits what we have been saying here. If a church is a "welcoming" church and finds that single adults are being incorporated into the life of the church at various levels, ministry is taking place, and there is less pressure to create programming for programming's sake.

Single Adult Ministry Is Built on Targeted Programming
It has been said that if you aim at nothing, you will hit it. It is also true, that if you aim at everything, you will hit nothing.

That adage is true of church programming as well. And it is important to understand when you think of the myriad of needs reflected by the single adult population in your church and community. No one program will be able to effectively meet all those needs. However, rather than discourage, that statement should encourage because now we can be free to be intentional and targeted. We can be "purposeful" in our programming efforts. And it should relieve us of the intimidation that we need to "minister to everyone." Only you can know what areas your church can be effective at targeting, and that process begins with need assessment and evaluation.

My advice? Try involving others in the process of assessment, planning, and implementation. And don't be afraid to fail. No program is sacred, so if it doesn't work, you can always try again.

This chapter began by saying that knowing the reason "why" creates the necessary foundation for an effective "what." Effective ministry is built on an effective philosophy of ministry and strategy. We mentioned three issues that are important to such an effective philosophy. And it is important to continually be reminded that single adult ministry should be owned by the single adults, that an effective ministry begins with the congregation, and that effective programming is targeted. If we don't remember, we can too easily do ministry by default, or build a program structure that is destined for failure because it was established on a weak foundation.

38

Terry Hershey
Executive Director of Christian Focus
Irvine, California

An an author, speaker, consultant, and singles pastor at the Crystal Cathedral, Garden Grove, California, Terry has had a great deal of experience developing and assisting other singles ministries.

SINGLE ADULTS GOD HAS CALLED US TO

▪ ▪

6. THE SINGLE ADULT IDENTITY

"Singles may find themselves going through various seasons or stages of singleness. Some might be in their season of single parenting. Many are pursuing their season of education or career. Hopefully all are seeking healing and growth in their season."

Carolyn Koons

Single Adult Identity: Uncharted Territory

Few men and women actually set out to be single, yet close to 65 million adults in America find themselves in this new uncharted lifestyle. Many feel that singleness was thrust on them by a death or divorce, and feel ostracized or branded. Others look at singleness as something to be avoided, and try frantically to alter their status. Many are teased about being single: "I can't believe you're not married yet!" And to others singleness is a provocative, sought-after, and flaunted lifestyle. Overall, singleness is often misunderstood.

The American culture is a highly educated, well-informed society which understands human growth and development. Psychologists, sociologists, family therapists, and educators have been able to study human growth from conception to death. Each discipline describes growth by identifiable stages, phases, and benchmarks, producing thousands of books on the topic.

Developmental theories are based on a marriage model. Traditionally in America, it has been expected that 97 percent of the population would grow up following all of the "normal" developmental stages through high school into the next steps of dating, courtship, marriage, and children. With the rise of the singles phenomenon, more than 50 percent divorce rate, and other sociological effects, these developmental patterns no longer apply to millions of never-married, divorced, or widowed adults. Stages of single adult development are not the same as developmental stages of married adults. This developmental gap helps contribute to the misunderstanding, stereotypes, and myths surrounding singleness, and the growing gap between single and married adults in America.

Major sociological and psychological literature states that serious research about singles is noticeably missing from the field of family sociology, though there are a few studies dealing with divorce. While not completely ignored by most writers on the family, singles are defined in terms of their relationship to marriage (the expected "norm" or "normal lifestyle"). Social psychologists are accustomed to referring to singles as "those who fail to marry," or as "those who do not make positive choices."

If singleness is discussed at all by these writers, it is generally in terms of stereotypes and assumptions. They see singles as hostile toward marriage or toward persons of the opposite sex; not having cut the umbilical cord from their parents; possibly being homosexual, unattractive, or having physical and psychological reasons for not finding a mate; afraid of involvement or commitment; lacking social skills for dating; having unrealistic criteria for finding a spouse; unwilling to assume responsibility. And the list goes on.

A divorced person is defined as someone who failed at marriage, could not adjust, or is unable to relate. No wonder approximately 80 percent of divorced people remarry within the first two years following their first divorce.

A New Awakening

America is changing. We are living in a time of transition. The singles phenomenon is a large part of this change. The statistic of over 65 million single adults is staggering as it has many implications for the American culture. Trends predict that more than 50 percent of adults today will spend some significant time during their adult lives as divorced or widowed singles. One fifth of all U.S. families are single-parent families. There has been an increase of 80 percent in single-parent families in the past 10 years. And there are over 11 million blended families in the U.S. today. Robert Weiss, in his book *Going It Alone* (Basic), states that "one half of all children being born today can expect to spend part of their growing-up years as members of a single-parent family."

Our concept of family is being redefined, reevaluated, and expanded to include singles, single parents, extended families, expanded families, and blended families. These individuals are looking for programs and ministries to assist them with the course and journey of their lives.

The Who of Singledom

It is important to understand that singles do not fall in one large group called "single adults." Today's single adult belongs to one of four very different groups, each with its own subgroups, varying needs, pressure points, and social and emotional concerns. Approximately 54 percent of today's singles are never-married; 22 percent are widowed; 18 percent are divorced; and 5 percent are separated. It is important to identify and understand the unique needs of each of these groups in order to minister effectively to them.

Why So Many Singles?

The increase in the number of single adults is a complex phenomenon, some of which is related to the reasons why men and women marry. Some of the reasons for marriage include the bond of love or sex, mutual aid in the struggle for existence, and the desire to have children. In today's urban and industrial age, modern conveniences, career emphasis, changing role of the family, increased divorce rate, changing lifestyles, women's rights movement, and fewer available men have made marriage less imperative as a means of providing love, aid, or children.

Though single lifestyles still carry a lot of uncertainty and conflicting messages, singles today are learning more about themselves and the world around them. As they live the single experience, they are able to identify three primary reasons for their current singleness: commitment to career, independence, and not having met the right one.

Some Challenges of Singleness

Singleness and marriage each have their own rewards and disadvantages. Edwards and Hoover, in *The Challenge of Being Single,* contrast general advantages of being single with those of being married.

SINGLE	MARRIED
Privacy: Being able to think and create without interruption in a peaceful atmosphere.	*Companionship:* Being held and loved; feeling another's presence; hearing another's voice.
Time: Having time to travel; cultivate talents; relax; entertain; be entertained.	*Family:* Having children and sharing in their care; having grandchildren as you grow older.
Freedom: Being able to choose; to make decisions; to form friendships; to use your time as you wish.	*Help:* Sharing the work; having another point of view when making decisions.
Opportunity: Being able to extend borders of friendship; develop skills; move to new jobs and places.	*Care and Security:* Having someone to look after you; having greater financial support.

When singles describe the benefits of or reasons for their single status, they include more privacy; freedom to pursue their own interests or careers; lack of readiness for marriage and family; desire to travel; freedom of movement, choice, and lifestyle; more time to read, seek, and achieve their potential; more opportunity for adventure; more opportunity for friendships, especially with the opposite sex; less stress, and more peace and quiet. These list but a few of the reasons.

This same lifestyle carries with it some definite struggles as well. These include dealing with loneliness; a search for identity in the context of a married society; a tendency toward or preoccupation with self; developing a pattern of going it alone; and outside pressure or criticism and misunderstanding from family and friends.

Singles list five struggles that seem to take precedence in their lifestyles. The biggest frustration and struggle is in "being left out" or "not included" by couples because of their singleness. Singles want to be part of the church, families, events, and leadership. They do not want to be thrust into singles-only groups. As Britton Wood states, "Singles want to be the church too." They want to be included equally as whole, growing people.

The second struggle for singles is the area of finances, especially if the single is a parent and head of a household. Seventy-five percent of single-parent women find themselves on welfare in order to survive. There is also no potential for two incomes. Singles also can get caught in the "me-now" syndrome, buying and doing things for themselves—now. Good financial counsel is needed.

Finding rewarding friendships is a third struggle for singles. A rewarding friendship is where they can share, be honest, laugh and cry—not a friendship with constant pressures to be paired off in an opposite-sex relationship, nor of questions about a same-sex relationship. Maybe one of the biggest challenges facing the church today is to understand the concept of community and friendship for both marrieds and singles, young and old.

The fourth struggle singles indicated is that of children, for both the custodial and noncustodial parent. Balancing work, parenting, parenting alone, and financial pressures, at the same time as maintaining some form of social life and friendship, is a major challenge.

Finally, fifth in order of priority, singles have to deal with their sexual frustrations and pressures. They indicated that the aforementioned four struggles consumed so much of their time and energy that they put sexual pressure considerably below those four. However, let us remember that singles are not dead! They admit to some sexual frustration, but that "being restricted sexually had tended to make them more creative and active in other ways." Also, it needs to be noted that marriage does not preclude sexual frustrations.

Seasons of Singleness

The lack of developmental information concerning singles and their lifestyles, combined with singles' questions about their goals, needs, and identities, encourages many singles to avoid singleness. Some fear that singleness might be for a lifetime, leaning toward the fallacy that "the grass is always greener on the other side." Singleness needs to be viewed more as a season of time. A season is unpredictable, without a specific length, and with various opportunities. And indeed this season, for some, may be for all of life.

A season of singleness provides freedom to grow, a time for healing and renewal. Perhaps this is a time to celebrate or reflect. This can be a time of seeking understanding, perhaps to deal with some painful scars and memories of the past. For some this season may feel like winter, but perhaps that is needed for growth.

Seasons have beginnings, middles, and endings. Singles may find themselves going through various seasons or stages of singleness. Some might be in their season of single parenting. Many are pursuing their season of education or career. Hopefully all are seeking healing and growth in their seasons. These seasons may overlap each other, but each has its own distinct characteristics. There may be the inclination to move through the season too quickly, trying to change it, not understanding it, or not seizing the opportunity set aside for growth and change. The greatest challenge for singles and those who walk beside them is to understand the season in which they find themselves, and seize the challenge for growth, change, and becoming God's whole person.

Carolyn Koons
Executive Director for the Institute for Outreach Ministries
Azusa Pacific University, Azusa, California

Carolyn is currently involved in doctoral studies in human development with an emphasis in single adult identity. She is also the author of two bestsellers, and is an adjunct professor at Talbot and Fuller Theological Seminaries.

7. SINGLES—THE NEVER MARRIED

"No doubt one of the most difficult groups for the church to reach is the under-35, never-married single adults. For many, it is often only after they go through a divorce, have children, or reach their 40s and 50s that they will recognize or admit any spiritual needs in their lives."

Jerry Jones

According to a front-page article in the *Wall Street Journal* (May 28, 1986), the proportion of never-married men and women in their late 20s and early 30s more than doubled between 1970 and 1985.

According to the U.S. Census Bureau, there are 20.5 million males and 16.4 million females who have never been married—a grand total of 36.9 million people. That comprises nearly one fourth (21.5 percent) of the total U.S. adult population.

Is this growth in the number of never-married single adults just a fad? That's not likely. According to *American Demographics Magazine* (Feb. '87, pp. 62-63), "The total number of people who *live alone* [which includes many never-marrieds] should grow by 50 percent between 1985 and 2000, from 21 million to 32 million." (This is compared to the projected 11 percent growth among married couples for the same period.)

Why Are There So Many Never-Married Single Adults?

Since 1970 there has been a dramatic, noticeable shift in the U.S. population. According to the U.S. Census Bureau, women are marrying later during the 1980s than during any other previously recorded period of American history.

The proportion of people putting off marriage in the '80s is even greater than the increase of the '70s. In 1985, 58.5 percent of women aged 20-24 had never married, up from 50 percent in 1980. Men have postponed marriage at least as much as women. The postponement of marriage is also creeping into the older groups ages 35 and up.

Do Single Adults Want to Get Married?

In most cases, yes. For example among never-married women in their 20s, according to a 1983 study, fully 36 percent expect to marry someday, but say they are glad they are single now. Only 26 percent of those who expect to marry wish they were married right now. Another 21 percent expect to marry, but are unconcerned one way or another about their current marital status. This leaves a balance of 6 percent who aren't sure if they will ever marry, and 10 percent who plan to stay single (*American Demographics,* Oct. '85, p. 16).

Why Are They Postponing Marriage?

A significant demographic shift. Today there are simply not enough single men to allow every single woman to marry. As researcher Peter Francese says, "There are now 6.3 million more women than men; by 2000 there will be 7 million more women in America than men" (*Single Adult Ministries Journal,* June '87, p. 2).

Called to ministry. Within the church there are single adults who sense a deep calling to some area of ministry. And oftentimes they are unable to find someone who shares their calling. Or they simply choose singleness so that they might focus more single-mindedly on the ministry God has called them to.

The growing number of career women. Women are participating in the workforce like never before. For example, women in the American labor force have increased significantly in the last 70 years.

From 1960 to 1982 women's representation in schools of medicine, law, and architecture jumped from 5 percent to 32 percent (*People Weekly,* March 31, 1986, p. 30).

Along with career comes the opportunity for greater financial independence. Women no longer need to rely on a husband for survival. (Most career-oriented women—if they marry at all—postpone their marriages an average of seven years after completing college.)

Furthermore, many men are threatened by women who earn as much or more than they do. Unmarried men and women in their late 30s not only face fewer options but also become pickier.

Personal freedom with no accountability. Another reason many adults have postponed marriage is an unprecedented craving for personal freedom. As job opportunities have broadened and incomes risen, baby-boomers in particular have chosen to seek the good life alone.

Unrealistic expectations. Many single adults say they are still single because they cannot find the right partner. It's not that they are not trying. According to a 1986 ABC news special, since one decade ago, dating services have grown from 300 to an estimated 5,000.

What is behind these unrealistic expectations? Here are two viewpoints.

(1) Their dates are never good enough. Some mental-health professionals say that the inability to connect with an appropriate partner is the main reason single people in their 30s seek counseling. "Every day I hear the same old story," says an analyst at Columbia University Center for Psychoanalytic Training and Research whose practice includes many single patients. "People's dates are never good enough. They're always a little too short, too thin, too shy, too aggressive. Yet patients tell me they are 'desperate' to get married. It's ridiculous! If they wanted to be married,

they'd be married" (*New York Magazine*, Aug. 20, 1984, p. 24).

But other professionals would say the situation is not so cut-and-dry.

(2) They have missed the "launch window." One of those who believes the answer is not so simple is Dr. Pepper Schwartz, a sociologist and coauthor of *American Couples*. According to her, these singles have missed what she calls the "launch window." "In college, people connect on the basis of shared backgrounds and interests. Adequate leisure time nourishes friendships, and many of these develop into romance. Today, 30-year-old professionals operate on tight schedules . . . and frequently judge one another on the basis of a 45-minute conversation. Under these circumstances, only the most attractive make it beyond the first round" (*New York Magazine*, Aug. 20, 1984, p. 25).

Furthermore, the older one gets, the harder it is to date. As one single adult put it, "When you get older, it's harder to bounce back from rejection."

Lack of commitment. The church is not the only one who believes the inability to make commitments has had a profound effect on this generation. Dr. Arthur Parsons, chairman of the department of Sociology and Anthropology at Smith College, has completed extensive studies of the 1960s and believes that much of its predominant ideology has hampered the development of long-term relationships.

"Marriage requires self-sacrifice," he explains. "But that concept was alien to the baby-boom generation, which was more interested in discovering the true essence of life within."

Yet, as Parson says, the quest for self-fulfillment was ultimately unfulfilling. "Marriage provides intimacy that people crave. But it also carries responsibilities, which interfere with self-fulfillment. . . . When the infatuation level begins to wear off, there is a major letdown. But instead of taking the relationship to the next step, they proceed to the next relationship" (*New York Magazine*, Aug. 20, 1984, p. 26).

The Peter Pan syndrome. Psychologist Dr. Dan Kiley popularized this term in his book by the same name. According to Dr. Kiley, this syndrome is a narcissistic, adolescent-like attitude which primarily afflicts educated urban unmarried adults who refuse to face the psychological and financial demands of growing up.

Two earmarks of adolescence are the beliefs that time is limitless and choices are unnecessary. Many singles in their 30s have adopted that same attitude. In the past, there were certain developmental tasks, like marriage and child-rearing, that signaled one's adulthood. In today's urban culture it's acceptable to postpone those tasks for as long as possible.

Lax sexual standards. No longer do two people need to marry to be sexually involved. In fact, according to a study conducted by the University of Oregon, from 1970 to 1980, couples living together before marriage increased from 13 percent to 53 percent. The study further found that this pattern is not limited to young adults but it cuts across all demographic lines and age-groups. Finally, the study reported that people who live together postpone marriage by at least one year or more (*Journal of Marriage and the Family*, Summer Quarter, 1986).

Other reasons. (1) Shyness. For some it is simply too difficult to meet other people and to develop ongoing relationships.

(2) Taking care of sick and/or elderly parents. Sometimes this is necessary and proper. But unfortunately in some cases, parents place undue guilt on an adult child in order to keep him or her in the home.

(3) Living in rural areas. This especially affects those who are involved in farming, ranching, or lumber. Their occupations require that they live far from metropolitan areas where the majority of available single adults are to be found.

(4) Handicapped. Some people never marry due to emotional, mental, or physical handicaps.

(5) Sexually transmitted diseases. The risk of getting a STD is greater than ever. More than 10 million people in the U.S. get some form of STD each year (from the book *Play Safe: How to Avoid Getting Sexually Transmitted Diseases,* p. XV, 1985). Many of these people are single. Oftentimes they simply choose not to marry for fear of infecting a partner or child. Furthermore, many of them are even afraid to date due to the possible rejection they may face once their partners find out.

(6) Homosexuality. It is estimated that approximately 4 percent of all single women and 10-15 percent of single men are gay. Most of these will not marry, at least in the traditional sense.

What Are Some of Singles' Attitudes and Characteristics?

Where they spend their money. Up to 63 percent of their food dollar goes to eating out. Other popular ways to spend money are: fitness equipment, high-quality home furnishings, premium lines of frozen food, and microwave cookware to make fixing food quick and easy. Furthermore, singles are the biggest subscribers to fashion magazines, attend more theatre and movies than any other group, are into tennis, skiing, sunning at the beach, jogging, bicycling, racquetball, backpacking, and walking their dogs. And believe it or not, they are even more likely to go bowling than marrieds.

Sexual habits/attitudes. Though sexual attitudes are still very liberal among most single adults, there has been a conservative, more responsible trend in the 1980s. The AIDS epidemic along with other STDs have helped bring this about. According to an article in *USA Today*, "Casual sex in the U.S. has declined dramatically since the freewheeling '60s and fear of sexually transmitted disease is a major reason, a long-term study shows" (Feb. 19, 1986, p. 10).

Even prior to the more recent AIDS scare, the "swinging single" was more alive in people's imaginations than in real life. In one study conducted by *People* magazine, of the singles surveyed (age 40 and under) 55 percent said they had had fewer than three sex partners in their entire lives.

Redbook magazine reports that 54 percent of all single women still believe premarital sex is wrong.

Church attendance. Single adults continue to express their attitudes toward the church most conspicuously by their absence. For example, in 1958, almost 50 percent of adults under 30 attended church. By 1980, the number dropped to 30 percent (*Single Adult Ministries Journal*, May 1986, p. 1). As early marriages have declined, so has church attendance for the under 30s.

According to author and church consultant Jack Simms, "The statistics are staggering. The average baby-boomer goes to church 6.4 times a year. The other 45.6 Sundays a year he is sleeping in, working out, or spending time with friends and family" (*Single Adult Ministries Journal*, May 1986, p. 1).

No doubt one of the most difficult groups for the church to reach is the under-35, never-married single adults. For many, it is often only after they go through a divorce, have children, or reach their 40s and 50s that they will recognize or admit any spiritual needs in their lives.

Singles and mental health. "Flying solo isn't necessarily a lonely ride," says Duane Alwin, a University of Michigan expert on single living and mental health. A large body of research indicates that unmarried people suffer more from depression, anxiety, and ill health than their married brethren—the theory being that close relationships protect the married against stresses the unmarried face alone. But Alwin argues that solitary living itself can't be held responsible. People need strong ties with others to be happy, he says, but it can't be assumed that living alone prevents those ties from forming.

Most experts agree that, to be content, single adults have to work especially hard at forging bonds with friends and family. "Personal contact in which we feel understood and accepted—there's no more powerful gift," says Ken Druck, a San Diego psychologist who specializes in working with singles. "If this need isn't met, it translates into health problems and hampers success and productivity at work."

Conclusion

As we move toward the year 2000, it is increasingly important for the church to recognize the changing social landscape of the communities which make up America. As we have discussed in this chapter, one of the most significant is the number of adults who are postponing marriage or are not getting married at all. No longer can the mission of the church be primarily built around the traditional nuclear family of the 1950s. Christ is calling us to make the Gospel relevant to *this* generation.

As mentioned earlier in this chapter, single adults must have strong ties with others to remain mentally and emotionally healthy. There is no better place for the never-married person to find love, acceptance, and the sense of family than in the body of Christ. Rather than building walls to separate us from those we don't understand or those who don't fit into traditional patterns, we are called to embrace them, affirm them, disciple, love, and nurture them. That is both our opportunity and challenge.

Jerry Jones
Editor and Publisher of *Single Adult Ministries Journal*
Colorado Springs, Colorado

Jerry is a never-married single adult who has had a significant contribution and ministry to single adults. He is author of the book, *First Person Singular*, Zondervan.

8. SINGLES—THE SEPARATED

"Do you view the needs of the separated as urgent and important? Do you view them as people to be reached with the Gospel right where they are? We must remember Jesus' response to the woman at the well."

Bud & Kathy Pearson

Separated people are in a place where identity is particularly difficult. Some view them as married while others see them as single. The truth is that the separated person is married but must now function as a single. It is because of this that separated people often seek the company of other singles and find their way into singles groups.

What We Need to Know about Separated People

It is important that we know what is being experienced by the separated person. For him, the feeling of loss is an every-moment experience. The person feels guilty about his part in the separation, and anger with self or spouse or both. He is frustrated over what to do now as well as how to cope with the added practical responsibilities that have come.

Separated people feel a sense of blame—either toward themselves or their spouse—for the break-up. They have a fear of the future because of changes and uncertainties. They worry that finances will become a major problem. They are sometimes faced with the task of explaining to their children what has happened and then with dealing with the parent/child relationship in new and different ways.

We also need to know how other people are treating the separated person. Parents often have a lack of understanding and can add to feelings that are already devastated. Friends may be incapable of coping and portray that they are rejecting the separated person. Coworkers or colleagues frequently lack sensitivity and are unable to be supportive.

This all results in the separated person feeling even more alone and alienated, opening the opportunity for a caring ministry.

Anxiety and fear prevent people from opening up to God's plan for them. Therefore, an atmosphere of acceptance where love and forgiveness can be experienced is much needed.

Provide an opportunity for the expression of hurts and feelings. This can be provided by personal counsel and/or in small groups where a nonthreatening atmosphere is evident.

The separated person needs godly counsel. Help in being objective without being manipulated or controlled is imperative. Counsel that is carefully and prayerfully given can bring excellent results. Practical counsel on marriage, finances, child care, job placement, housing, relationships, and more is needed.

Attitudes about Separated People

The attitude of the senior pastor is crucial in ministry to the separated. His view will be the guiding hand for all the church's ministry. The singles minister or director needs to spend adequate time with the senior pastor to inform him of the total picture in singles ministry including the needs of separated people.

The attitude of the church governing bodies will be molded by many things, but the senior pastor will be the key to their openness to singles ministry and all who are a part of it.

The attitude of the congregation is important. They provide the atmosphere of acceptance that makes any single feel comfortable and needed.

The attitude of the singles minister or director must be one of seeing the necessity of educating the entire church about singles ministry.

Theological background will influence the leader's attitude. If one cannot see that "the letter kills, but the Spirit gives life," it will be hard to welcome separated persons.

Openness will depend on people's ability to see the needs of the separated person and the ministry that can bless the person with those needs. Care and compassion will reach out with God's love.

To rightly (biblically) accept separated singles, a few questions must be answered. Do you view the needs of the separated as urgent and important? Do you view them as people to be reached with the Gospel right where they are? We must remember Jesus' response to the woman at the well in John 4:1-26. Jesus ministered to her as she was.

Do you want to risk including separated people with marrieds, as well as never-married, divorced, and widowed persons? This is the central issue and it can be resolved by realizing that all people are welcomed into the presence of Jesus. The church belongs to Him and His welcome sign is out.

Goals for Separated People

Help the separated person pursue a reconciliation with his or her mate. This cannot be manipulated. Often a separated person does not even wish to consider this. It is a process. We must offer biblical counsel and encouragement. Help the separated person avoid romantic or emotional relationships. Urge them to wait by impressing on them the need to consider a reconciliation as foremost. Share the need to wait, to deal with hurts, feelings, and needs before becoming involved in a relationship. Recovery takes time.

Help the separated person to focus on a relationship with Jesus Christ.

Christ is the way to wholeness and security (Pss. 37:4; 147:3 and Matt. 6:33). He is the One who has promised to bring gentleness to the heart and lighten the burden (Matt. 11:28-30).

Recommend books, tapes, and counselors. These are often provisions that help bring healing and hope back into the life of one who is in great need.

When divorce is inevitable, accept that fact and point the separated person toward the help that is needed.

Each situation is unique and one must listen to each person to understand his or her special needs. We are to bring God's love to hurting people so that His healing can lift and restore and set the course for new hope and new life (Ezek. 34:1-31).

Bud and Kathy Pearson
Bud is a Senior Pastor
Orange Coast Community Church, Orange, California

Bud and Kathy authored the book, *Single Again,* Regal Books. Bud is the former singles pastor at the Crystal Cathedral in Garden Grove, California.

9. SINGLES—THE FORMERLY MARRIED

"Most important, many formerly married are people in transition, wandering for the most part in a no-man's land without a map of the territory, searching for support, guidelines, and wisdom."

William White

Statistics and Trends

In 1960 the percentage of those divorced in the United States was 2.3. Divorce has steadily increased. The National Center for Health Statistics reported 2,425,000 new marriages in 1985 (down 62,000 from 2,487,000 in 1984); and 1,187,000 divorces in 1985 (up 32,000 from 1,155,000 in 1984). Based on these figures, the prediction is that by 1990 or earlier the percentage of those divorced will rise to 12 percent. As the chart indicates, there will also be more single adults than there will be married adults. There doesn't seem to be much on the horizon to reverse the trend.

Who Are the Formerly Married?

Formerly married people are people of all ages, including those in their late and mid-teens, with various backgrounds, vocations, incomes, and values. They are people who have differing religious persuasions. The intensity of their commitment to those beliefs determines to a large extent their ability to cope with loss. The more commitment, the more resources available; hence, the more effective the coping. They are people who are "single by decree." They have been before a judge or affected by a court's decision. Lawyers and judges have been involved in their lives. These professionals usually see and treat marriage as an economic partnership rather than one motivated and controlled by love and commitment. Formerly marrieds are people, having been separated from once-loving relationships, who are at different stages of their adjustment to loss. Those stages range anywhere between the time of divorce to time of recovery, remarriage, or on into retirement years. Some are raising children and teenagers in single-parent homes (custodial parent) and from a distance (noncustodial parent). This causes constant stress for some because of the continual contact with the former spouse as they comply with visitation rights. Some have been married and divorced more than once. As a consequence, if children are

Marital Status in U.S.

In Percent

Prediction

	1970	1980	1985	1990
Divorced	3.2 (4.3 mil.)	6.2 (9.9 mil.)	7.6 (13.1 mil.)	12.2
Widowed	8.9	8.0	7.9	7.8
Married	71.7	65.5	63	49.9
Never Married	16.2	20.3	21.5	30.1

involved, they may not be related in the traditional sibling relationships. This poses a unique and challenging setting of half brothers and half sisters. Most important, many formerly married are people in transition, wandering for the most part in a no-man's land without a map of the territory, searching for support, guidelines, and wisdom.

What Are Their Needs, Feelings, and Actions?

The needs, feelings, and actions of those formerly married vary, as one would expect, from individual to individual. However, there seem to be in most adjustments some common needs and feelings related to the (1) early weeks and months after the divorce, (2) the first two years, and (3) time after two years. The distinctions are not hard-and-fast, however, and one may vacillate within the structure.

In the early weeks, formerly married people are facing a crisis and are needing "now" time. They are in desperate need of and are looking for support. During this time irregular behavior may be obvious. Buying unneeded things, running up a high credit bill, and forgetting appointments would be just a few. They are coping (some better than others) with loneliness. (This is a constant throughout the adjustment.) They are struggling during this time with blame and anger. They are having a difficult time with their identities. If children are involved, they are straining with whatever energy is left (which isn't much) to relate in new ways to their children. There is a constant inner nagging put there by the question: Will my children be able to handle all this?

As time passes other issues begin to emerge, if they haven't already. If a formerly married person is a Christian, he or she may be searching for forgiveness (either from God, or quite possibly from himself or herself, friends, or even from a former spouse). It should be noted, however, that forgiveness is for those who are guilty. Many tried their best (some biblically and spiritually) to keep their marriages together but, without cooperation from the spouse (or others), it didn't work out. Therefore, they feel guilty. But the question is, what are they guilty of? They are also searching for answers to the biblical issues involved. What does the Bible really say about marriage, divorce, and remarriage? This is a marvelous opportunity for the singles ministry.

During this time, formerly married people are working through adjustments to transition and change, and the stigma of divorce and being single again. They feel like Hester Prynne in Nathaniel Hawthorne's *The Scarlet Letter*, wearing instead of the "A" a big "D," which they feel everyone notices. They are learning to live within a changed budget. For the majority, that means less. It would be helpful if church boards and committees could be aware of this as they plan events that cost money. Divorced people are attempting to answer the question: Who am I now that I'm no longer in a marriage? They are striving to let go of or hang on to their marriages. For many there is little chance of reconciliation (the former spouse has remarried or left the scene), but still some are holding on to the idea that the former spouse will be back. The question then becomes: How long is long? There is no easy, clear answer here. But at some point, after possibilities have been explored, one must quit the marriage and move on. There is the possibility that some will find restitution and reconciliation and possibly be remarried. This can and does happen by God's mercy and grace.

At some point in these months, formerly married people are leaving past relationships and developing new ones. There may be some conflict involved in holding on to past relationships. The question between those formerly married is: Who gets "custody" of friends? As with children, one spouse can turn former friends against the other with their blaming and accusations. The development of new relationships requires resurrecting or developing relational skills. Divorced people are also acquiring ways to deal with their former spouses and in-laws. In all this adjustment many formerly married people are reviewing their present value systems and quite possibly establishing new ones.

As time passes, beyond two years after the divorce, things are settling down. Things are beginning to focus again. Most of the hate and bitterness has begun to subside or is gone. Dating, though still not without its problems, might become a part of life. If marriage hasn't happened it is almost a foregone conclusion that it has been thought about. This is a period for some to start establishing and meeting new goals. Some decide to start school; others begin saving for a big purchase; still others may plan a vacation; and yet others may begin a satisfying hobby that could even provide some income. There is a settling into a single lifestyle. By now, singleness is accepted as reality and most can look in the mirror and say with some sense of confidence, "It's OK to be single."

Some Conclusions

It is obvious from what has been presented that formerly married people are unique in their adjustment to transition and have some specific needs that are similar to others who have suffered loss and yet different because of their past histories and individuality.

These are some things of which we can be relatively sure: the population of formerly married will continue to rise; formerly married people are people in transition and in need of support; and there are some effective, proven ways tò be that support.

William A. White
Editor at Warner Press
Anderson, Indiana

Bill is a formerly married single who has had an extensive ministry in the local church as a layman with single adults. He has been a national leader, speaking at workshops, conventions, retreats, and conferences and is a charter member of NSL.

10. SINGLE PARENTS

> *"The single parent is a disciplinarian, cook, teacher,
> nurse, handyman, maid, mediator, program director, coun-
> selor, nurturer, and pastor to the children. Obviously, it
> may be difficult to wear all those hats."*
>
> Jim & Barbara Dycus

Who is a single parent? Well, obviously it is a single adult who is a parent! But that's not really definitive enough to design a program of ministry. Mother Goose is a bit more definitive:

> There was an old woman who lived in a shoe,
> She had so many children she didn't know what to do.
> She gave them some broth without any bread,
> She whipped them all soundly, and sent them to bed!

These four lines from a well-known nursery rhyme characterize one single parent.

This single parent is a she. She had housing problems, financial problems, discipline problems, and an overload of stress which had left her emotionally drained in her parenting responses. Today she might even be labeled an abusive parent!

In order for us to know whether this is a good profile, we need to take a closer look at who today's single parents are.

Defining Today's Single Parent

It is predicted today that by 1990 less than one third of all families will be the traditional one-home, two parents, two kids, and a dog kind of home.

The 1982 census gave us some amazing statistics regarding the single parent.

There were 6,839,000 single-parent households in the United States. Mothers were the heads of 6,147,000 of these homes. Divorced mothers numbered 2,841,000, 1,548,000 were separated, 1,168,000 were never married, and 590,000 were widowed.

Fathers headed 692,000 single-parent homes; 386,000 fathers were divorced, 88,000 widowed, 68,000 never married, and 150,000 were separated.

Seven million one-parent homes represent a lot of unique situations. If we add the approximate 4-5 million parents without custody, we discover we are attempting to minister to approximately 12 million single parents. That sounds like a herculean task, doesn't it?

We need to take a closer look at these people. Take the example of the old woman in the shoe. If she were divorced, she would have additional issues to deal with that the widow doesn't. And if she were separated, it would not have helped to treat her as though she were a never-married single parent.

Divorced parents. The greatest majority of single parents are parents who have divorced. More than 1 ½ million divorces occur annually in the United States, and approximately 70 percent of these involve children. The single parent experiencing divorce must deal with the pain divorce causes in both his own and his child's life; at a time when the pain is most acute and many times without an adequate support system to help. Our ministry has to be twofold: we have to help "dry the tears" (cope with their responses to the pain), but we also have to help ferret out and discover the real source of the pain.

Widowed parents. Death is an unwelcome guest in any family. But it brings with it a permanence that is a tangible focus point for the family to move ahead in setting goals for family life.

Widowed parents will grieve the loss just as the family of divorce. But grief will move the family to recovery without the recurrence of that loss. The family of divorce may have compounded pain because it deals with flesh and blood—"living loss"—not "dead loss."

Never-married parents. This nontraditional group of parents has grown in number and social acceptance during recent years. Yet, it has its special loss to deal with too. If the old woman in the shoe were a never-married parent, would that knowledge elicit different reactions from you than if she were a widow? Attitudes of judgment on a person's past must be dealt with by all of us.

Adoptive single parents. This is a newer phenomenon of which little has been made known. But, they are also special people to be included, supported, encouraged, and honored.

Single parents without custody. While this group of parents is smaller than the previous groups we mentioned, their loss is many times greater. It is family life itself that they have lost. Whether that be by personal choice or not, they have a loss to deal with. It would be unfair to lump them all together into one predictable profile. Their special circumstances are as varied as the colors of their dresses or suits. The great majority of these parents are dealing with divorce, the "living loss," and the focus for their lives is how to implement divorce between the parents without experiencing "divorce" within the parental relationship.

Single parents with shared (joint) custody. Many divorcing parents today are opting for a form of shared or joint custody. These parents will need to make their own unique adaptations to this form of family life.

What Are the Special Needs of Single Parents?

Knowing the needs of single parents helps us design ministry to meet their needs. Perhaps the greatest need of all single parents is developing the capacity to look ahead! But that is difficult to do when things behind or to the side have grasped the attention.

What did the woman in the shoe need most? Baby-sitter, new job, bigger house, more money, counselor, or disciplinarian expert for the kids? All of these would help, but she needed the ability to look ahead! To be able to set goals and objectives for her life and her family's life, which would give her the thread to stitch her ripped-apart family back together.

She needed to believe Jeremiah 29:11: " 'For I know the plans I have for you,' declares the Lord, 'plans to prosper you and not to harm you, plans to give you hope and a future.' "

Needs of single-parent mothers. Female-headed single parent families are the fastest growing group of families in the United States today. Current statistics indicate that this group is growing 2 ½ times faster than traditional husband/wife families.

What are the special needs of the single-parent mother? Perhaps we can understand her needs by looking at her responsibilities. The single-parent mother is disciplinarian, cook, teacher, nurse, handyman, maid, mediator, program director, counselor, nurturer, and pastor to her children. Obviously, it may be difficult to wear all those hats. Statistics point up some of her needs:

● The median income of the female-head-of-household is one half that of male-headed families (U.S. Dept. of Labor, 1980).

● While 80 percent of all mothers with custody have been awarded child support, only 47 percent receive full support, 27 percent receive partial support (usually less than one half), and 26 percent receive no support at all (U.S. Census, 1983).

● There are over 100,000 custody battles per year within the court system. (Many other custody battles never make it to court.)

Needs of single-parent fathers. While the single-parent father with custody may fare better than mothers, he has problems she will never face. He must provide for and still nurture his brood of children. Providing for his family comes naturally, but nurturing is a task that many fathers find they are ill-equipped to do.

Needs of both. Both mother and father share the following needs in single-parent head-of-household homes:

● Dual-role responsibilities.
● Financial differences. This includes financial problems in the home as well as job pressures and demands which create financial difficulty.
● Custodial issues. This is where the "living loss" is most acute. The pain that family members suffer in a continual custody battle paralyzes growth beyond the pain.

- Establishing effective discipline and meaningful communication within the home, and between the homes.
- Handling stress overload. The stress in single parenting precipitates a host of other problems including child abuse, physical illness, and even childnapping by the other parent.

What Are the Single Parent's Personal Challenges?

Emotional recovery from the loss. In order to recover emotionally, the parent will need to deal with issues such as: understanding grief, letting go, forgiveness, dealing with depression, loneliness, accepting change, and diffusing anger.

Adjustment to singleness. Handling sexuality, learning to build positive relationships, and becoming whole as a single are adjustment steps to singleness just like the more tangible steps of managing a home alone and providing materially for your child.

Planning for the future. Moving forward out of yesterday toward tomorrow is a challenge to the single parent. Setting goals for family life, growing as a disciple of Christ, mapping out a life management course for the family are exciting prospects for the single parent. They will aid recovery and will focus family life on positive pursuits.

These are the people called single parents to whom the Lord has given us the privilege of ministry. They are a special group of people, capable of great success beyond their loss.

God's Word says, "He [God] has also set eternity in the hearts of men; yet they cannot fathom what God has done from beginning to end" (Ecc. 3:11). Knowledge that God knows, cares, and can make sense of all the change can become one of the key foundation stones for coping. The church, with God's Word and God's people, can be the bridge!

Jim and Barbara Dycus
Jim is Director of Ministry to Single-Parent Families
Calvary Assembly of God, Winter Park, Florida
Barbara is a free-lance writer and workshop leader

Jim and Barbara have been pioneers in developing one of the first programs in the church ministering to the entire single-parent family.

11. CHILDREN OF SINGLE PARENTS

"It is important to remember that one-parent families cannot be stereotyped. These families differ in motivation, resources, opportunities, and, especially, past circumstances. There is mounting evidence that these families can be viable, healthy, growing families."

Carolyn Koons

The American Family: For Better or Worse

Single parenting was the focus of a special issue of *Newsweek* in July 1985, stating that "by 1990 half of all American families may be headed by only one adult" (a single parent). The reality is that single-parent households have already exceeded the 50 percent mark in major cities. Nationally, one out of four households with children is headed by a single parent. The impact on society is only now being measured, but the trend is already redefining our concept of the all-American family.

A variety of circumstances bring about the single-parent household. The death of a parent is an unexpected loss, traumatic for a child as well as the remaining adult. Divorce is a second circumstance, bringing with it a painful and unique set of problems, confusion, and anger for the child and custodial and non-custodial parents. An increasing number of unwed mothers creates single-parent households as more women choose to keep their children rather than considering abortion or adoption. And then there are literally hundreds of thousands of older, often racially mixed or handicapped children who are being adopted by healthy, happy singles starting their own families. It is important to understand the diverse circumstances of single-parent homes as each has highly different emotional needs and motivations.

Assumptions of Single-Parent Families and the Children

Most groups within society carry with them certain assumptions, and single-parent families are no exception. It is frequently assumed that because one-parent families lack a second parent, they are "inevitably dysfunctional." It is also commonly assumed that many of the families' needs go unmet, or at least are poorly met, when the family has only one parent. In order to dispel some of these negative assumptions, a longitudinal study was launched to look at children in several families, half of which were one-parent families and the other half were traditional two-parent families. Researchers monitored the children's emotional and social growth, adjustments in school with peers, and relationships with family members. The interesting result was that the researchers could find no significant difference between those children raised in one-parent families and the children raised in two-parent families. The healthy adjustment of the children was connected with the *quality of parenting* in each group. They found children under tremendous stress, failing in school, showing emotional and social problems where the parents were neglecting the children, or not modeling good parenting. This was the case in two-parent families as well as one-parent families. In conclusion, it was not just the number of parents present in the home but the quality of parenting that made the difference.

Current studies of single-parent families are indicating that children in healthy single parent homes are actually beginning to excel over children in traditional homes in the areas of "individual decision-making" and "ability to work alone on a project or problem." This may be true because the children do not have two parents to go to or make decisions for them.

It is important to remember that one-parent families cannot be stereotyped. These families differ in motivation, resources, opportunities, and especially past circumstances. There is mounting evidence that these families can be viable, healthy, growing families.

The Effects of Divorce and Loss on Children: The Children Suffer Too

Divorce is a serious and complicated experience facing children today. The special problems and needs of children of divorced parents have received relatively little professional attention. There is no question that broken marriages inflict trauma and a series of crises on millions of children each year. It is important for us to understand the broad impact divorce has on parents and children.

Some determining factors in the child's adjustment following the divorce include the environment before and after the crisis, the circumstances of the crisis, and the emotional characteristics of the parents. Most children make healthy adjustments within a few years following the divorce, but the time of transition and adjustment is often quite traumatic.

There are certain characteristics associated with this period of adjustment. The response to the divorce varies according to the age of the child and the conditions surrounding the divorce. It was assumed that the younger the child, the more damaging the effect of the divorce. Therefore, some couples planning to divorce eventually stayed married until the children graduated from high school and left home. In studying children of divorced parents, the younger children went through trauma and showed signs of stress, but after a couple of years they appeared quite adjusted to this new single-parent lifestyle.

Some of the characteristics associated with the response of younger children vary with their age. Children, ages 1-3, sense stress and tension in their world. Everything seems fuzzy and doesn't make sense to them.

They can become fearful, ill, or show loss of appetite. At ages 4-6, children begin to withdraw, become silent, timid. They may have trouble sleeping, may be grumpy, and may retreat into fantasy. Elementary school children, ages 7-11, may show their reaction to the divorce by their grades dropping, having trouble sleeping, daydreaming, denial, aggressive and hostile behavior. They may feel guilty, thinking that somehow the divorce must be their fault.

The greatest adjustment and trauma of divorce seems to be impacting the older high school and college-age children. Being older, they understand the reality of the loss of the relationships, and the tensions and adjustments surrounding the decision to divorce. Special care and counseling need to be given to teenagers and young adult children of divorce.

Following are some predominant problem areas and characteristics of children of divorce.

It's their fault. The number one issue with children is that they are very confused about what is going on. They are often not told about the divorce until it happens, and because they have often sparked or been in the middle of arguments, they overwhelmingly feel that somehow it is their fault that the divorce has occurred. It is extremely important that parents sit down and explain the situation, and own their own responsibility for the dissolution of the relationship.

Grief. Divorce brings depression and a time of grief will follow, as if a death had occurred. It is often expected that the parents will go through this grief cycle, but it is important to recognize that the children will need to go through the same process. They will need help along the way.

Anger. Anger is a normal and painful part of the divorce process. The children feel cheated. They feel they deserve a normal life, and somehow this has been taken away from them. They feel anger against the parent who left and the parent who stayed. And they may show anger against God for not keeping their family together.

Abandonment, rejection, fear. One parent has left; are they not loved? Will the other parent leave too? They are afraid, and many questions arise internally that set off a chain of insecurities. Who will protect me? Who will take care of me? More than ever the child needs continual assurance that someone will continue to care for him.

Powerlessness. The children often watch the divorce play out before them and realize they have no control over the situation. They are powerless and have a tremendous sense of helplessness. They try desperately to get the parents back together, yet there is nothing they can do.

Decisions and choices. The children are hurt, confused, and frustrated. Decisions and choices may be difficult for them to make during this period. This is not the time for them to feel pressure to choose between parents or where to live. It will be difficult for them just to choose what clothing to wear today.

Sense of rootlessness. Divorce brings change, not only in the marital status and family living arrangements, but in areas that impact the well-being of the family and stability of the children. This rootlessness sometimes influences logistics: Where are we going to live? What school will we attend? Rootlessness affects education, and for a couple of years the children may not do well in school. Rootlessness also reflects economic changes: less income, new jobs, or perhaps going on welfare to survive. This sense of rootlessness may affect children socially as to how they adjust and relate to others.

Warning Points
Most children, to one degree or the other, will display some of the previous characteristics. Through these painfully tough times of adjustment, most children will recover and live healthy, productive, challenging lives. On the other hand, some children may become locked in this tumultuous time, which may cause emotional problems in their childhood and later in their adult lives. Anyone who has lost one of his parents as a child is more likely to experience some form of emotional problem later in life. Therefore, it is important that these warnings be recognized early and professional help sought.

Most single parents do not recognize the relationship between the crisis experience and their child's behavior. Once the cause of the behavior has been established it becomes easier to work toward a healthy solution. The warning points are: regressions (caused by guilt and anger); continual headaches or stomachaches; suffering in schoolwork; daydreaming; change in behavior and moods (withdrawal or aggressive behavior and fighting); disobedience and moodiness; lethargy (no energy, always weak or tired); driven desire for physical contact (clinging); inability to function in a group; and diminished self-esteem.

Children may experience a few of these characteristics, to some degree. If they are displaying too many of them, too long, with too much intensity, professional child and family counseling and therapy may be indicated.

Helps for Children of Divorce
Talk. The best therapy for children of divorce is open and honest communication. Get them to talk! Talking alleviates guilt.
Relationship-building. Build relationships within the family, among relatives, and with close friends.
Comfort. Give comfort and understanding.
Admit struggles. As a single parent, don't try to have all the answers. Sometimes it is good to let your children know that you too have questions and struggles, so that they do not feel they are alone.
Love. Love them. This is the most consistent and greatest gift we can give children of divorce.
Include. The church needs to rethink its traditional views and models of the family so that they do not eliminate single-parent children. The church

needs to offer special single-parent seminars geared to the specialized needs of this group. Help single parents be a part of the family—the church family and individual families.

Single-parent families are viable, growing, and contributing families. They require a lot of work and support.

Carolyn Koons
Executive Director for the Institute for Outreach Ministries
Azusa Pacific University, Azusa, California

Carolyn is the single parent of her adopted son, Tony. She is the author of the bestseller, *Tony, Our Journey Together,* and *Beyond Betrayal,* Harper and Row.

12. SINGLES—THE NONCHURCHED

"Most nonchurched singles do not differ much from church-attending singles in their basic need and desire to have meaningful relationships. The difference, many would argue, is in the establishing, nurturing, and depth of those relationships."

Georgia Coates

The average nonchurched single is *not* a low-life, love-'em-and-leave-'em, druggy gang member! He or she more likely drives a sporty Toyota, wears preppy clothes, goes to T.G.I. Fridays where he hopes to socialize with friends and work associates, and develop a relationship for a sexual encounter, new friendship, or a potential mate. By the "world's" standard these singles would be "honest," good people with life goals, responsible jobs, a close circle of at least a few friends, and avid viewers of the "Cosby Show" and "Cheers."

Does this sound vaguely like the average church-attending single that you know? It probably does. Whether white-collar, blue-collar or "new-collar," the average unchurched single adult is just like most of us. They too are searching for a comfortable level of happiness, success, intimacy, security, and the all-American quality of life. And like all of us they experience disappointments, problems at work, pain, and selfishness.

Plight of the Nonchurched

In America most people have *some* experience or exposure to the church. Taking a look at the "church" through the eyes of a non-Christian, nonchurched single we see many misconceptions but also judgments based on bad experiences. Sadly, many singles interviewed had gone to church at some point but had not personally accepted Christ. Others had only "visited" a few times. Yet both groups felt that they had "tried church" and some did not want to return. One successful single woman, fairly satisfied with her life and relationships, said, "I attended a church; I even went to their singles group. The people I met were friendly but very superficial. In the singles class, they were discussing some issues in small groups. Though I tried to interject some questions I had, they just wanted to talk about themselves and the problems they were having. When I left there I longed to be back with my other [non-Christian] friends who seemed more interested in things that really matter and in finding answers, not in dwelling on themselves!"

Several others had comments like this young, urban, professional man. Though "yuppie" is now a passé term, this person would fit the description. When asked about Christians he had met at work he said, "We try to be nice to them. We ask them to join us for a drink after work, and it's not like they *have* to order alcohol, but they won't come with us. They keep to their little 'clique' and read their Bibles at lunch rather than join us in the staff room."

Looking for Relationships
Most nonchurched singles do not differ much from church-attending singles in their basic need and desire to have meaningful relationships. The difference, many would argue, is in the establishing, nurturing, and depth of those relationships.

Books on relationships are by far the fastest-selling nonfiction hot item! According to publishing statistics, single women are the first in line at the cash register. Media, peer pressure, personal desires, and the "biological time clock" push singles in their quest.

Ticking of the Time Clocks
In addition to the "biological clock," the "matrimonial clock" is a concern of nonchurched men and women today. The "matrimonial clock" seems to tick loudest when they attend the weddings of friends or read inflammatory statistical "evidence" which echoes mothers and aunts who have reminded them, "You're not getting any younger, Dear." Both of these clocks seem to tick loudest in the dark apartment at three in the morning. They advise against waiting, warn against choosiness, and caution that the world does not offer infinite possibilities. They instruct that not choosing is a choice and that inaction is an action.

Will I Ever Get Married?
Paul C. Glick, an eminent demographer predicted a 1980s "marriage squeeze" in 1959. In 1970, for every 100 women ages 20 to 24, there were only 67 men ages 22 to 26. By 1985, for every 100 unmarried white women aged 38 to 42, there were only 77 white men a couple of years older. *But* the sex ratio had roughly evened out for white women in their early 20s. In fact, in the next decade the tables could be turned as men start to greatly outnumber women, according to William Novak in his book, *The Great American Male Shortage.*

Where and Who Do They Meet?
Cosmopolitan magazine surveyed 65,000 women readers on where they meet people they date, and the following are some statistics from their findings:
- 42 percent meet at parties or get-togethers with friends
- 31 percent meet at work

- 26 percent meet at singles "hang-outs"
- 18 percent meet at classes or clubs
- 2 percent used personal ads or blind dates
- Those surveyed said men seem to be less romantic today than "old-fashioned men," and they missed it.
- 81 percent of the women said that the men they meet are still playing the field and enjoying it (as compared to 36 percent of the women).
- 44 percent of couples said that most squabbles are over how leisure time is spent and disagreements over money matters came in a close second at 42 percent.
- 30 percent of those dating said that their men don't have close male friends and 37 percent said that the men were often jealous of close relationships between female friends of the women they date (Claudia Bowen, "What Are Men Like Today: Survey Results," May 1986, pp. 263-268).

The "Me" Generation

Making commitments is a difficult concept for many baby-boomers. Marriage, which provides the intimacy that most singles crave, carries also self-sacrifice and responsibilities. This short-circuits the individual freedom and self-expression of the "me" generation.

Most nonchurched singles, even those divorced, still cling to the belief that marriage is the ideal and they expect and desire a marriage to last forever. Yet the vast majority of nonchurched singles interviewed were critical of their parents' relationships, even though most of them were still together after 30 or 40 years. "My parents are non-intimate companions. I want more than that!"

The Perennial Adolescent

Some experts link this narcissistic attitude to the emergence of a new breed of unmarried adults: the perennial adolescent. This syndrome tends to afflict educated urban singles who refuse to face the psychological and financial demands of growing up. Psychologist Dan Kiley called it "the Peter Pan Syndrome." "Maybe I'm a victim of arrested development," says a 32-year-old TV executive. "But I don't feel old enough to be married. Right now, I just want to concentrate on my career and enjoy my life."

"Traditionally, two earmarks of adolescence are the beliefs that time is limitless and choices are unnecessary," says Dr. Ava Siegler, a psychotherapist who specializes in adolescent psychology. "Many singles in their 30s have adopted that same attitude. In the past, there were certain developmental tasks, like marriage and child-rearing, that signaled one's adulthood. But in today's urban culture, it's acceptable to postpone those tasks for as long as possible" (Patricia Morrisoe, "Forever Single," *New York*, Aug. 20, 1984, pp. 24-31).

I'll Think about That Tomorrow

This "Scarlett O'Hara" attitude came through in the actions of a non-Christian single. After confessing that she had had a long relationship with a bisexual man, she was asked if she thought she should be tested for AIDS. "No, I'm afraid of what the results might be!" Even with this suspicion, she continues to have intimate relations with her current boyfriend, refusing to tell him of her past. This, "I'll think about that tomorrow," response relieved her of any responsibility toward herself and her boyfriend, at least for the moment.

The Church's View of Singles

A study conducted in 1957 revealed that 53 percent of the American public believed that single people were "sick," "immoral," or "neurotic." The '50s proved to be the most family oriented decade of the century, with 96 percent of the childbearing population married. Yet, this social condition has dramatically changed since then and so should the church's view of singles. *Unchurched* singles today are not only non-Christians living immoral, rebellious, godless lives, but also includes many PKs (Pastor's Kids), those raised "in the church," and "practicing Christians" who, for various reasons, are not attending a local church.

A Prodigal Son of the Church

A survey was taken among singles who were actively involved in a church singles group. They were asked if there had ever been a time, after they had become Christians and had been growing in their faith, when they stopped attending church. If so, why, how long, etc. About half said that they fell away from the church for a time. Most, *but not all of them,* felt that they had also fallen away from God's pleasure.

One man, who admitted that he had eventually walked away from God, said that he first left the church because he didn't "fit in" as a single. After a broken engagement he was shattered and angry. He felt awkward and out of place in his church where most of the couples had expected him to get married "to such a nice Christian girl" and join their "couples group." There were very few other singles in his church and none of them were close friends. Lonely and frustrated, he stopped attending.

It was several years until he began to regularly attend a church where he found an active singles group and a warm acceptance of single men and women. "A prodigal son (of the church)" came home to a warm welcome.

Georgia S. Coates
Founder and Director of Christian Singles United
San Diego Evangelical Association, San Diego, California

Georgia has ministered with Campus Crusade for Christ for 15 years and helped pioneer a singles ministry in London, England. She is actively involved in the business community as an effective witness for her faith in Christ.

13. SINGLES IN THE CHURCH

*"Adults who happen to be single are not more important
than any other group in the church, but they are as important.
They are not in a 'hallway' unto marriage but in a 'living'
room full of potential and possibilities."*

William White

Singles in the church are *adults who happen to be single,* similar in many
ways to adults who happen to be married. So, as we speak of singles we
are addressing ourselves to adults, within an age bracket that spans out-of-
high school to the oldest person in the congregation, who happen to be
either never married, separated, divorced, or widowed.

These adult singles are perceived in many different ways by married
adults. Within the church, singles who have never married are sometimes
perceived as nice people but who have something wrong with them or they
would be married. If they are at the younger end of the age bracket, they
are usually perceived in a "hallway" unto marriage, and it will just be a
matter of time before they will be married. A divorced woman usually fits
into the category of one who is available and often a threat, particularly to
a married woman who doesn't feel secure about her marriage. A divorced
man might be seen as somewhat untrustworthy and who, in some ways,
shows a lack of responsibility.

Divorced people are sometimes viewed as "sinners," out of the will of
God. A widow receives support (which sometimes comes across as pity),
but only for a short time because she is soon forgotten and expected to get
on with her life. Even though she is single with honor, she is now different
and often difficult to communicate with because of lack of skills on the part
of married friends. A widower, on the other hand, is seen as one who can
take care of himself. He probably has (or can acquire) some financial base
so that he has that sense of security. However, a "good woman" would
help. (If a congregation is large enough there may be one or two who feel
it their "gift" to be matchmakers, pairing widow with widower.) Those
who happen to be single after having been married more than once are
viewed with some suspicion. They are seen as unsettled and/or unaware of
the meaning of commitment. They are sometimes viewed as prone to take
the easy way out.

Not every married person recognizes adult singles in these ways, but it
seems to many singles that those who do outnumber those who don't.

How does all this make singles feel? The following words surfaced (as a majority opinion) from a group of singles of all ages and circumstances in Florida at a retreat. They responded to the question: How do you feel you are perceived in your local church? The responses were, "Isolated, necessary evil, ignored, irresponsible, fifth wheel, second-class citizen, judged, overworked, and overused." A small minority, however, did feel accepted, supported, listened to, and had a sense of "family." So, we can assume that not all churches are alike in how they perceive single adults. However, far too many churches help singles feel negatively about who they are.

So, single adults with whom God has called us to minister are probably feeling a bit negative about who they are and where they fit into the scheme of things in the local church. Ministry to and *with* them will blossom when:

(1) They are seen as adults of all ages and circumstances and growing in number.

(2) They are perceived as adults searching to identify their gifts and talents and for a place to share them in the body of Christ. (One pastor I know commented that the singles in the church he serves were "pacesetters" in sharing their gifts and talents.)

(3) Those who are Christians are seen as "ministers" capable of serving on program committees and administrative boards.

(4) The single lifestyle is accepted as valid and normal, realizing that for whatever reason some single adults will remain single for the rest of their lives, and that's OK.

(5) It is discovered that they are adults trying to put their singleness in spiritual perspective and find their completeness in God.

(6) It is recognized that they are adults trying to come to terms with some of the misconceptions about their singleness (not normal, odd, and so on).

(7) It is discovered that they are adults who are community members ready to contribute to those communities something of themselves to make their lives count.

(8) They are recognized as adults who may or may not be committed Christians.

The ministry and mission to adults who happen to be single (which is the same to adults who happen to be married) is to: proclaim the Gospel to all persons, nurture Christian growth in all persons in their individual situations, and equip all persons for servanthood. Each person, as well as each group, has some general needs common to most and some very specific needs that are uniquely theirs. Local churches would do well to work out a balance here. Program planning boards need to make sure plans are made with both singles and marrieds in mind. Adults who happen to be single are not more important than any other group in the church, but they are as important. They are not in a "hallway" unto marriage but in a "living" room full of potential and possibilities, which may or may not have an entrance leading to marriage but has many doors that lead to ministry.

Single adults are adults. They are single. They are in the church of Jesus Christ. We must see them as God sees them—His children and ministers of the Gospel message.

William A. White
Editor at Warner Press
Anderson, Indiana

As a single adult active in the local church, Bill has also had an extensive ministry with various Christian organizations. He has also led numerous workshops on singles ministry in many churches from coast to coast.

14. SENIOR ADULT SINGLES

*"Senior adult years can be the most rewarding years for
many men and women if loss and grief are acknowledged as
normal and are addressed initially in the ministry to the
senior adult single."*

Dan Lundblad

As disciples of Jesus Christ and ministers of His Gospel message, it is not
so uncommon to hear statistics regarding the dramatic increase of senior
adults in our society today. It is also not so uncommon to hear of churches
developing specialized ministries to the increasing numbers of senior adults
that have been part of the church family for many years. Seminars on
aging, fellowship opportunities for seniors in our church, and the development of retirement communities across the country attest to this fact. The
new development in our churches today is the awareness that the senior
adult who is single comprises approximately 37 percent of the 28.5 million
persons 65 years or older. Who are these 10.5 million men and women? If
God has called us to minister to the senior adult single as well as the
younger single adult, how are we to meet this challenge? What are the
similarities and unique needs of the senior adult who has never married, is
widowed, or is divorced?

Statistics
A Profile of Older Americans (1986) was recently prepared by the American Association of Retired Persons (AARP) and the Administration on
Aging (AOA), U.S. Department of Health and Human Services. They
found that people 65 years or older, married and single, numbered 28.5
million in 1985. They represented 12 percent of the U.S. population.

The number of older Americans increased by 2.8 million or 11 percent
since 1980, compared to an increase of 4 percent for the under-65 population. From 1900 to 1985, the percentage of Americans 65-plus has tripled
from 4.1 percent to 12 percent; i.e., from 3.1 million to 28.5 million.

The older population is expected to continue to grow in the future. This
growth will slow down somewhat during the 1990s because of the relatively small number of babies born during the Great Depression of the 1930s.
The most rapid increase is expected between the years 2010 and 2030
when the "baby-boom" generation reaches age 65.

By 2030, there will be about 65 million older persons; that is, two and
one half times their number in 1980. If current fertility and immigration

levels remain stable, the only age-groups to experience significant growth in the next century will be those past age 55.

By the year 2000, persons 65-plus are expected to represent 13 percent of the population, and this percentage may climb to 21.2 percent by 2030.

Specific Statistics of the Senior Adult Single

In 1985, older men were twice as likely to be married as older women (77 percent of men, 40 percent of women). Half of all older women in 1985 were widows (51 percent). There were over five times as many widows (8 million) as widowers (1.5 million).

In 1985 divorced people represented only 4 percent of the number of older persons. However, numbers of those divorced increased nearly four times as fast as the entire older population did in the preceding 10 years.

About 30 percent (8.1 million) of all non-institutionalized older persons in 1985 lived alone (6.5 million women, 1.6 million men). They represented 41 percent of older women and 15 percent of older men. Older people living alone increased in number by 64 percent between 1970 and 1985, about one and one half times the growth rate for the older population in general.

These statistics emphasize the necessity for the local congregation to expand its vision to meet the needs of the senior adults, especially single senior adults. What needs should be considered before launching a ministry to the senior adult single?

Meeting the Needs of the Senior Adult Single

Psychologists tell us that all humans are born with one overriding purpose: to survive. Beyond survival, we have the potential to grow and develop our spiritual, intellectual, social, and psychological selves. Growing older challenges one's ability to survive, and thus it impacts the potential to live fully. A normal part of the aging process is loss, so people have to successfully work through the various stages of grief.

Losses include:
• children moving away from home
• death of a spouse or close friends
• retirement
• decreased health
• decreased financial resources
• lack of purpose in living
• inability to contribute to community spirit
• loss of pride

These various losses bring about change at a time when change is more difficult to handle.

Addressing the issues of loss and grief does not imply that ministry to the senior adult single is characterized by comforting the bereaved until the time of their own death. On the contrary, the senior adult years can be the most rewarding years for many men and women *if* loss and grief are acknowledged as normal and are addressed initially in the ministry to the senior adult single.

The study of human behavior has shown that men and women are able to reach their potential by satisfying three basic needs:

- to belong and be loved
- to learn
- to contribute

The ministry to senior adult singles must acknowledge these basic needs.

To belong and be loved. Older persons have the need to be significant to someone else. The loss of their "significant other" by death or divorce leaves an emptiness that can be met by a single adult ministry. Involvement in various programs gives the senior adult single someplace to belong so the need for intimacy can be met.

To learn. Retirement and/or a change in lifestyle because of death or divorce, provides the senior adult with a valuable resource that seems to be in short supply during years of working and raising a family. That resource is *time*. The senior adult now has the time to satisfy the basic need of learning more about his world through reading, studying, and traveling.

To contribute. Comfortable feelings, a sense of belonging, significance to others, knowledge about one's surroundings, and contributing to meaningful, purposeful, tangible projects all complete the cycle of belonging—learning—contributing. This enhances a person's self-esteem.

Specific Needs

The single senior adult who has never been married needs acceptance from the church body as being a "whole" person and not a "half" person because he has not been married. He also needs acknowledgment that singleness is not a status to be pitied but is a gift with options for ministry within the body of believers.

Also the senior adult single needs acceptance into the fellowship of couples and their families. A sincere open door that says "welcome" must be extended to the senior adult who has never married. Whereas the widowed and divorced senior adults may have some kind of family, the never-married senior may have no family after the death of his parents. Plus, we live in a transient and mobile society where many miles may separate family members. Church equals family in their eyes.

The widowed senior adult comprises the greatest percentage of the ministry to senior adult singles. Their needs include: support at various stages of the grief process, learning creatively to use one's solitary time, encouragement so they won't feel alienated from the community they were part of when their spouse was alive, counseling in making decisions about remarriage, the opportunity to share their story with others in a support group for their healing and for encouragement to others recently widowed, and the opportunity for service where their efforts will be acknowledged and appreciated.

The divorced senior adult used to be a rarity; however, with their numbers increasing over four times as fast as the older population as a whole, attention must be focused on their special needs which include:

- learning to forgive
- understanding one's anger
- coping with growing older alone
- resolving the "myth" of the golden years
- dealing with the judgmental attitude of general community and family; i.e., "After all these years, why couldn't you keep the marriage together?"

Opportunities for Ministry with the Senior Adult Single

A ministry of most any size may develop support groups. Groups can be small or large. They may be structured with materials shared or unstructured for personal interaction. One-on-one may be the desired "group."

Support groups may be developed for individuals who have lost a spouse to death. Monthly meetings for fellowship and regular seminars on grief recovery will establish an environment where men and women can grow as they work through their pain. Connecting people who have grown through pain and loss with those recently widowed can be of great support.

Groups are also helpful for individuals who have experienced a divorce later in life. Involvement in a regularly scheduled divorce recovery workshop will be beneficial. Individual discussion groups for divorced senior adults will allow their special concerns to be shared. Personal support through new friendships will be invaluable.

A group can be started for individuals who are helping to care for grandchildren being raised in a single-parent family. Many women today are being asked to care for their grandchildren while their divorced son or daughter pursues employment and/or education. Basic "how tos" can help encourage the child of divorce and give the senior adult single a sense of purpose and success.

Those considering remarriage or who have already remarried need support too. Again, a course, small discussion/prayer group, or a one-on-one support group can make the difference.

Organize one-day or extended bus trips making sure the cost is kept at a minimum so everyone can take advantage of this exciting opportunity for fellowship.

Establish a ministry of lay counseling where the wisdom and maturity of senior adults can be utilized.

Facilitate senior adult singles getting together at meal times in homes, restaurants, or at church.

Develop service projects where talents and special gifts of senior adult singles can be utilized to benefit:

- Single parents involved in child care
- Grandparents
- The church body
- Missions

(Remember that contributing to others is a basic need of us all.)

Organize a "needs board" where senior adult singles can list areas where they need help, and then seek to meet these needs through the larger church body.

Five Ways to Begin Developing an Exciting Ministry to Senior Adult Singles

A key leader must serve as an enabler to a resourceful, creative committee of senior adult singles. Recruit members from all areas in never married, widowed, divorced.

Draw on the senior adult singles' vast experience to develop unique programming ideas. Ask for their opinions and take time to listen.

Foster a spirit of interdependence between older and younger segments of your single adult ministry. Don't allow a spirit of isolationism to occur within the body.

Appoint a coordinator of the senior adult singles group and develop, with them, a calendar of activities that includes time for fellowship, healing, and personal spiritual growth.

Establish outreach as a focal point of your ministry. A group that becomes ingrown or exclusive will die a slow death. A group that constantly welcomes new senior adult singles into their various programs will be characterized by excitement, commitment, and love. This is a great ministry to share the Gospel message and reach the unchurched.

God has indeed called us to minister to all people. The challenge of ministry to vast numbers of singles is indeed great. It is only with God's help and direction that we will be able to successfully meet this challenge. But we must be willing and available.

Dan Lundblad
Pastor to Single Adults and Director of The Counseling Center
Colonial Woods Missionary Church, Port Huron, Michigan

As a member of the National Association of Social Workers and The Academy of Certified Social Workers, and as a minister to singles, Dan has a broad scope of ministry experience and understanding. He is a workshop leader and author.

15. WIDOWS AND WIDOWERS

"The church must monitor and uncover the needs of the widowed. There should be a mobilizing of the membership to respond to and meet the initial needs. . . . The church and singles ministry must develop listeners and produce a climate of genuine welcome."

Robert A. Featherstone

General Characteristics of the Widowed

Grief. This is certainly the first and most obvious characteristic. The grieving time can vary in length from two months to six years. This is a period marked by vulnerability, repressed feelings, and stress. Self-sufficiency is doubted and social life is usually diminished if not totally cut off. Another evidence of the grieving process is disorganization accompanied by health risks due to a lack of personal care and a lower immunological level. There is a great need for at least one sensitive and caring friend. Each grieving person must be treated as very special, unique, and respected for their present pain.

Fears. Fears grow and develop after the loss of a mate. Fear of the unknown, financial anxieties, and fear of being unable to cope top the list of many fears. Often with the loss of a mate is the loss of "couple" friends. This loss is accompanied by a fear and alarm of detachment with a fear of rejection. The fear of isolation grows especially when one is at home ill and no one is there to help. Other fears include: fear of meeting the opposite sex, fear of violence at home or on the street, fear of making decisions.

Sex and intimacy needs. These needs represent the widowed person. Certainly there is often a lack of desire for sex during the grieving process. Yet, there is a strong need for intimacy, someone to listen, someone to understand and provide comfort. After a period of time there is a sexual vulnerability and often widows/widowers are seen as threats to other marriages. Unfortunately, even in healthy relationships, motives often become suspect. The negative fallout is that most marriages of widow/ers within 18 months of widowhood fail.

Self-pity. This is seeing self as less fortunate and more deprived. This characteristic becomes selective in memory reconstruction—forgetting the good and recalling the bad. This can attribute the lack of understanding to others. The antidote is sharing self with someone else in need.

Depression. This is to be expected to some degree. This is part of the mourning process and can be a normal part of the recovery process. But, there must be some control. One of the mistakes is seeing oneself as "half a couple" rather than a whole person. The debilitating effect is boredom and a lack of growth stimuli. There must be a plan for compensation during the "down times" and the "down places."

Anger and hostility. These are again normal, but can be harmful. The view is that the deceased "escaped," and there is a sense of great resentment. Also, there is a view that God "snatched" the loved one. This is accompanied by the same level of resentment. These feelings of rejection and resentment engender defensive stances. The result is being bogged down by new responsibilities and continued resentment for many other things and areas of life.

Money. This means net worth. But it also means self-worth to many people. The formerly married often have difficulty with finances after losing a mate. Income changes and so do expenses. Care needs to be exercised in spending habits and the use of credit. Provision of income must be determined. Insurance needs and budgets must be reevaluated. There is a great necessity for objective financial counsel.

Loneliness. This is a characteristic that requires a strategy to use it to one's advantage. One of the dangers is a loss of self-confidence and self-esteem. First the widow/er needs to separate loneliness from worthiness. Next, he/she needs to begin the journey back to self-acceptance, self-responsibility, and self-assertiveness. Indeed there can be a passive shunning by others in society that is aggressive toward high achievement so that the widow/er is left alone in the slow and quiet state of mourning.

Intrapersonal and Interpersonal Needs

Devotional life. A devotional life is needed to develop and restore a love relationship with our Lord. There is a need to return to church fellowship as soon as possible—immediately. God's love must be shared with others. The widow/er must learn to relinquish to God unfulfilled needs along with the acknowledgment of an initial time of being too stunned to have any devotional life. The single can be encouraged to read biographies of bereaved people. Singles must learn to trust God with an aggressive daily dependence.

Sharing dependencies. This sharing means diffusing one's dependencies by moving away from reliance on the former spouse and becoming more independent and self-directing. Here is where relying on "significant others" without losing self-identity is important. Participation in a loving and caring support group is most helpful. Coping skills can best be developed through a structured approach to each day.

Social contacts. These should be encouraged to increase their involvement in social support groups through the local church and other para-church organizations. Help them recognize that their new flexibility can be used to permit more socializing. They must anticipate that friends will move out of a widow/er's life. Teach and train the single to improve personal skills in communication. Help them recognize that they provide society with an unwelcome reminder of its mortality.

Lifestyle changes. These will include: being a "solo" parent, more personal discretionary time, the possibility of more or less dollars to work with, the need for new skills of managing the home, and a residence. The point is that life will now be different and change is evident. Help the single see and welcome change as a friend. Help them through their fears so that they will see the newness that God can provide.

Transitions. These will come along with changes. There is a basic transition from marital dependence to single independence and often back to dependence with another. A great deal of evaluation is required before entering into a new relationship. Mental health, emotional stability, and spiritual growth are very important before building a new relationship. The single must understand that the courtship is greatly accelerated before a second marriage. Also, there are inherent difficulties with the children being able to accept the new spouse. Often the parent can become angry at the child for being critical of the parent's choice in dating.

Family and children. There is a need to continually share the memories and experiences of the life of the deceased with each other. A "memory book" of pictures and other mementos can aid the adjustment of children and others. Family events should be encouraged along with shared events with other families and relatives. These efforts should be made in the beginning days and months after the loss. Grandparents can provide a great stabilizing role for the remaining spouse and grandchildren.

The Church's Role in Helping the Widowed

An atmosphere of awareness. The church must monitor and uncover the needs of the widowed. There should be a mobilizing of the membership to respond to and meet the initial needs beyond providing lunch at the funeral. The Christian Education Department as well as the board members should be well informed and equipped to respond. The church and singles ministry must develop listeners and produce a climate of genuine welcome.

Deacon responsibilities. Assign widow/ers to certain deacons or shepherding individuals in the church. Regular contact is essential. Communication lines need to be open to meet the many changing needs. Deacons and other care givers should receive frequent briefings and instruction on caring techniques.

Provide counseling to help the widowed. It is important to "strike that delicate balance between a yesterday that should be remembered—and a tomorrow that must be created." The singles leader and church staff will do well to learn counseling techniques for the bereaved. Also, develop a system of referral. Some need clinical and professional services to help with stress and abnormal grief. Support groups provide a great ministry to singles. Family connections can be lifesaving.

Devise a Christian ethic of the body. The body needs to recognize that God has given it a role, and that each member has a part in the healing and growing process. This includes the widow/er. The body is not to be seen as a "soul's tomb" (Plato), but an instrument linking person with reality. *Subsume special days.* Father's Day, Mother's Day, Valentine's Day, etc. can be very difficult for the remaining family members. Be sensitive! Use a broad "Family of God" emphasis. Be careful not to exclude.

Other helping roles.

- Develop a Sunday School class session or Bible study geared to the widow/ers' needs.
- Include the children in singles and church events.
- Expand your church's definition of the "family."
- Foster godly self-esteem.
- Develop a "buddy system" with other people keeping in touch with the widow/er.
- Provide a trouble "hot line" where singles can call in case of a personal emergency.
- Plan a retreat and special events just for the widow/er, as well as inclusion in other singles and church events.
- Stop using loaded words:

Not	But Rather
Alone	Individual
Uniform	Unique
Separate	Particular
Unsupported	Unattached
Isolated	Distinct

Remember God's good Word to the body of Christ. "Religion that God our Father accepts as pure and faultless is this: to look after orphans and widows in their distress and to keep oneself from being polluted by the world" (James 1:27).

Robert A. Featherstone
Retired Seminary Professsor
Asheville, North Carolina

Bob experienced the loss of his wife to death several years ago and is now married again. For 23 years he has produced the syndicated radio spot "Think About It."

NEEDS AND ISSUES OF SINGLES MINISTRY

16. SELF-ESTEEM

*"When a person goes to the Scriptures to see who he/she is
and to find God's plan for life, there will be improvement in
the single's behavior and self-esteem."*

Jim E. Towns

The term "self-esteem" is used to bridge the gap concerning a long list of
"self" words such as self-value, self-dignity, self-worth, etc. Therefore,
self-esteem is simplistically defined as the human longing for the divine
dignity that God intended when He created us in His image.

In contemporary society, self-esteem is a key issue for single adults.
From Madison Avenue advertising to *Gentleman's Quarterly* to *Mademoi-
selle* magazines, singles are told what they must wear, drive, buy, and be if
they are to be acceptable. This phenomenon has caused severe pressure
and attacks on esteem. People in ministry must realize that the Madison
Avenue philosophy of self-esteem is unattainable. As the population of
single adults grows, this presents potential for growth in the ministry of
the church. Thus, there is the desire to understand several factors about
self-esteem and single adults.

Perceptions of Self
Images of people are perceived in at least seven interacting ways.
My image of myself. This is the image I have of myself and results in how I
see myself.
Your image of yourself. This is the image you have of yourself and is how
you see yourself.
My image of you. The image that I have of you is my perception of you.
Your image of me. The image that you have of me is your perception of
me.
My image of your image of me. This is what I think you are thinking about
me.
Your image of my image of you. This is your interpretation of how you feel
that I perceive you.
God's image of you. This is what God had in mind when He first thought of
you. In other words, it is how our Creator sees us through the Scriptures.
When we commit ourselves to God, then we begin to see ourselves as He
sees us.

The pastor and/or counselor has a wealth of resources in single adults as
he helps them develop key areas of esteem.

Key Areas of Developing Esteem

A single person must develop a sense of wholeness in his/her singleness. Traditionally, this has been extremely difficult to accomplish since our society puts a high premium on marriage as an indicator of one's worth. Many single adults are not affirmed in their identity because of a negative self-concept. One of the saddest quotations in literature is Thoreau's, "The mass of men lead lives of quiet desperation." So many singles are living in quiet desperation and devoid of developing a positive concept in the following key areas.

Develop a meaningful personal sense of singleness. Properly adjusted singles are not anyone's "better half"; they are their own well-balanced whole. Marriage must not be an "escape" from singleness, but a time to develop personhood.

Develop an ability to be alone without being lonely. Most singles need to find help in adjusting to aloneness and dealing with loneliness. Loneliness happens when a person lacks the inner resources to be alone. In other words, there is a longing for companionship or a feeling of isolation when away from others. Some people enjoy being alone, while others dread it. Aloneness is that "quality time" when we can enjoy our own company.

Develop life goals and fulfilling vocations. Immediate goals are those things you want to accomplish within 1 year. Long-range goals usually refer to 5 to 10 years in the future. If a person is not fulfilled in his job, there will be frustration in other areas of life. Since we spend so many hours at work, it is imperative that we find our "niche" in the "workaday world."

Develop a financial plan to achieve security. Singles should develop a financial plan concerning income, expenses, and savings. The way singles use their material resources might give evidence to their priorities in life and levels of commitment. So within the "nuts and bolts" of a practical "down-to-earth" budget are the values of what one really believes!

Develop proper attitudes toward dating, commitment, and possible marriage or remarriage. A single may not know if he/she will remain single all his life, but should accept marriage if it comes or singleness if it stays. Both marrieds and singles appear to be suffering from a kind of "grass is greener on the other side of the fence" syndrome.

Develop a biblical purpose of life. This is where the ministry can be of great assistance. When a person goes to the Scriptures to see who he/she is and to find God's plan for life, there will be improvement in the single's behavior and self-esteem.

Dealing with the Single Self Realistically

The first step in single-awareness is to become aware of how one relates to God, self, and others. The positive result of single-awareness is single-acceptance. A great deal of work has been done in the area of self-acceptance. In a capsule, the single must accept self in four areas.

Appearance. Physical appearance of the body is usually why a person accepts or rejects oneself. There are physical characteristics that each person desires to change about himself/herself. I must do the best I can to make my appearance as attractive as possible, but to realize that the body is only the container for the "real person" inside.

Abilities. Physical and mental abilities interact in the acceptance or rejection of oneself. One should not capitalize on what he cannot do, but what he *can* do! In other words, I must do the best I can with what I have in the given time.

Parentage. Some people think they are somebody because of who their families are or are not. Those with rich, famous, or normal family roots perhaps feel acceptance, while the poor and abnormal feel unworthy. This societal perspective is inadequate.

Environment. The surroundings in which one finds himself/herself will usually cause good or bad feelings about self. The affirmation is to change what you can for the best and learn to live with the rest.

What the Church Can Do to Help the Single

The church has a role in helping the single adult to become aware and accepting of self. The goal is to become overcomers of low self-image. First, through self-analysis, the minister or leader can suggest individual counseling as well as some small groups geared to meeting needs of several people at one time.

Second, the church can assist the single in learning how to make a self-commitment. Whether individual or group counseling, the result of the work must be found in the principle for self-esteem—it is not by what I *think* or *feel*, but by an act of my will that I choose to be self-accepting.

Pastors can enhance self-image of single adults if they will invite them to be on planning committees and task forces of the church. There is a wealth of resources for the church which can be found in single members.

Last, a single adult must be able to see as God sees. He must learn about and accept his new identity as a believer in Jesus Christ (2 Cor. 5:17; John 1:12-13; Eph. 1:3-14).

Jim E. Towns, Ph.D.
Professor of Communications
Stephen F. Austin University, Nacogdoches, Texas

Jim is an author of 10 books and numerous articles including *Singles Alive,* Pelican Press, and *Life: Joy in Being,* Convention Press.

17. INTIMACY

> *"We want to be real, to understand intimacy, to give and receive love. At the same time, we fear our nakedness, vulnerability, and incompleteness."*
>
> *Terry Hershey*

Too often we perceive intimacy as a "place to arrive" rather than a journey. Are we so focused on the "destination" of "intimacy" that we have forgotten the journey? Are we so tempted to have the "right answers" that we forget how to ask the right questions? Are we so "goal-oriented" that we miss the process?

Psychologists tell us that we all have two fundamental needs: the need to belong and the need for significance. The message is clear: we are created to function in relationship. We are indeed "people who need people." Without even defining the word, "intimacy" is something we want. At the same time, we find ourselves making choices and decisions, and behaving in ways that lead us away from the very relationships we desire. We are all drawn to such relational characteristics as honesty, respect, vulnerability, trust, communication, reliability, and acceptance. And yet, we continue to approach our relationships with one arm extended as a protection against the reality that, in fact, we do need one another.

Our need for intimacy—for closeness with another, for affirmation, for touch—also exposes our fear. We are all afraid of the shadow-side—the brokenness. Nowhere is that more apparent than with the subject of intimacy. Neither our trivialization nor our sophistication has eliminated our fear of being exposed. We want to be real, to understand intimacy, to give and receive love. At the same time, we fear nakedness, vulnerability, and incompleteness. We want to be intimate, "But can't I wait until I've got my 'act together'?"

Many singles will wait too long. The singles leader must teach and live out the intimate relationships that are ours in God and His Word. So where do we begin to unravel the dilemma of human relationships—the approach-avoidance dilemma of intimacy? Our tendency is to look for more precise definitions, as if intimacy is something we can possess. And many of us teach about intimacy as if it is our job to "give answers." Unfortunately, there are no simple "answers." Yet, in leading adult singles, God gives us the intimate picture of His relationship with us through His Son, Jesus Christ. The picture is seen in His Word and experienced by His Spirit making us real and open as "new creatures" in Christ.

It is true, intimacy cannot be made "nice and neat," as if it is something that can be controlled and admired and added to our relational resumés. Because nice and neat doesn't do justice to real people with real hopes and real pain, who desire someone with the courage to give them permission to be "fully alive," even in their incompleteness.

Intimacy as a Journey

George Leonard, a 63-year-old black belt in aikido offers these observations about our predicament: "We are in an impatient society, dedicated to the quick fix. . . . For 10 years I've run an aikido school near San Francisco. I'd had the striking experience of watching students show up the first day with excited eyes, only to drop out quickly, at an alarming rate. Only 1 or 2 percent might make it to black belt. Most of the casualties are young men who are mainly concerned with looking good. They are usually preoccupied with overnight progress, with getting ahead without the necessary long-term practice. . . . We've got to accept the fact that mastery . . . is a journey, not a destination" (*Esquire,* May '87, p. 15).

That's good advice. Intimacy . . . is a journey, not a destination. Our temptation is to want a shortcut, to want to short-circuit the process. We want intimacy without significant emotional investment, joy without pain, friendship without time investment, and love without risk.

Is it possible to begin to see intimacy as a journey? Where do we start? What does the journey look like? Where is intimacy "born"? I wish it were a simple task. But the agenda has already been determined by the world in which we live. We cannot begin this subject with the naive assumption that intimacy can be neatly defined. Our primary task is not one of learning but of unlearning, a task involving realism. In fact, intimacy must be rescued from the illusions that precede it. Which means that the first step in our personal growth and in our teaching is honesty. Honesty about our need for comfort ("Are we there yet?"), and about our temptation to find solace in cultural counterfeits.

Intimacy's Myths

What are those myths that cloud our perspective? What are the counterfeits that seem so tempting? What are the illusions that prevent healthy relationships? Many singles are looking for intimacy in the wrong places and in the wrong ways. We need to help them. Here are five myths to help single adults understand many misunderstandings of "God's best" in an open and loving relationship.

Intimacy is magic. Because we live in a Polaroid culture, we expect our relationships to "develop" instantly. It is our hope that intimacy will "just happen," as if there is a feeling or a mood that signals our arrival. We are sure that if we create the right "intimate atmosphere," or read the right book, or attend the right seminar, intimacy will follow.

But such is not the case. There is no magic wand. There is no guarantee. There is only an invitation to work at relationships, and to keep working—the journey of continual work. We are hopeful that someone can "make us" intimate, as if we could be a "victim" of intimacy. But the characteristics of healthy relationships—honesty, trust, respect—are a result of choices, not magic or victimization.

Intimacy is ecstasy. Living in a culture where the values are dictated by Madison Avenue, singles are bombarded daily by the myth that if they are living life to its fullest, they will be in ecstasy most of the time. And TV does its job parading before us the "beautiful people"—where else is a culture so taken by the "Lifestyles of the Rich and Famous"—as a model for us to emulate. And as a culture we have been inculcated with a fear of ordinariness—old age, stretch marks, introverted personalities, and being "out of style."

The pressure this creates on relationships is inevitable. Every date needs to be the "end all and be all" of life. Unreal expectations are placed on all relational encounters, hoping to avoid any appearance of being normal, ordinary, or worse yet—boring. One fear is that we learn to equate adventure—fullness of life, pleasure, intimacy—with "non-boredom." Our cultural language implies that adventure equals ecstasy. Ecstasy is essentially a power issue. The absence of ecstasy equals powerlessness. Contentment becomes less and less easy to embrace. More is never enough.

And in our world of "hype," it's too easy to give in to "what's new"—ecstasy, excitement, entertainment. Perhaps we've lost sight of "what's best."

Tim Hansel learned what was important to his sons when he asked them, "How do you know Dad loves you?" He assumed the response would have something to do with Disneyland or Christmas presents. He was surprised by the answer, "We know you love us when you wrestle with us!"

Intimacy is romance. There's an implicit assumption that intimacy has to do with relationships with the opposite sex. This assumption is fueled by the church when it declares: "When God created you, He created one more person on this globe just for you! Your job in life is to find that person! And God's job is to keep that person hidden for as long as He can!"

It's no wonder we enter relationships with the opposite sex with such tension and unreal expectations. "Hi there, you lucky person. You don't know this, but you get the job of making me OK."

Merle Shain is right: "Our society isn't very big on friendship, really. We think of friends as people to spend time with when there isn't anyone else around who really matters. And sometimes when we have a vacancy for lover or spouse, we look for someone to fill that slot instead of seeing what there is, and miss what might have been" (*When Lovers Are Friends*, p. 84, Bantam).

The irony, of course, is that when you look through the Bible for examples of intimacy, you discover models very different from this equation with romance: Naomi and her daughters-in-law, David and Jonathan, Jesus and John, Jesus and Mary Magadalene. All of them were relationships practicing intimacy, but none of them were held together by romance.

Intimacy is a status of marriage or sex. Often, we see the word sex used as synonymous with intimacy—as in one Christian book warning its readers against "premarital intimacy." Such an equation is unfortunate. For reality tells us that it is far easier to take off one's clothes than it is to take off one's masks.

The issue at stake here is not sex, but our misunderstanding of intimacy. And as long as we assume that the issue of intimacy is resolved with sensual touch, then we avoid the real work of honesty, communication, conflict resolution, and commitments.

Neither a sexual encounter nor marriage guarantees intimacy. Again, we are hoping to become a victim of an experience or another person as a way of avoiding our own need to make choices and take responsibility for the "health" of the relationship.

And it is ironic that many sexual encounters are used as a defense against intimacy with the argument that, because we encountered each other sexually, we touched each other personally—as if sexual involvement were some kind of shortcut to "real" intimacy.

Intimacy is "out there" somewhere. "Intimacy will happen when the 'right person' comes along," one young woman told me, probably secretly hoping it was really true.

The fact remains, however, that if I am not in a small way learning to respect, trust, care for, and be vulnerable with the people who are in my life today, what guarantee do I have that the right person will walk into my life in six months. In truth, all of my life is lived behind an "if only." If only I were married, if only I hadn't had so many hurts, if only I had had a good family life, if only my children would leave home.

Life and relationships are something that are always "just around the corner," and always something that "the other guy has." And all the while we gradually harbor a resentment against life itself, living as if "life is guilty until proven innocent." We blame our parents, our circumstances, our past, our looks, our missed opportunities, and all the while hoping against hope that "real life" is going to begin soon.

Intimacy—honesty, trust, respect, vulnerability—begins today. We can all continue to hold out for magic, or for prolonged ecstasy, or for perpetual romance, or for that nirvana-like sexual experience, or even for the right person to charge into our lives. But that's just it. We will wait. And wait. And God's best for our lives will pass us by.

To know God, to really know God, is to know intimacy, because He intimately knows us. To grow in our openness and relationship with Him is the foundation and beginning of openness and intimacy with others. Dispel the myths. Begin the journey. Draw close to Him and others (Heb. 10:22-25; James 4:4-10).

Terry Hershey
Executive Director of Christian Focus
Irvine, California

Terry has authored four books on singles ministry, including *Intimacy: Longing of Every Human Heart,* Harvest House, and *Beginning Again,* Thomas Nelson.

18. DATING AND MARRIAGE

*"Most single adults struggle at some point with dating,
though some have simply chosen to respond more creatively
than others. Help your single adults see dating as an opportunity rather than a problem."*

Harold Ivan Smith

Dating has been labeled the scourge of modern single adult society; few singles have positive affirmations of the process. After all, many don't want to be dating in the first place—they'd rather be married.

The Big Question

I have an acquaintance who opens every conversation with one question: "How's your dating life?" The previous conversation could have been on trivial aspects of the levitical Law or on car prices; his curiosity is undaunted. Many single adults get annoyed by similar questions from married believers: "Dating anyone these days?"

There's a classic toothpaste commercial: "How's your love life?" The "beautiful person" with a mouth full of sparkling teeth sounds off a list of superlatives: "Great! Super! Incredible!" Then the announcer sternly demands: "How's *your* love life?" Reluctantly our single pal confesses, "Awful." (And there are a lot of nods in the audience.)

Fortunately there's hope for the guy: consistent use of brand X toothpaste will make him very dateable. The commercial closes with our hero wandering into the sunset with a beautiful woman at his side (probably late for a Bible study). The suggestion to single viewers: use *this* product and you won't be sitting home watching this commercial.

Once upon a time, dating was relaxed, fun, adventuresome, even inexpensive. There were set rules that assisted the process toward the inevitable: marriage. Supposedly, someday when one least expected it (that's why grooming aids are so essential), Prince/Princess Charming would come sweeping into one's life to the strains of "Ah, sweet mystery of life, I found you."

Furthermore, dating was goal-centric: "And *they* lived happily ever after." (Just fill in the appropriate names for "they.")

So why are single adults still dating?

For many single adults, the most troublesome aspect of adult dating is the memory residue from adolescence. Have you ever drunk a glass of milk, then noticed the filmy residue on the glass? Because most adolescent dating left a lot to be desired, some single adults have tremendous scar tissue which complicates dating as a single. Furthermore, by this point, parents and extended family may have become impatient.

Some single adults complain that dating is like dividing up for softball in the third grade. "Somebody pick me, *please*." Softball wasn't much fun when the two captains argued, "You take him!" "No! You take him!"

The Big Picture

There are realities that have to be faced if adult dating is to be understood. Some singles leaders have constructed intense "biblical systems" of dating. Unfortunately, dating was beyond the comprehension of Moses, Abraham, and most of the biblical authors. Proof texts won't be helpful to everyone.

However, I would suggest the following.

Face the reality of dating. Adult dating can be the pits or ecstasy. Singles cannot pretend that they are not adults or are not single. Nor can they avoid the basic need for relational living. Single adults are not designed to be relational lone rangers. Even the masked man had his faithful sidekick, Tonto.

Enlarge your understanding of dating. You can help single adults "defuse" some of the frustrations in adult dating. Most single adults struggle at some point with dating, though some have simply chosen to respond more creatively than others. Help your single adults see dating as an opportunity rather than a problem.

Express and work through negative feelings. Some single adults have a dating life that leaves nondaters envious. Many insist on sharing tidbits over the coffee and donuts on Sunday morning. As a result, "So how come I don't date?" will be the question in the singles' minds all during your session. The reality is that a single can tithe, teach Sunday School, have an incredible figure and personality, live at the best address in town, have the correct doctrinal conclusions on everything, and still be dateless!

They will respond, "It's not fair!" Your response may be little more than, "Life isn't fair." Some singles will cry, some will be depressed, others will perhaps covet their neighbor's dating. Help them work through the negative feelings by appreciating the pain of datelessness.

Give up the grand illusions. By this time in one's life, expectations of Prince/Princess Charming may have changed. Some are tempted now to settle for the discount; some are motivated by desperation. On the other hand, the single may be more emotionally and spiritually mature and more likely to be Prince/Princess Charming to someone.

The Big Reality

What then are the realities that single adults face in dating?

The old rules don't apply. Maybe singles want dating referees in striped shirts to keep the process moving and fair. You can help the newly single make sense of the bewildering changes in dating practices. Many divorced and widowed people have been stunned by the sexual expectations in dating today. Help the single adult confront that reality.

Some professional teams have difficulty early in a season with the new rules. Rules change. Today women do ask men out. Certainly that frightens many traditional males. So they hibernate.

For yuppie-oriented singles, dating must be squeezed into a busy work schedule. Some prefer to date people who are in the same or similar line of work. Moreover, there is more spontaneous dating, which doesn't mean the asker is taking the askee for granted.

A lot of people aren't dating. It's safe to take bragging about dating and divide by four. It's easy to exaggerate about one's dating. It is equally easy for some single adults to be oversensitive, to be too negative on themselves. Have them ask: "Am I really the only person in my neighborhood who isn't dating?"

Some dates aren't worth the hassle. Too many single adults live by the notion: "A bad date is better than no date!" Wrong. That notion may explain the significant increase in what is termed "date rape"—when a date turns into a wrestling match and ultimately into rape.

Just how creative is the dater? In singleland there are psychopaths, neurotics, abusive personalities, people who "hate" the opposite sex. The more desperate one is to date, the more likely one is to encounter one of these.

Too many single adults have put themselves into "situations" and then prayed for deliverance. There are singles who are so focused on themselves that they do not have time to get in touch with another person. How many first-person-singular monologues can a single survive?

Finally, some singles think that X expenditure of funds on a date automatically entitles them to a corresponding portion of intimacy. Too many do not understand the word "no" or "NO!"

Finances are important. There is a common but dying tradition that males should pay for the date. That may have been true in adolescent dating, but in today's world, a single who insists on maintaining that standard will watch a lot of TV reruns, dateless.

Many single men are not, contrary to popular opinion, rolling in the dough. Rent, taxes, insurance, car expenses, utilities, take a disproportionate share of any person's income (especially if you add child support/alimony).

Dating can be expensive for those who are trying to prove something to someone.

Women who reach for the check—who seriously offer to pay—and men who are not threatened by such, date more.

When/then thinking is unproductive. Some singles think, "When I lose 25 pounds, then I'll date," or, "When I get a new job," or, "When I change singles groups, then. . . ." This thinking makes dateless evenings a little easier to handle by suggesting, "It's really my fault that I am sitting here, dateless."

Possessive dating is the discount of dating relationships. A lot of dating is a "flea market" for bartering fringe benefits. Some singles become so attached to the fringes that they cannot terminate unwholesome relationships.

A lot of men want to date women who can cook or sew or clean house. Some women "use" men for home maintenance, automobile repair, or security consultations.

Possessive dating means: "I don't have to worry about Friday night—we'll do something."

Some manipulate as a basic survival tactic. But with the fringes come the strings that become ropes.

Help your single adults develop skills to carefully evaluate the "emotional" portfolio of individuals they date.

Some are Mama's boys. In a world where "macho" is important, some men are desperately confused by the new rules and expectations of women. Some are looking for a mother rather than a wife. Some men become prisoners to shyness to such a degree that a date is an incredible psychological hurdle. Some men do not know how to treat a woman. They envy the finesse of their friends; others self-indict—"Who would want to go out with me?"

Some desperately fear rejection.

Remember, for bonafide Mama's boys, Mama has home-court advantage and a decisive headstart.

The Big Confusion

If a single is tightly clinging to a fantasy of Prince/Princess Charming, and has heavily invested in that fantasy, what does one do to "tide oneself over" until the tardy Charming arrives on the scene? Just as a snack may reduce one's cravings for food until mealtime, so there are individuals who seek "relational snacks" or minirelationships.

So, the individual invests enough to keep the door ajar, but not enough to be inclusive. "I won't commit myself to you long enough to see if there is potential for a lasting relationship. Besides, someone 'better' may come along and it would be difficult to dump you gracefully. So, let's just be friends, OK?"

Many single adults want riskless, hassleless dating. Some become comfortable with the uncomfortable. But the essential element in relationship-building and maintenance is risk.

One difficulty with relational snacks is misunderstood intentions. One concludes, "*If* I keep giving and giving, eventually he/she is going to fall in love with me."

A lot of single adults have pals and "special" friends. Some proclaim to the married world that that is one of the luxuries of singleness.

Agenda dating is unproductive. Some singles only do presort dating—i.e., dating people they would seriously consider marrying. Dating should enhance friendships, and friendships are a good way to evolve into marriage.

Transitional Christians confuse everyone. There are a lot of undisciplined Christian single adults who have accepted Jesus as Saviour but not as Lord of their dating. So, they walk in both worlds, but not firmly in either one.

Finally, Christian singles who date have a commitment to wholeness in Christ Jesus that they do not wish to compromise.

Christian singles who date must be alert to "snowballing" relationships. They cannot hesitate to ask for a "time-out."

Christian singles who date must watch their relational language. They do not prematurely say, "I love you," without understanding the significance of the phrase and the potential for misunderstanding.

Christian singles who date must realize that those they date are equally loved by Jesus. Therefore, any manipulation or exploitation is unthinkable.

Christian singles who date realize that other single adults compare their witness on Saturday night (and any bragging or commentary on dating) with what they profess on Sunday mornings.

Christian singles who date cannot ignore realities, but through faith in Christ, they can deal with those realities redemptively.

Harold Ivan Smith
Executive Director of Tear-Catchers
Kansas City, Missouri

As a single adult, Harold is sensitive to the needs of singles in our culture. He has authored several books, including *Jason Loves Jane but They Got a Divorce.*

19. GOAL- AND CAREER-PLANNING

"Many singles tend only to schedule their appointments or commitments where other people are concerned. However, they will accomplish their personal tasks far better if they also schedule in blocks of time to do certain tasks in which only they are involved."

Jon Clemmer

The biblical model for goal-setting and planning is set by God Himself. It is evident that God establishes clear personal tasks and goals for Himself and He always accomplishes them (Eph. 1:11).

God has also laid a solid foundation of goals and plans in the way that He administers His will and designs through His children (2 Cor. 4:7; Eph. 3:20). God then continues this principle by holding us personally accountable for our time usage and talent development (Matt. 25:14-30).

God has ordained that the Christian life is not neutral in the service of Christ. God does have an action plan for our lives that we must endeavor to discover and follow (Jer. 29:11-14). We must resist the enemy in the pursuit of Christ-honoring goals and objectives (1 Peter 5:8).

Goal-Planning

Types of goals one should set. (1) Long-term goals. These are goals that involve one's whole life and every aspect of it. They tend to reflect our *values* in terms of what is important or not important to us as far as the big picture is concerned. These should include all the major areas of one's life such as: personal, developmental (including spiritual), social, family relations, vocational, recreational, financial, and community. Singles need to think in terms of long-term goals because so many of them tend to put life on hold until they marry.

(2) Intermediate goals. These are goals that involve every aspect of one's whole life over a specific period of time. Three years is a good length of time within which to accomplish intermediate goals because three years seems long enough to notice significant progress but short enough that an individual can manage personal life choices during that time.

(3) Short-term goals. These are goals that can involve every aspect of one's life or one certain aspect of life at the present moment. The question has been asked, "Suppose you were to find out today that you only had six months left to live. How would you change your life?" Asking this question can force a person to weed out the insignificant goals and priorities in his

current lifestyle and refocus on the truly important things. Or, there may be one need, dream, or commitment that requires special attention. It alone may become the short-term goal.

Seeing dreams become realities. The secret to getting large tasks done is to break them down into smaller, manageable increments. There are classically three levels or strata of planning necessary to accomplish larger goals or tasks. They are:

(1) The objective. The objective is the vision, event, large task, or idea which one wishes to see become a reality. An objective can almost never be accomplished by completing one task alone. (E.g., My objective is to hold a weekend retreat for 200 single adults at a resort two hours from the church.)

(2) The goal. One of a limited number (3-10) of tasks which, when all accomplished, will guarantee the accomplishment of the objective. A goal can rarely be accomplished by one task alone. (E.g., My goal is to line up a retreat location for 200 single adults, 2 hours from the church.)

(3) The action step or strategy. One of a limited number (1-10) of tasks which, when accomplished, signal the completion of the step. These are small enough increments that each can usually be accomplished by one task alone. (E.g., My action step is to call five different conference and retreat centers and inquire as to cost and availability.)

Setting priorities in personal daily, weekly, and quarterly goal-planning. Planning is key to success. Many singles have large amounts of discretionary time and, as a result, often waste large chunks of it and then feel guilty. Singles especially need to consider the following principles of time usage:

(1) Planning your time. Just as you plan your money (set up a budget) or plan your vacation (line up friends, transportation, and accommodations) so you also need to plan your time on a quarterly/weekly/daily basis. I personally recommend three hours for the quarterly planning session, one hour for the weekly session, and one half hour for the daily session. But, regardless of the time spent on planning, the point is to plan. Each should be made in light of long-term, intermediate, and short-term goals you have already established as well as your priorities within each category. Such planning will give you confidence in making and keeping personal time commitments.

(2) Planning your tasks. Many singles tend only to schedule their appointments or commitments where other *people* are concerned. However, they will accomplish their personal tasks far better if they also schedule in blocks of time to do certain tasks in which only they are involved (e.g., personal devotions, doing laundry, paying bills, etc.).

(3) Prioritizing your tasks. In the classic little pamphlet on time management called *Tyranny of the Urgent,* Charles E. Hummel states, "The urgent things of life often crowd out the important." How true this is for all people—and especially singles. One way to keep the important tasks on

the top of our list is to prioritize your To-Do list. Each To-Do list, whether kept on a daily, weekly, monthly, quarterly, or annual basis, can be prioritized item by item, so that the most important items get done first. To do this, you can use the A-B-C system. In this system an "A" placed next to a numbered item on a To-Do list means it is crucial, vital, absolutely essential, must be done, and that it will pay high dividends in terms of goal accomplishment when completed. A "B" placed next to a numbered item means that it is important and worthwhile but not vital. This is an item that, if left undone, would *not* create serious problems. A "C" placed next to a numbered item means that it is of limited value. "C" items are often there merely for future reference and can often become a "B" item and then an "A" item as time changes priorities. Beside the A-B-C method of prioritizing, a check mark (√) is very crucial to denote an urgent item that calls for immediate action and which cannot be left undone. The check mark allows me to go back and reemphasize some priorities as time passes and they become more crucial. Again, the point is not *this* system of numbers, letters, or checks, but *some* system of writing things down and maintaining order and balance.

(4) Evaluating your priorities. It is good to set time aside weekly, monthly, and annually to see if you really are accomplishing your goals with the priorities set. This can be a time of real encouragement or chastisement as you see whether or not you have disciplined yourself to follow a plan.

We all need assistance in planning and setting goals. The singles leader can be a great model to the singles. The result is fulfillment and satisfaction of growth and maturity. This is a marvelous ministry that many singles will benefit from.

Career Counseling

A prevalent concern. There is indeed great concern on the part of many singles about career goals and the destination of their lives in a vocational career. Career counseling is near the top of the list of issues that a singles minister deals with on a regular basis.

Many singles are very young (age 18-25) and are just embarking on new career adventures, yet there is a high level of concern and doubt about "this job being the right one." Some singles enter the job market with an already high level of dissatisfaction in life. Therefore, the job is added to the same list of life's frustrations and question marks.

Singles are on the move. Many are not planted geographically or relationally. Their options for friends and scenery are wide open. Their career is not always a number-one priority. Added to that is the lack of financial commitments. As a result, career transition and mobility are more likely.

Other singles need to work just to survive. Some are recently divorced and have to reenter the job market. Education and skills might be few. Counsel is needed.

Pastoral counseling and careers. When counseling single adults on issues surrounding career choice, evaluation, and change, try to focus in on the following issues:

- Discerning God's will according to biblical principles
- Including personal enjoyment as a criterion
- Handling inappropriate pressure from parents and friends
- Evaluating past experiences in the job market
- Soliciting the opinions of close friends and relatives
- Getting sophisticated *personality* testing done through a reputable Christian counselor
- Getting sophisticated *vocational* testing done through a reputable counselor
- Considering any limitations in ability or education
- Determining whether further training is needed
- Getting the hard facts regarding the current job market
- Keeping your walk with Christ strong (see James 1:6-8)
- Knowing the principles behind a call to full-time ministry

Resources on career counseling. There is a wealth of material on the market dealing with every aspect of career-planning. Many professional singles will read these books or seek out and attend specialized seminars and conferences on the subject. Therefore, you don't need to be an expert in the literature. But it does help to be able to point a single to some books that will help him get started. The two books I recommend are:

What Color Is Your Parachute? Richard Nelson Bolles, Ten Speed Press, Berkeley, CA, 1984.
The Three Boxes of Life, Richard Nelson Bolles, Ten Speed Press, Berkeley, CA, 1981.

The final and most valuable resources are the leader's prayers, encouragement, and perseverance with the single in transition. Your support and possibly a support group of God's caring and loving people are most significant.

Jon Clemmer
Pastor of Single Adult Ministries
Church of the Saviour, Wayne, Pennsylvania

Jon has had broad experience in career and goal development through counseling singles, leading seminars, and personal experience.

20. FINANCES AND HOUSING NEEDS

"Part of the responsibility of the church is to walk through the process of financial assistance with singles so they know it's OK to experience special needs."

Andy Morgan

Divorce is considered one of the most traumatic and stressful experiences a person can encounter. Therefore, there is no doubt that when people go through a divorce, they will face major emotional, psychological, spiritual, as well as physical changes. Add to that the trauma of relocating, paying bills, possibly changing careers, upkeep of home and automobile, and perhaps raising children alone or "long-distance."

This chapter deals specifically with some of the financial and housing issues that the divorced person faces. The basis of this chapter is the result of surveys and conversations with over 400 single adults. The purpose is not to be exhaustive or scientifically accurate; instead the chapter is intended to inform, to help make us aware of certain areas of need that a single adult may face, and give some concrete suggestions that can be used by ministers, churches, counselors, and the single adults themselves.

Some suggestions will be able to be put into place with little effort—just a few phone calls; whereas other suggestions may involve a major effort by the church or a particular ministry.

Of the many problems that the single adult may face, finances and housing may cause the greatest amount of stress. Housing came up over and over again as the main financial need when experiencing a divorce, because a house or rental payment is usually the largest payment anyone makes in a month. Coming up with a security deposit was also mentioned, that amount is usually needed over and above the usual monthly payment.

What Singles Have to Say

Though the financial side of finding a new residence is extremely impor tant, the housing issue brings some emotional problems: "We've shared this home all our married life. How can I possibly move out?" "How can I take the kids out of school in the middle of a school year?" "All my friends live in this town. How can I move where there are only strangers?" "A three-room apartment after a seven-room house? What will I do with all my things? . . . These and memories are all I have left." Many, too many, major decisions have to be made . . . usually in a short amount of time, adding stress to an already stressful situation.

When people's financial pictures change, they also face a grief process from loss, and an identity crisis. Their identities, their esteem, their confidence, their feelings of security all will change when their financial pictures begin to change.

Housing is the "biggie," but there are also several other financial needs that have to be dealt with, any one of which can cause the financial structure to come tumbling down like a house of cards. A home without heat, lights, or water is not considered much of a home in America—home of the "free and the brave." Utilities need to be paid every month. Thankfully, some of the utility companies are willing to help people work out a payment plan, so that discontinued service does not take place.

Putting good food on the table three times a day is another area where changes may have to be made. Shopping becomes a chore—sometimes a nightmare—because you now have $35 to spend on a week's groceries and you used to have $135. Name brands may have to go; and that '29 Depression story about "adding another potato and some water to the soup," now becomes true again in '88.

Automobiles and insurance are also part of the "American way." You must get a job if you didn't have one before, you must be able to drive to that job, and your car must be insured. Do you borrow from relatives? Just when you think you have your monthly budget worked out, one of these "six-month biggies" comes around and throws it all out of whack. If you're lucky, the kids' medical bills are still covered, but your six-month checkups with the doctor and dentist may have to be postponed for an extended period of time.

Clothing is another area of concern. Again, your thoughts, your values, your ideas on "being in style" may have to change. You may have to start "making do" with last year's models, rummage-sale bargains, and hand-me-downs from relatives and friends. Pride takes another step backward.

So far, all we've discussed are "basics for survival." What about vacations? Spending money for the little extras? Savings in the bank for a rainy day? (Overnight *all* your days may become rainy days!)

Though there are no absolutes, most often the noncustodial mate is able to take the kids someplace special for vacation. And you are happy for them . . . almost. "Santa Claus Dad" and "Disney World Mom" aren't just cute chapters in books anymore. They've moved into (or out of) your house. Often the custodial parent is just getting into the full-time job market, and hasn't had time to acquire a paid vacation. So the competition for the kids' hearts, the jealousy, the "this is not fair" syndrome sets in at the same time as all the other financial worries.

If you are fortunate to be able to get all the basics under control, often there isn't much, if anything, left over. "Fun" times become creative, because movies and dinners out and bowling and concerts are too expensive. Walks, bike rides, puzzles, minitreats at McDonald's, and trips to the park all take on a new meaning.

If your sense of security was wrapped up in mutual funds or savings accounts, you literally may be forced to move it out of the bank and into the hands of God. The story of Job becomes precious. If you're strong and can hang on long enough, you can say, "If he could do it, so can I."

When asked what organizations helped the most when facing the financial, housing, and emotional trauma of a divorce, it was surprising how few people found the help they needed through the church. This is a shame because Christ said, "Religion that God our Father accepts as pure and faultless is this: to look after orphans and widows in their distress and to keep oneself from being polluted by the world" (James 1:27). The widows and orphans (fatherless) of the 20th century include our divorced people and their innocent children.

What the Body of Christ Can Do
The church can, and more importantly *should,* take a very active role in helping to restore a person's life to a sense of wholeness and stability in the midst of one of the major traumas of life. To do this the body of Christ needs to first open their hearts and minds to areas of ministry that are unique and challenging. Second, it is important that they know the resources that are in their community that can help by setting up a lay counseling system and to possibly work with a bank for financial advice and credit counseling.

There are many ways that the church, or a particular ministry, can help. The main tool would be a committee that would handle the "networking" involved. In times of great stress, it can be very difficult to know where to turn. There are so many questions and seemingly so few answers. The church, through this committee (possibly only one person in a small church), could be the "pool" where those who are dying of thirst could come get a drink. This pool should be full of refreshing water and surrounded by many cups.

One cup could be "housing." There could be a network within the church of people who have short-term housing available. "How many rooms?" "Are children and/or pets allowed?" "How would expenses be handled?" are all questions that could be asked of people who were willing to open their homes. An index file would be kept and referred to as needed. Perhaps people vacation in Florida every winter and would appreciate having someone in their home for 6 months to "take care of things." Others might have a room or two that they would like to rent out for as long as necessary. This "housing cup" could also contain a directory of the different types of homes/apartments that are available in the area and a contact person in the real estate field who would alert the church to places as they became available.

A second cup could be a "food/utility" cup. Again, knowing where to get help is sometimes as important as being able to do it yourself. "How does one apply for food stamps?" "I hear about government programs that help the needy. Where are they? How do I get in touch with them?" "Food pantries, cheese and milk programs . . . how do I connect with them?" "I've received notice that the gas is being shut off. What now?" If the church had the answers to these questions, the distressed person could avoid the countless headaches and the days and weeks of "letting your fingers do the walking" that it might normally take. When even getting out of bed becomes a chore, facing numerous organizations, all asking numerous questions, can be overwhelming. And frightening. And humiliating. And just plain difficult.

Another cup would be labeled "maintenance." Homes and cars and furnaces and water heaters have a way of breaking down—always at a bad time. The church could possibly work out a deal with a local mechanic who would work on cars through their referral at a discounted rate. Another file or "yellow pages for the church" could be kept on people who would be willing to help when a divorced person in their church had a "breakdown" of a mechanical, electrical, automotive, or plumbing nature. They could also host a seminar on "basic car maintenance," or be able to recommend such a class through their community adult education program or junior college.

The fourth cup could be the "benevolence" cup. Every church should have an emergency fund, monies set aside for just that purpose: groceries, doctor bills, rent, utilities, whatever is deemed an emergency. Most churches have a few (even one would help) people who are interested and willing to give extra financial support. Missions should begin in your own backyard, and I believe that the local church would be willing to help if they knew the money was going toward real needs. Or the church could build right into its budget an "emergency account." A percent of the weekly offering or a special offering could be set aside for certain emergencies. So in addition to supporting its buildings, staff, and programs, the church would be, in a very real sense "looking after orphans and widows in their distress."

A "resource" cup is number five. In addition to housing and food and maintenance resources, additional support could be offered through valuable resource contacts: a banker who could offer financial counseling; a lawyer who could offer legal advice; a list of phone numbers and prices of the local day care centers; names and numbers of those available for baby-sitting; crisis center and hot-line numbers; a list of classes offered by the community colleges that are geared to helping singles get back on their feet; women's resource centers, etc. Most metro areas have church-related agencies that can help. Find out what they are. Keep a file on them. Find a dedicated person in your church who has a heart for the hurting and help him keep this file current.

As the old saying goes, "Last, but definitely not least," the church should have a "healing" cup. Having financial needs met will relieve much of the stress of a divorce, but certainly not all. The emotional pain cuts deep. Healing of the heart takes longer than healing of the broken-down water heater. Where should a person turn then? First, last, and always to his church family. As in the other areas, the church can have much to offer.

One of the most difficult aspects of facing crisis and change can be tied in with emotional embarrassment. When a person who has been accustomed to buying the best cuts of meat and the softest toilet tissue now has to apply for food stamps, a tremendous amount of emotional upheaval erupts. Some would rather starve themselves than have to face this type of embarrassment. Part of the responsibility of the church is to walk through the process of financial assistance with singles so they know it's OK to experience special needs; that it's OK to receive help. Then, and only then, will the church be able to support singles emotionally as well as physically to work through the process of starting over.

Churches can offer a support group with individuals who will walk through the issues/problems with the hurting person. They could provide counseling within the church, or have a network of counselors/services who can deal with identity and crisis issues. They also need to help the divorced person form a new base of security. Something God asks of all of us (but is often ignored unless we are forced into it through a crisis such as a divorce) is that we move from our materialistic mentality to a spiritual/relational mentality. How is this accomplished? Through spiritual counseling and teaching people that they need to focus on their relationship with Christ, who is their only true security. Human beings being what they are, it is easier to trust what they can see and feel and touch—their homes, their jobs, their retirement accounts, etc. When these artificial supports are knocked away, it's time to take a good hard look at faith. How strong and deep is it? Is it real? Can God be trusted? A church should be able to guide a person to the answers to these questions.

None of these suggestions for how a church helps its hurting through housing and financial and emotional needs are difficult. They just need a little organization and a person or two who are very dedicated to answering God's call to serve in love; people who are not called to judge or condemn or belittle, but to love.

Andy Morgan
Minister with Single Adults, Single Point Ministries
Ward Presbyterian Church, Livonia, Michigan

Andy has had 10 years of experience developing a variety of housing programs for adult singles in several different economic areas. Andy is on the executive board of NSL.

21. GUIDING SPIRITUAL GROWTH

"Many people go to the Bible and demand that God fulfill the passage their way in their time. Many people think that if they pray 'hard' enough or 'long' enough, God will have to give what is demanded. However, spiritual growth begins with a desire to know the Blesser rather than trying to get a blessing."

Jim E. Towns

Many adult singles today might claim to be religious. Yet, there is a distinct difference between being affiliated with a religion and having a personal relationship with Jesus Christ! Spiritual life and vitality is sought by many who claim to be "Christians." They are seeking to know their Creator personally. However, many are confused. Others are thirsting for spiritual refreshment and guidance.

Nonscriptural Concepts about God and Spiritual Growth

Even though there is a need to know God, some people have immature concepts about who God really is. In addition there are several inadequate, nonscriptural concepts about spiritual growth.

Spiritual yuppiedom. If I have all the appropriate material possessions and position, then God will be happy to have me on His team.

Spiritual Santa Claus. God is keeping a list and checking it twice to find out who has been naughty and nice. If you live right, then only good things will happen to you.

Spiritual chance. God is perceived as a "slot machine in the sky." You put money in the offering, pull the prayer handle, and He will pay off sooner or later.

Spiritual computer. Some see God as a giant computer in the clouds that you feed your problems to, and He gives answers. Spiritual matters are treated like an IBM system. You punch your problem tape, run it through the computer, and God will kick out solutions at church.

Spiritual policeman. This damaging view sees God as a policeman who keeps you in line. God is watching and hoping you will "mess up" so He can crack you over the head with a club.

Formal Sunday event. Perhaps one of the most common misconceptions that people have about God is that He is a formal Sunday event. In other words, spiritual growth and vitality begin and end in worship, ritual, form, organ music, and sermons.

A Scriptural Concept of God Precedes Spiritual Growth

It is imperative that we communicate to our singles a scriptural concept of God. It is not possible to have an appropriate, healthy relation with God without having a scriptural understanding of who He is! An inadequate concept will bring a wrong response to Him. A distorted idea will cause a distorted response to Him. But a right response to God will come from a right understanding and knowledge of Him.

Scripture reveals God as Father-Son-Spirit. Throughout time, God has been revealing Himself. Scripture gives a progressive revelation of His nature. The first expression of God is God-Father: who is the Creator, Ruler, and Sustainer of the universe and me! In the Bible, God progressively revealed Himself as *Elohim*—the supreme, all powerful God; *El Shaddai*—the Almighty God; *Jehovah-Jireh*—the Provider; *Jehovah*—Redeemer and Lord; *Jehovah-Rophe*—the Healer; *Jehovah-Nissi*—the Banner of Victory; *Jehovah-Shalom*—our Peace; *Jehovah-Rohi*—our Shepherd and *Jehovah-Shammah*—our God who dwells with us! Therefore, God-Father loves us so much that He not only gave us life, but also provides for us.

The second expression of God is God-Son: Jesus Christ, Saviour, and Lord of those who trust Him. The greatest revelation of God is given to us through Jesus Christ. He came to tell us about our Father in heaven. But more than that, Jesus Christ came to provide the way for us to be united with our Father.

The third expression of God is God-Spirit: The illuminator of the Scriptures and enabler to perform His works through His people. Just as holy men of God were inspired to write the Scriptures, we must trust the same Spirit of God to illuminate us in order to understand spiritual truths. The Holy Spirit convicts us of our need for Jesus the Saviour and Jesus unites us with the Father.

To the Left, to the Right, Who's Right?

In the Christian faith there is a battle between legalism and libertinism. The carnal Christian boasts of his liberty. The spiritual Christian boasts in his slavery to Jesus. Love foregoes even legitimate liberties that would neglect or hinder other persons. Many singles will confuse legalism for fundamentalism, and libertinism for liberalism.

In legalism, people get caught up more with the "means" than the "end." To these people, the Bible is only a "rule book." These live by the letter of the law while often ignoring the spirit of the law. There is always a quick answer by quoting a passage of Scripture that may or may not fit the situation. There are those who make an oversimplification of scriptural truths. These live by surface responses rather than getting the deeper meaning of what God is really saying. Then there are some who give easy answers for tough questions. They have a list of 50 Scriptures and recite answers without thinking and praying. They spiritually "cop out" without really knowing a word from God on a specific situation. This is simply a

112

plea to consider the spirit of the law as well as the letter of the law.

In libertinism, people view the Bible as only a "guidebook" for freedom. There are several characteristics of the libertine perspective. This group seems to be "drowning in freedom." They say, "Once saved always saved, so I can do anything I desire." This group has the carefree attitude of, "I don't care what others think, we are not much anyway." This misses the point because it is not what others think of us but what they think of God because of us!

Guiding Spiritual Growth

Whether spiritual guidance is one-to-one or on a group basis, the wise minister/counselor will first realize that single adults are not overgrown youth. They are adults and must be treated as such! Yet, the leader has an important role and responsibility to provide spiritual guidance resulting in spiritual growth.

Some try consciously or unconsciously to manipulate spiritual growth. Sometimes through deliberate design, singles set out to try to *make* God do what they desire. We need to cease manipulating improper instant growth through the inaccurate uses of the following components of proper spiritual growth:

The Scriptures. Some people go to the Bible and demand that God fulfill the passage *MY WAY* in *MY TIME!* This is being presumptuous even to the "name it and claim it" perspective.

Prayer. Many people think that if they pray "hard" enough or "long" enough, God will *have to* give what is demanded. They go to the Bible and say, "God, You said it; You have to do it."

Praise. Some people try to manipulate God through praising. They feel that if they truly praised the Lord, He would have to change situations and meet demands.

Bargaining. Many people try to play on God's sympathy and make a bargain for spiritual growth. They say, "God, if You will do _____, then I will do _____."

There are many marvelous methods of Bible study, prayer, and praise. Excellent study guides and programs are readily available. However, spiritual growth begins with a desire to know the Blesser rather than trying to get a blessing. The "answer" for producing spiritual growth is not in formulas, conducting meetings, and so on. Many people seek to live off formulas for miracles, conducting meetings, fellowshiping, serving, etc. These singles may be "miracle hoppers" and "meeting jumpers" who are usually deeply searching but spiritually shallow. Spiritual depth is realized when God's truths and plan for living are appropriated.

In counseling/teaching/preaching, positive spiritual growth occurs when we let God be God in our lives. The wise minister/counselor will go beyond the "band-aid" approach. He/she will cover the basics of Christ's saving Gospel, being sure the single adult has trusted Jesus as Saviour and

Lord. Then helpful tools (Bible study, memorization, meditation, and prayer) can be given as helps to grow in a living, vital, personal faith in Jesus Christ.

Jim E. Towns, Ph.D.
Professor of Communications
Stephen F. Austin University, Nacogdoches, Texas

As a single adult, speaker, and author, Jim has devoted his life to the spiritual nurture of singles. One of Jim's 10 books is *Faith Stronger Than Death*, Warner Press, Inc.

22. THE SINGLE LIFESTYLE

"A Christian single is frequently identifiable by what he/she believes; by how he/she behaves; by where he/she belongs; and by how he/she budgets (spends) money and resources."

Harold Ivan Smith

It is one thing to be single or unmarried; it is quite another thing to develop a single lifestyle that is dynamic and meaningful, however long this season called "single" may last. Jesus, a single Adult, said, "I have come that they [single adults] may have life, and have it *to the full*" (John 10:10, italics added). Some translations say "abundantly."

Ultimately, lifestyle is a choice. Never before, however, have there been so many factors competing for inclusion in that choice. First, there are numbers. At the time this nation was founded, approximately 6 percent of the population was unmarried; a single adult was highly conspicuous in that society and, therefore, highly suspect.

Today, more than 36 percent of the population is unmarried. There is safety in numbers. Single adults are the trendsetters, particularly those who are yuppies or baby-boomers.

Second, materialism is a strong temptation in shaping a lifestyle. As a group, singles account for $330 billion in disposable income (18-34-year-olds claim half of that amount). Single adults make up 12.5 percent of the total consumer spending in the U.S.; 15.5 percent of eating out expenditures; 20 percent of liquor sales; 15.5 percent of automobile sales; and 15 percent of vacation sales. One in six home buyers in the U.S. is single. In fact, single women have emerged as the fastest-growing group of new-home buyers.

Third, single adults are mobile. They may find themselves living, by their choice or an employer's choice, halfway across the continent from their families. In a strong consumer-oriented subculture, how are they to shape their lives?

Three Basic Lifestyles

I believe there are three basic lifestyles common for singles, some of which are like circles and overlap.

Mate-seekers. This single adult is committed to the notion that life begins "when I get married." The agenda of singleness is to find a mate, and some would add, "the sooner, the better. " Singles events and groups are places "to meet someone." The mate-seekers often define themselves by their dating (or deep desire to date).

Self-seekers. This single adult is committed to "getting ahead" or to concentrating on his career. This is typical among the host of young single adults labeled "yuppies" or young urban professionals. Singleness offers them a chance to take advantage of career or educational opportunities, as well as additional time to invest in their work or profession. They work longer hours, pursue more leads, make more sales presentations, and do more billings than a married person who has a family to go home to.

Some, who are not professionals, are still self-seekers, in that their lives revolve around them in first-person singular living. This individual is characterized by a commitment to "going it alone" and to a self-focus that borders on selfishness.

Kingdom-seekers. These single adults are committed to relational and spiritual development and maturity. Even if they perceive singleness as a negative (and few kingdom-seekers do), they realize it beats other alternatives.

Kingdom-seekers generally see their singleness as a season. Many kingdom-seekers become vitally committed to single adult ministry and other ministries in their churches. They take Paul's admonition seriously: "An unmarried man is concerned about the Lord's affairs—how he can please the Lord. But a married man is concerned about the affairs of this world—how he can please his wife—and his interests are divided" (1 Cor. 7:32-34).

This single adult would say that, if marriage happens, it will be a pleasant surprise. If it doesn't happen, it will not be a bitter disappointment.

Elements in a Lifestyle of a Christian Single
A Christian single is frequently identifiable by what he/she believes; by how he/she behaves; by where he/she belongs; and by how he/she budgets (spends) money and resources.

Singlestyles
There are distinctive lifestyles common among single adults. Some are transitional, others are more set, particularly in older single adults. (Adapted from "Personalities at Work," Michael E. Cavanaugh, *Personal Journal*, 64 [April '85], pp. 255-64.)

Joel/Josephine the right. This single adult has to always be right, to have the last word. Anyone who disagrees with this single adult is on a collision course. They have a strong need to be right—regardless of the subject.

Milton/Mildred the nice. This single adult wants to be nice because you are more likely to like him/her if he/she is nice. This single never complains, never finds fault, and never says no to any request. The Miltons/Mildreds keep many single adult groups surviving. They have a strong need to be liked and will avoid choices that threaten their popularity.

Arthur/Alice the sensitive. This single adult has feelings that can spill over

116

(or erupt) with the slightest jar. Many have a permanent chip on their shoulders. This single adult has unfinished business and unresolved conflicts.

Ben/Beth the successful. This single adult equates one's self-worth (at the moment) with his latest success or coup in business or relationships. The more successful he or she is, the better he or she feels. Some see it as a "dog-eat-dog" world. They are willing to do almost anything to get ahead or to climb the ladder. Sometimes, the need to be successful is stronger than the need to be ethical or have a correct view of the source of their self-esteem.

Dan/Dinah the attention addicts. This single adult needs a lot of attention to ward off loneliness, anxiety, and boredom with their single status. Some are hypochondriacs. They would rather get negative attention than be ignored. They deal with details and expect you to listen to long recitals of problems and insults. This single adult can be a disruptive influence in a group because they alienate emotionally healthy single adults.

Steve/Sally the strong. This single adult has to perceive himself/herself as a "strong" individual, who really doesn't need the group. They view other single adults as either strong or weak. They push themselves to the max, whether at work or with a "friendly" game of tennis. The need to be strong may be misperceived by others as aloofness or arrogance.

Paul/Pris the spiritual. This single adult is a "Christian's Christian." They toss around Greek nuances and C.S. Lewis quotes. This single adult keeps a running tally on everyone's spirituality. Many carry "a burden" and are "glad to do it!" They have a strong need to be publicly recognized as spiritual persons.

Chris/Cynthia the intellectual. This single adult prides himself/herself on knowing where everyone stands on every issue. They have never once said, "I don't know." They have an opinion on everything and can be very verbal. This single adult does not want to be caught "unaware" or "uncertain" on any topic.

All of these single adults have enormous potential. They become a challenge to the single adult leader: How can I reach them? Unfortunately, some leaders focus on, "How can I CHANGE them?"

The leader should urge them to work for balance and vulnerability in their lives. For some singles, their success or intellect or strength is a shield behind which they hide. They will only let down that barrier and allow themselves to be known and loved in response to the persistent kindness of a leader.

Formulating a Christian Lifestyle

To develop a distinctively Christian lifestyle, one has to face several challenges.

Learn to reject the materialistic hedonism of contemporary single culture. "I am more than what I own, drive, wear, possess." The single adult must

constantly evaluate the "trinkets" so prized by a single adult subculture.
Learn to define oneself by other than a vocation or job. The first question
many singles ask is, "What do you do?" Some professions gain immediate
status, while others do not.

Learn to treat all people with dignity. It is easy to be a "with-it" single in a
single adult fellowship or group, to consider oneself slightly "superior" to
others in the group. The attitudes of racism, ageism, elitism, and sexism
die slowly among single adults.

Learn to be a good steward of one's talents and resources. Single adults need
to be aware that God has expectations of how they can share those
resources in kingdom-building. Paul wrote, "Therefore, as we have opportunity, let us do good to all people, especially to those who belong to the
family of believers" (Gal. 6:10).

Learn to extract good from every situation. Some single adults seemingly
have accumulated more than their fair share of life's lumps and bruises.
Some have social, financial, psychological, or emotional handicaps of some
degree. Some let others continue to use them as doormats. Some have
never learned to defend themselves.

But every "situation" can either be perceived as a problem or an opportunity. The single decides.

Develop a network of cheerleaders. The single adult is not called to be a lone
ranger. Rather, he needs other single adults and married adults for a
strong balance in his life. Single adult ministry offers a laboratory, of sorts,
to examine and fine-tune one's lifestyle.

Single adult groups have been tremendous motivators for change and
growth. But growth always occurs more expediently and orderly in the
climate of affirmation.

Questioning a Lifestyle

A single adult group must lovingly call into question its lifestyles, whether
individually or corporately. Alfred Montapert (*The Supreme Philosophy of
Life,* rev. ed., Books of Value, 1970, p. 89) has formulated some questions
which are a good resource for such an examination or evaluation.

- Am I doing the things that make me happy?
- Are my thoughts of noble character?
- How can I simplify my life?
- What are my talents?
- Does my work satisfy my soul?
- Am I giving value to my existence?
- How could I improve my life?

To that list I would add this question: Is Jesus Lord of my singleness?
Am I seeking *first* the kingdom of God? (Matt. 6:33)

Paul's words summarize the need for guidance in building, maintaining,
and evaluating a lifestyle. "Make it your ambition to lead a quiet life, to

mind your own business, and to work with your hands, just as we told you, so that *your daily life* [or lifestyle] may win the respect of outsiders" (1 Thes. 4:11-12, italics added).

Harold Ivan Smith
Executive Director of Tear-Catchers
Kansas City, Missouri

Harold's ministry is a consulting firm that deals with the single adult in the workplace. Two of his books published include *Pastoral Care for Single Parents*, Beacon Hill, *Tear Catchers*, Abingdon.

23. SEXUALITY AND MORAL CHOICES

"A healthy approach to decision-making in the area of sexuality will require a willingness to ask questions, to struggle, to live with ambiguity, and to look honestly at our fears, hopes, desires, and insecurities."

Terry Hershey

Slave or Free

Today's single adult lives in a world bombarded by sex. The moral decisions that they have to make are influenced by strong voices with a New Age philosophy. The pressure out there is great. The pressure inside of the single adult's life can be even greater.

Sex. We view it with alarm, we laugh about it, we feel guilty, we get excited, we sense a presence of dread (with the AIDS crisis)—but have we come to terms with our sexuality? Where do we turn for perspective? Is it possible to be a Christian and "sexual"? Is it possible to make healthy decisions in a world inundated with sexual stimuli? Is it possible to make healthy choices without simply resorting to a "list of rules"? The temptation is to reduce morality and sexuality to a nice, neat formula—a list of do's and don'ts, something akin to a seminar handout. Others have attempted such a simplistic view, but I cannot. To understand decision-making in our modern age, we cannot afford to pretend that life is either easy or simple. This chapter assumes that life is difficult. Decisions are complex. Single adults are not exempt.

A healthy approach to decision-making in the area of sexuality will require a willingness to ask questions, to struggle, to live with ambiguity, and to look honestly at our fears, hopes, desires, and insecurities.

What we can do in this context is to begin to create a framework that makes dialogue possible, that allows for personal reflection and change through the freedom to struggle with real concerns—a context that doesn't make the subject trivial or unreachable by single adults. Let me offer three principles that can begin to create such a context for singles to dialogue. The Pharisees discovered that there was another level to morality. Jesus said, "Your righteousness must surpass that of the Pharisees." On a behavioral model, that statement seems impossible. The point is relatively simple—morality must go deeper than behavior. It must touch the "heart"—or one's "belief system."

Moral choices begin with our identity. As the ad sponsored by the Humane Society—interested in encouraging people to open their homes to homeless animals—articulated boldly, over a full-page picture of a puppy and kitten, "It's who owns them that makes them important!"

In the same way, our moral choices are built on the foundation of "who owns us." In this case, identity and intimacy—not sexuality—are the primary issues. My decision-making with regard to my body becomes clouded when I fail to understand my need, addiction, and drive for intimacy. I can become easy prey to the unspoken promises of a modern generation sex-ethic.

The question becomes: "Who or what owns me?" (The Christian single has been bought by Christ through His blood.) Therein lies the impetus behind our decision-making. To answer that question requires honesty and a healthy introspection. I can be owned by my need to be needed, my need to rescue, my addiction to the "high" of a sexual experience, or even my addiction to the "high" of the "conquest," my need to be "held," my need to prove my masculinity (or femininity). It is in coming to terms with this area of neediness that we begin to successfully address the issue of our decision-making. For change will not be effective if it is strictly behavioral; it must touch "who I am"—which includes my fears, my drivenness, and my neediness.

A lasting change, however, can never be external. It must be internal. If morality is who and not what, then change comes when we learn to live life "from acceptance" and not "for acceptance."

Moral freedom is based on personal love and responsibility. Morality that is built on the foundation of "who owns me" encourages personal responsibility. And personal responsibility is frightening—especially if we are loved (by God and others) for reasons that have nothing to do with our actions or accomplishments. It takes our control away.

It is no wonder that we prefer to be "legalists." We feel powerful because legalism defines life by rigid limitations. There is a "line" that divides right from wrong. The assignment is to stay on the right side of the line—for there we are affirmed for our virtue. We seek to be exonerated by the rules. The question is no longer, "What is right?" but, "What can I get away with and have God still love me?"

"If we are ever to enter fully into the glorious liberty of the sons of God, we are going to have to spend more time thinking about spiritual freedom than we do," Robert Capon writes. "The church, by and large, has had a poor record of encouraging freedom. She has spent so much time inculcating in us the fear of making mistakes that she has made us like ill-taught piano students: we play our songs, but we never really hear them because our main concern is not to make music but to avoid some flub that will get us in dutch. She has made us care more about how we look than about who we are" (*Between Noon and Three*, Harper and Row, p. 148). Or, about "whose we are."

121

Why does responsibility unnerve us? Won't people take advantage of the system? Aren't there any standards? What criteria should we follow in exercising responsibility? To help answer those questions, let's look at the third principle:

Morality is about investment—personal commitments are the foundation for our choices. Whether we like it or not, our identities are made up of the commitments we have made. If we are "responsible," we can "make commitments"—or covenants, or pledges. Such commitments assume that we are not "victims" of life.

With regard to morality, we are confronted with this alternative: either we have choices and can make commitments, or we are at the mercy of our feelings, hormones, urges, and drives. We can approach life as a "gallant fighter" or a "victim." Our relationships can be "personal," and do not need to be merely "functional."

There is a two-step process at work here. The first is our need to come face-to-face with that expansive reservoir of sexual drives and needs that makes up our identities. And it is here that we need to stop and clarify our working definition of sex and sexuality. Simply put, sex is not intercourse. Sex is more than what happens with our bodies. It is the full range of what it means to be a male or female, the full range of emotions, needs, and drives. It means taking responsibility for all of what it means to be a body-person. In addition, sex gives us permission to "get to know" that part of our identity—namely our needs, insecurities, drives, and urges—that has remained for the most part hidden or repressed. If my sexuality means embracing the full range of my humanness, then I am compelled to get to know the hidden self—the irrational needs, the impulses, the obsessions. And God still loves me regardless of what He sees in the hidden self.

Is it possible that my emotions, feelings, drives, and urges are "user-friendly"? Can I befriend them? Can there be other options than repressing or ignoring or acting out?

Making Right Choices

The second step of this process is the permission to choose behaviors that are healthy for us and for those around us. The key word here is "choose." The foundation for choice must be God's Word and His moral choice for us. We are not just "at the mercy" of people, feelings, or life itself.

In other words, if morality is based on who (and not what), then the source of my identity declares that I am not only free "from," but free "to." Our freedom comes when we respect our boundaries and our bonds—those commitments established by choices we have made.

The alternative is to feel victimized, or overwhelmed, or caught "off guard." By not making choices in favor of previous "commitments"—namely, intimacy, mutual nurture, fidelity, celibacy, wisdom—my underlying desires "take control," and I feel as if I am "victimized" by them. ("I

122

just couldn't say no," we confess.) All the while, we are feeling guilty, or confused, or wishing for "more discipline," or working harder at repressing what is already there.

At this point, it is important for us to note the close connection between our morality and the "addictive process."

Our identities have been co-opted by a person or behavior or substance that promises (albeit through our projection) to insure our okayness and security. It provides us a source of "life"—while at the same time protecting us from and removing us from the very life it promises to provide. And we feel stuck, unable to escape our "predicament"—on the one hand, wanting release; on the other hand, believing we "need the fix" to be OK. Guilt only intensifies the craving for the addictive substance, activity, or person.

It is pointless for us to continually reprimand, or even encourage more discipline with a person who is locked into an addictive behavior pattern. What are the symptoms: repetition of negative behavior patterns, belief we can "handle" our problem, need to lie.

What's the solution? Listen to Sam Keen. "The cure for addiction lies in developing the witness self. . . . When I invite all that I am into awareness I realize that no one substance, activity, or person has the capacity to satisfy me fully" (*The Passionate Life*, Harper and Row, p. 140).

In other words, if we are loved, we are "free" to make choices that are healthy for us—not for fear of punishment, or for hope of reward—but because we are free to be "committed to health."

So where do we go from here if we want to be effective in communicating in the area of sexuality and morality? I recommend the following:

(1) Don't be a moral policeman. Your reputation is not at stake. There is no need to relieve people of responsibility. For it is the decision-making process that creates the relationship, and God wants responsible children, not clones.

(2) Teach biblical principles and truth. Allow for dialogue and debate. Use case studies and role playing as teaching devices.

(3) Support structures are a must. We set ourselves up for trouble when we make decisions in isolation. We need relationships to remind us of "who owns us," to provide perspective, to avoid myopia. Small groups are the best thing we can use to deal with the issue of sexuality and morality in our churches and single adult groups. Why? Because morality is developed in the context of relationships, not lectures.

(4) Practice forgiveness. We represent the God of second chances. The God of hope. The God who gives permission to be different, but godly.

Above all else, never assume the issues are "resolved." Keep the communication lines open. It is not our job to "have the answers." It is our job to love people, and to let them know that God never quits on them, and that maybe that will make a difference in the way we make decisions.

Terry Hershey
Executive Director of Christian Focus
Irvine, California

Terry's book, *Sex and the Choices We Make,* Group Books, was written from personal experience and pain as a minister of God's good grace. Terry is a charter member and former executive board member for NSL.

24. BATTERED AND BRUISED— THE WOUNDED SINGLE

"We must help the battered come to grips with their responsibility for health and wholeness in an attempt to allow them to gain control of their lives."

Dennis Miller

"A man was going down from Jerusalem to Jericho, when he fell into the hands of robbers. They stripped him of his clothes, beat him, and went away, leaving him half dead" (Luke 10:30). How often have we seen a single who has been left in this condition? They have been stripped of that which once had been dear. Their lifestyle has gone through extreme change and they have suffered rejection or failure. The emotions are charged with hate and hurt. They find their way to us, often as a last resort. How do we help? Here are some guidelines in our ministries.

Identify How They Have Become Battered
Everyone has a story. The truth is that the stories we hear do not always contain enough reality to help. Some people come to our ministries for pity. Others will want to continue the outpouring of hostilities by bringing new people into the picture. As you attempt to identify how the battered have become that way, it may be helpful to draw others into the helping process. Learn to gain permission to call on people who have been instrumental in the wounded person's life. The abuse and breakdown of relationships can be traced over a long period of time. We must help the battered come to grips with their responsibility for health and wholeness in an attempt to allow them to gain control of their lives.

All Pain Is Not Bad
A great deal of time and energy is spent in the avoidance of pain. Many people in the helping field have bought into this philosophy. The Bible points out a different attitude toward pain. James tells us that we are to be thankful when our lives have difficulties for it brings us to growth (see 1:2-3). Most of us, when faced with a tough situation, want out. We will do anything to avoid the pain. We will even seek out a helper to enable us to avoid what we must face if we are to grow. God offers a gentle leading that encourages those who help to lean into the pain as they listen rather than to avoid the pain along with those who suffer. This requires listening

to God, a light touch, and a willingness to be frustrated. Karl Rahner writes in *Encounters with Silence* (Christian Classics), "And what do these men want of me? Sometimes it's material help. Sometimes just the consolation of a sympathetic heart. Or if it's not that, then they look upon me as some kind of celestial insurance agent, with whom they can take out an accident policy for eternity, to make sure that You never break in upon their lives with the omnipotence of Your holiness and justice."

We Offer More Than They Want!
I believe that we can lose sight of God's calling on our lives. If we are to take people out of the wilderness, we must take them to the place that God has for them. I am sure that the wounded one spoken of in Luke 10 was a better person because of the help that he received. We know that the Good Samaritan did all that he could do. We need to do all that we can by realizing that our job is not done until we share the total love of God to those that He brings to us. The wounded and hurting are often verbal in telling us what kind of help they need. We must not be controlled by what people tell us they are willing to listen to. There will be those who will walk away from us because they do not want our kind of help. This is difficult to experience but cannot always be avoided (see Mark 10:17-22).

Encourage the Wounded to Do the Right Things
"For the sorrow that is according to the will of God produces a repentance without regret, leading to salvation; but the sorrow of the world produces death" (2 Cor. 7:10, NASB). There are many resolves the broken make as their wounds begin to heal. Some of those decisions are appropriate only if they are made for the right reasons. Learn to explore the "why" of each decision that is made. "Am I using God as a vending machine?" "Is my decision to move motivated by wisdom or anger?" "Is my faith helping me or am I using it to fuel my hurt and anger?" These and many other questions must be explored if the wounded and hurting are to find health and peace in their decision-making. Sorrow that is according to God, or used by God, will always ultimately lead an individual to strength and hope.

Give Them a Safe Place to Grow
When the Apostle Paul warned Timothy about the last days, he spoke of those who enter households and captivate weak women (2 Tim. 3:6). He was speaking of those who, through their own sin, find people in a place of weakness and capitalize on their pain. The bruised and battered need safety in our ministries. This subject needs to be addressed in our groups as a whole. Men should be the key contacts for men, and women for women. Our hurting and wounded brothers and sisters need people to pray with them and not people who will prey on them. It will take much time and sensitivity to build a safe place but it must be one of our primary concerns. We will often talk about the fact that our people are adults and

we cannot take responsibility for every aspect of their lives. This is true, but we must remember that they are wounded adults. Their capacities are reduced in many cases. Speaking of the divorce process, Jim Smoke writes, "Adjustment sometimes means that you have to make very important decisions for yourself, family and future while you are at your emotional worst" (*Growing through Divorce,* Harvest House). If this is true, then we must help our wounded in decisions about relationships as their wounds heal.

Healing Is a Process

Oftentimes, doctors will allow a patient with a large incision to heal from the inside out. They simply wire them shut and let the body do its job. There is often the urge to congratulate someone on a quick recovery when there is still a great deal of work left to be realized. We can place people in areas of responsibility too soon. We are tempted to see them move into close relationships before they are healed from the inside out. This is where it becomes helpful to encourage the hurting to keep a personal account of their growth, healing, and faith. Dr. Susan Muto writes, "Journaling enables us to keep track of those persons and events that really mean something to us. It enables us to lift out of life's flow those moments that have a forming effect, for better or worse, on our lives" (*Pathways of Spiritual Living,* Image Books). A journal also gives much to talk about when you find time to get together to share with a friend. Coming out of the confusion and pain that brings the hurting to us will be the personal sharing record that he/she has kept. You will be able to see more quickly and accurately the progress of those in your ministry. Someone else's journal must never be ours to read, but it is a great resource for the hurting and wounded to draw from as they share with us.

Don't Take Yourself Too Seriously

There are many despairing moments in ministry. It hurts to come on one that is not helped by our methods, prayers, and those solutions that have worked elsewhere. Oftentimes, we become angry at ourselves because we cannot find the key. We feel that we must do the whole job. This may not be possible for us at times. Remember, it is given to one man to sow, another to water, still another to reap, but God causes the growth (see 1 Cor. 3:7). We must learn to be content in letting God be the One to decide how helpful our help will be. God has told us that His ways are not ours and His thoughts are not ours (Isa. 55:8). I believe that a greater trust in God than in our own skills causes us to be more relaxed as we come into the presence of those who are already troubled.

Begin to Build Multiple Help Systems for Hurting Singles

This is one of the particular beauties of the church. We have so many different resources to draw on. Small groups, worship gatherings, personal friends, pastoral counseling, and many other ministries will allow the hurting to find constant support and guidance. This takes time for the hurting as they must build trust in each area. Constant encouragement from you will be most beneficial.

Build a Lending Library of Both Books and Tapes
It is a sad but true commentary on today's society that many people do not read. I have a wealth of help in my library that I cannot share with some. They have never learned to read or to concentrate on their reading. I have found it useful to duplicate the help from the books with corresponding tapes in each area. This also helps with the single parent who is too tired at the end of the day to read, but could find time to listen in the car while driving to and from work.

Set Aside Food and Funds
When all of the people were hot, tired, and hungry after following Jesus all day, the disciples were ready to send them away for food. Jesus said, "You give them something to eat" (Luke 9:13). We must not depend on agencies that are finding less and less funds. Encourage people in your ministry to share from their supplies. It doesn't take a great deal of sacrifice to stock a food pantry or have limited funds set aside for help. A group will grow in impact if, along with counseling, you can take a person to a food pantry and send groceries home with your prayers and advice. This kind of help can become a great encouragement to the hurting and wounded. It helps them to believe more in the provision of God.

Continue to Work on Your Own Faith and Walk
It is sad to see helpers become tired or burned-out in ministry. We must find ways to stay in touch with the Spirit of love, discipline, and power that called us into the ministry in the first place (2 Tim. 1:7). Our greatest calling is to stay faithful to our Lord as we work with people who have been let down by so many other areas of life. Seek to keep honest people around you who will help you stay in balance. Learn all you can about single adult ministry but stay in touch with the deep spiritual issues in your own life.

Dennis Miller
Minister to Singles
Grace Community Church, Tempe, Arizona

After 10 years in youth ministry, 10 years in the senior pastorate, and now as a singles pastor, Pastor Dennis has had many ministry experiences with battered and bruised singles.

25. DEALING WITH THE FORMER SPOUSE

"The divorced person must accept the fact that he or she is not responsible for the attitudes and actions of the former spouse. One cannot make a good relationship happen."

Bud & Kathy Pearson

Many divorced single adults need help in their attitudes and ways of functioning with their former spouses. In a singles ministry there is seldom the opportunity to work with both parties in a divorce situation. Therefore, minister to the one who is there with the goal in mind to help him or her develop the right attitude toward the other. This will also include providing information on ways to relate that will contribute to bring healing and help, so that parents, children, grandparents, and others will benefit. This must begin with each person taking responsibility for his or her own attitudes.

The Divorced Person Is Responsible for His or Her Own Attitudes

Dealing with the former spouse begins with dealing with oneself. The easiest thing to do is to focus on how bad life has become and to live in denial of where one is at this time in life.

Help the person accept where he or she is, not where they would like to be. Some single adults never accept their singleness, thinking of themselves as married even while they are not. This usually leads to a hurried remarriage that seldom works. Accepting their single status opens up the possibility of growth and wholeness as persons.

Help the person see the need for receiving and giving forgiveness. The past cannot be redone. God's way of dealing with it is through forgiveness. We can do the same; it is God's way. Each person needs to receive God's forgiveness for his or her part in the divorce. The single adult often places guilt on the former spouse because of guilt within. Facing one's own guilt and having it cleansed by the blood of Christ frees one to project forgiveness to the former spouse and others.

Either through verbal contact or by writing, one can ask forgiveness and express forgiveness to the former spouse. It may or may not be accepted readily, but the one doing it will have a new attitude and a new freedom.

There might be negative feelings toward parents, in-laws, or friends.

True forgiveness will bring release and open the way for moving ahead in life.

Dealing with the Former Spouse Involves Facing One's Past in the Divorce Realistically

Seldom is divorce the responsibility of only one party. The divorced person needs to get over the "blame game." Each person, honestly asking himself or herself why the divorce occurred, will quickly see that both parties played important roles in it. The divorced person who feels, "It was all my fault," needs to be released from that burden. This is as unrealistic as placing all the responsibility on the former spouse.

A more healthy approach is to accept responsibility for one's part in the divorce, realizing that the former spouse was also responsible. Forgiveness of self and the former spouse brings healing and a new attitude that opens one up to dealing with one's own need for growth and preparation for the future.

The Divorced Person Must Accept the Fact That He or She Is Not Responsible for the Attitudes and Actions of the Former Spouse

One cannot make a good relationship happen. Both parties must want a good relationship for it to be a reality. Often, this is not the case. The one who has a desire for it must realize that he or she is not responsible for the former spouse's actions. If the former spouse refuses to have a good relationship, it must be seen that it is his or her choice and responsibility.

The divorced person needs to avoid some things in respect to a former spouse who refuses a good relationship.

Avoid arguments that bring up old hurts and problems. "Love keeps no record of wrongs" (1 Cor. 13:5). Digging out past hurts is to be avoided.

Avoid trying "to make it better" when the other person refuses to do so. This adds fuel to the flame, just the opposite of what is desired.

Avoid trying to act as if things have not changed. This is a common approach that adds frustration to any attempt toward a better relationship. Accepting where both individuals are and working from there is the only plausible place from which to build.

Avoid self-help methods only. Be open to seeking professional help for yourself and the relationship when the need exists. Often a few counseling sessions will do wonders. This help might be a counselor, a mediator, a minister, or there might be a need for an attorney in certain cases.

Accepting responsibility for one's own attitudes is of utmost importance. Equally important is not accepting responsibility for the attitudes and actions of the former spouse. A growing person will be the result. One will not be held back by denial, anger, bitterness, or any other negative emotion when he or she has responsibly dealt with things as they are.

The Divorced Person, the Former Spouse, and the Kids

Divorce is always more traumatic where children are involved, for the parents tend to bring their own hurts into the lives of the kids.

The well-being of the children needs to be a top priority for a divorced couple. Children must never be used for the purposes of the parents in their struggle with each other. If one parent tries to use the children against the other parent, then the one who cares can choose not to respond.

The divorced parent must never say negative things about the other parent to the kids. In the tumult of separation and divorce, if careful thought is not given to what one says to the children, much harm can be done. It is easy to blame and talk about how no-good the former spouse is, and this is often done to children or in front of them. Children who are bombarded in this way will often be swayed toward the other parent, and especially when they are a little older and realize that the accusations are unfair or not all true.

A right relationship with both parents needs to be a priority. The former spouse is a parent too, and children will benefit by having a healthy relationship with both parents. They naturally identify with both parents, and always will, so their identities and self-esteem are related to these relationships.

There is a need for both parents to work out rules and goals for the children. The question needs to be asked: "What is best for the kids?" No matter what the cause of separation and divorce, parents need to communicate and cooperate for the benefit of their children. Divorce is traumatic for children just as it is for adults. But the children are at the mercy of their parents' attitudes.

Both parents, by caring and communicating, can establish the rules and goals for the children. If possible at all, write out the rules so that in both homes there is uniformity of expectations. Post them in a conspicuous place (like on the refrigerator) in both homes. This reduces the potential for conflict and confusion for all parties involved. The singles ministry can offer help by providing someone to sit with both parents and work this out.

Summary

There needs to be an awareness on the part of both parents that each person perceives what is going on from his or her own perspective. In counseling both parties, the counselor soon learns that each person sees the situation from his own orientation. This needs to be understood by both individuals. It can reduce the tendency to inflict wounds and helps each to refrain from name-calling and blaming.

The single adult minister or director who is aware can help divorced persons develop good attitudes toward former spouses and free them from feeling responsible for each other's attitudes and actions. The minister or director can also encourage cooperation between the parents for the benefit of their children.

The most important aspect in this is to teach the importance of trusting the Lord with one's life and the lives of children and former spouses. Prayer is the greatest resource—turning former spouses and children over to God and seeking wisdom for oneself to bring help and healing into everyday life.

Bud and Kathy Pearson
Bud is a Senior Pastor
Orange Coast Community Church, Orange, California

Bud and Kathy have had extensive counseling experience with hundreds of singles who struggle with the issues of divorce. They are authors, seminar speakers, and leaders in singles ministry.

MINISTRY
TO SINGLES

26. SINGLES HELPING SINGLES

"With proper direction and preparation, trained single lay counselors can help meet the real needs of their single brothers and sisters. Also, many single adults are gifted teachers and speakers and can lead Bible study classes geared to other singles."

Rich Kraljev

Where is single America anyway? You'll find them in restaurants, singles bars, clubs, and health spas by the thousands. Sundays you'll find them in the pews of virtually every church in America.

Unfortunately today this vast resource pool is going untapped in some respects by both single adults and the church. Many adult singles tend to minimize their own potential, and because of a lack of understanding, many churches are turning singles away because they don't fit conveniently into traditional molds and comfortable stereotypes. Because we are stewards of the gifts God has given us, single adults and Christian leaders need to be challenged to discover and put to good use such a deep well of talent and ability!

What does God say about single adults and their lifestyles? Jesus referred to the single state as a unique and special kind of gift (Matt. 19:11-12). He Himself had chosen this as His lifestyle. For those without children the single life can be a time of *simplicity* because of not being responsible for a family; of *energy* that flows with greater flexibility from available time; of *opportunity*—never before has there been a time such as now with so many singles. Today is a time that begs for the considerable energies and abilities that singles have to offer. For those with children, it can be a time of growing and receiving from many who can help.

What Do Singles Have to Offer to Each Other and the Church?

• In many cases, compassion and sensitivity to human need born from brokenness and subsequent healing.

• A profound and deep appreciation for the renewing grace of God forged from their own redemption and restoration.

• An ability to look at life with realism and a sense of humor.

• A variety of spiritual gifts and abilities for ministry given by God.

• Flexibility and creative energy within the single lifestyle.

• A desire for evangelism and discipleship designed to reach the unchurched singles of the community.

• A loyalty and dedication to Christ's church and its local leadership that manifests itself in commitment, follow-through, and faithfulness.

Here are some practical suggestions in the form of a shopping list of ministries that singles could be involved in.

Ministry One to Another
• Because many have experienced the break-up of marriages, singles who have healed and are trained can become adept at beginning and developing a divorce recovery ministry. Widows/widowers can help much the same way.
• With proper direction and preparation, trained single lay counselors can help meet the real needs of their single brothers and sisters.
• Small group ministries led by single adults in homes, the church, office buildings, and restaurants create a sense of continuity and community for single adults.
• Many single adults are gifted teachers and speakers and can lead Bible study classes geared to other singles.

Support and Healing One to Another
• Singles who have become successful at single parenting are ideal leaders for single parenting support groups.
• Support groups for those afflicted by eating disorders, sexual abuse, and compulsive behaviors are well within singles' abilities to provide help and facilitate discussion.
• Singles can pool their resources and be a real help to each other in cooking, auto repair, moving, house maintenance, and so much more.

Outreach One to Another
• Trained and organized into teams, single adults can be effective in personal peer evangelism.
• Singles can meet a great need in our society today with compassionate ministries to shut-ins and the hospitalized.
• Singles can fill a big gap by acting as friends and role models in Big Brother/Sister programs.

Having Fun One with Another
• Singles have deep social and relational needs. Single adults can plan and stage activities of a social nature that create great excitement.
• Camps, conferences, hikes, rafting trips, tours, and excursions near and far are all possibilities when singles are given leadership.

Building the Body of Christ Together
• Single adults are productive and fruitful. They can be biblical tithers and an asset to church finances.
• Singles are stalwart prayer partners to the church and each other.

- Many singles are skilled professionals in the business world and have much to offer administratively to committees and planning organizations.
- Singles can set the pace for ministry in many areas of the church.

The possibilities for single adults in ministry to each other are endless. The only limiting factor is lack of vision and willingness to use this great untapped resource. It's time to cease looking at singles as a liability and open our eyes to the great asset they can be to each other and the church.

Richard Kraljev
Pastor—Minister with Singles
New Hope Positive Singles, Portland, Oregon

Rich is a conference, workshop, and retreat speaker to singles, with over 12 years of single adult ministry experience.

27. MARRIEDS HELPING SINGLES

*"The first step is simple—opening one's home to single
adults. Inviting another person into the home, however, also
implies access to the lives of that couple or family."*

Doug Calhoun

In Christian ministry a gap often exists between adult singles and married couples. Age alone does not seem to be the cause of this separation. Marriage establishes a demarcation line between the couple and their friends who are single. Divergent interests and commitments begin to place them into two separate worlds. Children add complexity to the lives of couples, intensifying the already-present desire to have more time by themselves. How can there be a meaningful ministry between these two groups?

The concern of this chapter focuses on the important effect married couples can exert in the lives of the single members of the church congregation. Both marrieds and singles are *adult* members of the body of Christ first, with a specific relational status second. At least, it is argued, this is a fairer perspective than that which consigns singles to some stage of ongoing adolescence until they get married. Marrieds may not consciously perceive single adults in a "less-mature" status. It is simply the mind of the world seeping in and saying that married people are the responsible ones.

Recently a group of three singles and a young married couple met for dessert. Two of the singles were older than the couple. Yet on more than one occasion the married couple asked the singles, "What do single people think of. . . ?" as though they expected some nonadult response. The couple finally remarked, "We really are all the same age!" That discovery of mutual adulthood was somehow a surprise! Mutuality in Christ is a goal for all believers.

Why Help?

Scripturally, married people live under the injunction "to love one another." After a couple gets married, the tendency is to pull out of other relationships and to focus only on the marriage. The notion that love is a quantity that we must hoard prompts people to carefully invest their love in their marriages. The love that Jesus calls us to actually works on the principle that the more you give it away the more you possess (Luke 9:24-25). Somehow the married couple must think where they can serve beyond their own family unit, in order to enrich themselves.

Ecclesiastically, the complete segregation of people into age-groups or preference areas falls short of the true marvel of the redeemed community of the faith. Paul's grand picture of Christ's body in the Book of Ephesians constantly portrays the oneness and interdependence of the members of Christ (Eph. 2:11-22; 3:6, 10, 14-15, 20; 4:3-6). One of the strongest evidences of the power of the reconciling Gospel can be demonstrated when "natural" group barriers are broken down or ignored because of Christ. While recognizing the distinctions between marrieds and singles, the ability of each group to relate to and serve the other reflects the presence of God at work.

Many singles will end up being married. The interaction between the two groups allows important learning opportunities for singles to observe Christian marriage at work. How crucial this is today where a growing percentage of singles come from broken families and/or homes without a biblical basis. Modeling does not imply perfection; rather, it requires people who are willing to live their lives before others in a shared fashion.

Needs Necessitate Help

Transience hallmarks our generation, particularly the single person. Employers feel little regret shipping off one of their unattached workers to another city. The relocation costs are much smaller than for a married person and the "supposed" ease in uprooting makes for a quick transition. The business industry relies heavily on the young adult population to be mobile, flying between the major metropolises. Though strategically true, this attitude fails to realize the cost to these people. Such uprootedness usually results in being some distance from family and friends. The lack of roots in the community itself creates loneliness. Many such individuals have to live without any support system in their immediate area. A couple or family has their own enclave to rely on, but the single person must fend for himself.

Another facet of the single person's existence derives from their living arrangements. Most either live alone or else with other singles whom they rarely see because of schedule conflicts. This isolation suits the normal desire of this age for independence; but an equally strong, though conflicting, need for belonging remains unfulfilled. Perhaps the forced separation from home brings welcome relief, or perhaps not. Either way, many singles desire to have someplace where they can be a part of a family. Relating only to other singles can result in being unconnected with a broader scope of life. Knowing and being known still remain as key concerns of an adult single.

It should be noted briefly that marrieds have needs of their own which single people may help meet. For instance, a couple cannot fill each other's total need for relationships. They can become ingrown and unserving in their outlook. The freshness brought by a single person and the initiation to serve can bring a new vitality and appreciation to the marriage.

Ways Married Couples Can Help

From the start it is important to stress that a "program" is not what is needed. Rather, what follows is a description of a way of life, of building friendships. The first step is simple—opening one's home to single adults. Inviting another person into the home, however, also implies access to the lives of that couple or family. And that is just where mutuality is needed. The single person may need a place of refuge or rest from his own world. The focus may be conversation or games or politics or hobbies or study. Whatever avenue is used, there is opportunity for the building of relationships that will enhance all the people involved. Think for a minute how refreshing it would be to have the freedom to kick up your heels, relax, and forget your high-pressure job (or your lack of a job); to be able to frolic like a kid for a while. Or on the other hand, imagine the joy of being able to discuss issues that concern you and be taken seriously by those listening. In short, the fundamental idea is to develop acceptance of each other and to cultivate trust.

What may begin as a casual acquaintance between a couple and a single adult has the potential of becoming a meaningful friendship—with both the husband and wife. Being able to offer safe relationships with each spouse individually or together presents a unique opportunity for the single person to develop relationships uncomplicated by romance. If the couple is older, the pattern may resemble that of parent/child; if they are closer in age, it can simply be a strong peer relationship. These friendships can be very formative in interpersonal skills and self-evaluation. By creating a sense of belonging, the couple provides a place to know and be known safely.

Another arena of ministry arises from bringing adult singles without children into family life as a whole. If the couple has children, encourage the single person to develop relationships with them. Kids have a way of lavishing love and affection on anyone who takes the time to be with them. Parents already know the joy this love brings. Sharing this gift with singles who may be lonely can be like administering a life-saving drug; it can bring meaning and hope back into their lives.

All this indeed calls for a growing level of trust and communication between each person and a willingness to allow God to work. Sharing disappointments or resolving conflicts with each other are as important as any gift one could give to the other. The relationship cultivated between the single adult and the couple becomes a school for learning love in all its fullness. The reality of a lived-out marriage can correct the idealistic conception of marriage or redeem the shambles left from a broken marriage or a broken family in childhood.

The mutuality of this friendship appears in the ways people learn to give and to receive from each other. The ages of people concerned affect the avenues this mutual service manifests itself. Besides what is inherent in the previous suggestions, the couple can especially help by connecting the single person with the broader church congregation or the community. Explaining traditions or upcoming events, sitting with them at meetings, inviting them to participate in planning or putting on programs—all these are ideas to involve someone who is new as having difficulty plugging into the scene.

One other specific service is providing counsel for the single person. This should probably come about slowly in the relationship and at the request of the adult single. In any relationship, friends have to earn the right to be heard and to develop trust before they can speak the truth in love. A married couple can provide helpful insight for a single person. If couples are open to this, the opportunities will present themselves.

How Can Churches and Pastors Help?

The attitudes of the church leadership occupy a pivotal role in the life of its congregation. To build the kind of interaction discussed in this chapter will take effort on the attitudinal end as well as trying some program changes. Regarding attitudes, the manner in which comments are given about singles' events or congregational affairs can carry the connotation that singles are not really part of the whole church. The implication can be that singles are great to have around when the church needs a labor force, but not when it's considering leaders/board members.

For example, a church can sponsor a Dinner-for-Eight program on a monthly or bimonthly basis. Arrange to have two couples from the church and four singles meet for dinner. The interchange between the individuals creates meaningful relationships which might not have happened otherwise. In the Sunday School program, offer electives that are available to all adults plus some specifically targeted for singles or for marrieds. The same idea holds for small group Bible studies; try to provide a balance for the needs of both. Giving singles responsibility in the church affirms them and builds the church. Are singles on the governing boards? Singles certainly have more to contribute than simply being baby-sitters in the nursery or waiters at a banquet.

In the discipleship area, the relationships between singles and marrieds are key. Many singles want someone they can look up to in the faith. Many couples can learn much from adult singles. An older Christian can provide what the individual's parents were unable or unwilling to give him. Encourage the older women to train the younger ones in the Lord (Titus 2:3-5). Also in terms of general church activities, this may mean consideration should be given to specific publicity for the singles to be included. (E.g., "Church Family Night"—how can that be reworded to convey welcome to singles?) Are the singles meaningfully included in the planning and concerns of church retreats or summer "family" camps?

The wise pastor and congregation will sense the potential for the future of their church when looking at the younger singles, and will cultivate the interchange between marrieds and singles.

Cautions to Be Considered
Building healthy relationships takes effort and commitment. A couple can probably handle only a few (two or three) such relationships at any given time. The loyalty and perseverance they offer to a few people carries more value than many superficial acquaintances. To avoid overextension, each person needs to feel free to honestly communicate with the others. Asking too much too soon of the single or married person will dampen the enthusiasm for the friendship. It may be in order at the beginning stages to more explicitly spell out what is being offered or expected, without sounding too stiff. (E.g., if the couple or single has children who require attention early in the morning, explain why this puts a time limit on the evening's activity.)

The married couple (especially if they have children) will be tempted to see the single person only on the couple's own terms or timetable. While to some extent this may need to be the case, the underlying attitude fails to connote equality or mutuality. Similarly, people should resist a one-sided or one-directional approach to the relationship; namely, we, the married couple will now help this "poor" single person. Instead, both parties should try to engender a spirit of discovery and loving service to each other. The couple must guard against these relationships substituting for their own marital relationship. It may be easier to talk with that single man or woman than one's own spouse, but that is no excuse for failing to give energy and time to work on one's marital bonds. In the end, this kind of tension and its proper resolution will demonstrate the work involved with marriage, and that is a needed lesson for everyone.

One can easily see that the downside of this tension could be the start of an affair. Yes, it is possible. Hopefully, fear of what may happen will not hinder folk from building good friendships that honor God with the opposite sex. Spouses must discuss how they feel about the husband getting close to a single woman, or the wife to a single man. It may be helpful for the couple to agree together on a method of bringing this issue up for discussion before the pressure of the event itself. The single person also has responsibility to mention the dilemma if it is developing. Most of the time, the deeper relationships will form between members of the same sex; but the opportunity for opposite-sex friendships is important.

While there are many advantages to mutual caring, both parties should realize that this is not meant simply to be free baby-sitting, a laundry service, a hotel, or meal-dispensing station. Such things may be given to each other, but beware of any emotional blackmail to obtain them.

Conclusion
The ability and commitment to developing long-term and loyal friendships benefits all those involved and the church as a whole. Somehow Christ

always gives us more capacity to love and to give, even when we think we have reached our limits. To offer such care between singles and marrieds brings health, challenge, and growth in our obedience to our Lord, and a valuable perspective on life and marriage.

Doug Calhoun
Minister to Young Adults
Park Street Church, Boston, Massachusetts

Doug and his wife Adele have been ministering to singles in their home for the last 10 years through both a local church ministry and Inter-Varsity Christian Fellowship.

28. COUNSELING THE DISCOURAGED

"Accepting that the discouraged single is a unique unrepeatable miracle of God identifies him as one God loves and cares for very much. Identify God as One who draws near when we are discouraged."

Dan Lundblad

Categories

There are three categories of discouraged persons who seek out a ministry to single adults:

Those who are discouraged from losing a spouse by death or divorce. The crisis in their marriage has left them with many hurts, questions, disappointments, and problems. Walking into a single adult ministry is admitting, often for the first time, "I'm discouraged and I need some help."

Those who are discouraged from early environmental factors in their homes. Various situations and parenting styles instill within children an encouraged or discouraged sense of identity. Parenting styles that are highly autocratic produce an environment which is highly critical. Parents are often found to focus on mistakes, demand perfection in work, and fail to encourage the child with praise or positive feedback. Children are overprotected and fail to receive the support to establish a sense of independence and courage to face the world as an adult. Studies have shown that children growing up with an alcoholic parent may have difficulty developing a sense of trust with others and thus struggle at developing intimacy in relationships.

Those who have failed to have their goals and expectations in life met. They find themselves alone and without a real sense of purpose and direction in life. Unmet goals and expectations might include:

- financial stability
- satisfying employment
- academic pursuits
- lack of intimate friendships
- strife with parents and/or children.

Profile of the Discouraged Single Adult

Discouragement is a term used to describe a state of mind before depression. Though a discouraged person may have brief episodes of depression, the period of discouragement is characterized by a general malaise or feeling that life has let him down. Characteristics of a discouraged single adult are: a low self-esteem displayed in inability to belong to something or someone, inability to move beyond survival needs to satisfying one's full potential in life, and inability to contribute to the need of others. Another characteristic is a lack of confidence demonstrated by a withdrawn individual who does not relate easily with others. Confusion and bitterness over his situation is demonstrated by conversations carried on in caustic, argumentative, and judgmental fashion.

Discouraged people often use one of the following defense mechanisms. *Denial.* To deny one's feelings of worthlessness or feelings of anger at someone. Discouraged people who use denial usually try to present an image of, "I've got it all together," and usually believe they do. *Repression.* To repress one's feelings in an attempt to cover them up. Repressed feelings will usually reveal themselves in explosive behavior or psychosomatic illnesses. *Projection.* To project one's feelings onto someone else in an attempt to give up ownership of the problem and blame someone else. *Rationalization.* To justify one's behavior by giving some logical reason why something was done.

Guidelines for Counseling the Discouraged Single Adult

At the request of the individual, meet initially to demonstrate concern by listening to his story and offering your support to help *him* resolve *his* problem. You must avoid the temptation to carry the burden of the problem yourself and solve it *for* him.

Suggest involvement in one of the following options. Begin by encouraging involvement in a local single adult ministry to establish a sense of belonging and purpose. Next, establish a counseling relationship with this individual with identified goals for counseling and a predetermined number of sessions. Caution needs to be exercised regarding the longevity of the counseling relationship.

Development of your ministry could be stifled with many discouraged persons looking to you for their answers. Also, recognize that you may need to refer the person to another professional helper.

Start in your counseling where the individual is, not where you think he should be or where you eventually want him to be. Acknowledge with him that growth does not happen overnight—it takes time to make permanent changes.

Acknowledge the individual's worth in God's eyes and yours. Accepting that the discouraged single is a unique unrepeatable miracle of God identifies him as one God loves and cares for very much. Identify God as One who draws near when we are discouraged. "The Lord delights in the way of the man whose steps He has made firm; though he stumble, he will not fall, for the Lord upholds him with His hand" (Ps. 37:23-24).

Separate the individual's worth from mistakes and disappointments. We are all precious in God's sight; however, sin keeps us from doing everything according to His purpose for our lives. If we have God's Spirit living within us, mistakes and disappointments can become effective teachers directing us back to a right relationship with God and others.

Learn to recognize your limitations and refer to a more-qualified counselor, psychologist, or psychiatrist when necessary. If long-term counseling is indicated, refer early so the individual can develop a counseling relationship with someone he will work with for a while. Don't counsel beyond your training and set the counselee up for dealing with termination issues in order to be transferred to another counselor.

Therapeutic Qualities of a Single Adult Ministry

A place to belong. Many discouraged persons have come from families where strife was present in the formative years. "Family" often carries negative connotations and leaves individuals with no fulfillment of this need to belong to a family of significant people. The church offers people an alternative to "family" in the body of Christ. As one involves himself with the body of Christ known as the single adult ministry, significance is found in belonging to this body.

A place to be encouraged. Discouraged singles need an environment where they are encouraged to learn about themselves and the present situation. Whether the issue at hand is loss of a spouse, early environmental factors, or unfulfilled goals, the resources inherent in and available to a single adult ministry will bring healing to the lives of discouraged single adults.

A place to serve and share. Provide opportunities for serving others and sharing one's experience and knowledge with them. Emotional healing enables people to reach out and solidify their progress by sharing with others. The Apostle Paul wrote, "Praise be to the God and Father of our Lord Jesus Christ, the Father of compassion and the God of all comfort, who comforts us in all our trouble, so that we can comfort those in any trouble with the comfort we ourselves have received from God" (2 Cor. 1:3-4).

Eight Ways to Put Courage Back into the Life of a Discouraged Person

Give responsibility. Share the success of the single adult ministry with individuals who need to realize the benefits of investing their time in assuming responsibility in some small area of the ministry. The role may be as simple yet significant as:

- setting tables for dinner
- passing out name tags
- preparing coffee for class on Sunday morning.

Ask for individual opinion or advice. The feelings of the discouraged person will give new insight into the needs of a single adult ministry and affirm the worth of that person.

Avoid the temptation to rescue. Unless the individual has walked through the discouragement himself, he will miss the lessons that life has to teach. Learn to walk beside discouraged persons.

Acknowledge accomplishments. Once the discouraged individual makes even the smallest contribution, acknowledge it with a word of thanks and encouragement. Enhance, build up his reputation.

Concentrate on improvement, not perfection. Identify goals that can be attained in small steps. Learning to walk again comes with slow, steady improvement.

Stimulate independence. Encourage single adults to assume responsibility for a project of their own. Give them the freedom to fail and succeed.

Help develop a sense of interdependence between yourself and the single adult. Learn to be vulnerable with individuals who desire to grow through their discouragement.

Foster a spirit of cooperation between "healing" single adults. Facilitate ministry where singles have to work with and support one another with words of encouragement or a helping hand to accomplish a specific role, goal, or task.

The discouraged can be encouraged. God's Word and God's people can and do bring healing and help. Use all the resources of ministry to help those who cannot help themselves.

Dan Lundblad
Pastor to Single Adults and Director of Counseling Center
Colonial Woods Missionary Church, Port Huron, Michigan

As a social worker and pastor over the last 12 years, Dan has counseled hundreds of single adults going through crisis points in their lives.

29. COUNSELING "IRREGULAR" (DEPENDENT AND DOMINANT) SINGLES

> *"Educate the church body in accepting and helping the irregular person. The congregation must see even the irregular single as part of the entire body of Christ."*
>
> *Jim E. Towns*

Madison Avenue and mass media set a "cookie-cutter" normalcy for acceptable behavior. Positive singles are usually welcomed in the church. It is a wise pastor who realizes that God has entrusted singles—even some irregulars—to him to shepherd. Have you ever heard anyone say, "That's the way I am; I cannot help it"? Sometimes there is some truth in a statement like that, but usually it is a cop-out. It is easier for irregulars to ask others to adjust to their ways than to change their behavior.

Types of Personality Temperaments

Every human personality has a combination of characteristics. The classic Greek and Roman philosophers as well as contemporary writers have categorized characteristics into temperaments. Hippocrates, a Greek philosopher and physician, was the first to give some attention to this area 400 years before the time of Christ. The Romans continued to follow the Greek's ideas about personality. In the late 1700s, a German philosopher named Immanuel Kant was influential in popularizing a revised theory of temperaments in Europe. In contemporary times Tim LaHaye has familiarized America with the classic concepts of four personality temperaments. Most people seem to be dominated by characteristics in one temperament and strongly influenced by traits in a second or third type. An examination of temperaments will aid in understanding the difference in regular and irregular behavior.

Sanguine—Happy Harry—the extroverted optimist. Harry is lively and emotionally optimistically warm. By nature he is friendly and has a nice personality. He has a "happy good time" entertaining people. Harry is at his best when he is the life of the party. The sanguine is a good salesman since he is never at a loss for words. This type person is often envied by many people who are less extroverted. People with this temperament make good entertainers, salesmen, social workers, actors, and speakers.

There are possible weaknesses as well as strengths in each temperament. Happy Harry is often restless, disorganized, impractical, and egotistical. His noisy mannerisms make him appear more confident than he really is. The spiritual needs of sanguine persons are self-control, long-suffering, faith, peace, and goodness.

Melancholy—Weepy Wendy—the introverted pessimist. She is extremely selective, analytical, and thorough concerning life. As a deep thinker, her idealism tends to exaggerate the negative. Therefore, she is a perfectionist with a sensitive emotional nature. Wendy will find a great deal of meaning in life from some form of personal sacrifice. She is a faithful friend and has a deep appreciation for aesthetics.

Several philosophers have concluded that melancholy temperament has the greatest strengths. Yet, this positive potential is usually accompanied by some of the largest potential weaknesses. Wendy may be subject to moodiness, self-centeredness, rigidity, and vengefulness. If the melancholy is dominated by these weaknesses, she may become a neurotic, hypochondriac person who neither enjoys herself nor is enjoyed by others. If Wendy saw two people talking she would assume that they were saying something bad about her. The sanguine in the same situation would assume they were admiring her. Many of the great artists, educators, inventors, geniuses, and musicians are melancholy.

Choleric—Workaholic Wayne—the strong-willed, hard-driving person. He is the hot, quick, active, practical temperament. Usually he is self-sufficient and independent as he sets superhigh goals and works tirelessly to achieve. It is easy for him to make decisions for people. Since he thrives on activities; adversities only serve as encouragement. He does not sympathize or show much compassion toward others. He tends to use people for his own purposes, then ignore them. This sometimes causes him to be opportunistic. Through these negative characteristics, there are positive traits of leadership. Most of the world's great leaders, executives, idea men, and producers have been cholerics.

The greatest spiritual needs of the single workaholic include gentleness, meekness, goodness, and long-suffering. Some people in this temperament have yielded to the Lord God and have become powerful Christian leaders.

Phlegmatic—Straight Sam—the slow, good-natured person. Sam is calm, cool, well-balanced, and has an easygoing temperament. He is happy, unexciting, pleasant, and avoids excessive involvement as much as possible. This person never gets ruffled-up regardless of circumstances and seldom gets angry or laughs. As he keeps his emotions under control, he enjoys a dry sense of humor. Sam can keep people in "stitches" and never crack a smile. He is a big teaser who delights in poking fun at other temperaments. Straight Sam makes a good accountant, diplomat, scientist, teacher, leader, or a technician who is meticulous.

A study of personality and temperaments is primarily to be used for "self-analysis." A by-product of the analysis should be to become more understanding of the strengths and weaknesses of others. An irregular single may say, "My personality temperament hinders me." Many times irregulars are "locked in" to "hang-ups" and try to explain why they cannot relate to others in an appropriate manner. Victory is a moment-by-moment appropriation of the Word of God in every area of life.

Types of Manipulators
Your personality temperament is the innate raw product from which your actions and behavior become manifested. Irregular singles are the world's best manipulators. There are several fundamental ways temperament may reveal manipulative behavior.

A dictator. This person exaggerates his strengths. He likes to dominate and control people. Quoting authorities and giving orders is the dictator's pleasure. There are different kinds of dictators. Some of these are "boss," "rank puller," "godfather," and "God's junior partner."

A weakling. This person is the dictator's victim. He is directly opposite from the dictator. The weakling tries to develop skills in coping with the dictator. He exaggerates his sensitivity and is passively silent. Variations of the weakling are the "confused," "spacy," "worrier," and the "withdrawer."

A calculator. This person exaggerates his control. He tries to control other people by outwitting, deceiving, and lying. Variations of the calculator are the "poker player," "con artist," "blackmailer," and "seducer."

A clinging vine. This person exaggerates his dependency. He is the opposite of the calculator. He is one who wants to be taken care of and led around. He is glad to let others do his work for him. There are several variations of the clinging vine such as the "parasite," "helpless," "hypochondriac," "crier," and "baby."

A bully. This person exaggerates his aggression and cruelty. He loves to control other people by implied or direct threats. Pushing people around is a favorite game. Variations of the bully are the "tough guy," "threatener," "nagger," and "humiliator."

A nice guy. This person exaggerates his love and caring. He kills everybody with kindness. At times this person will almost make you "sick of niceness" when you are around him because he seems too "sugarcoated" rather than real. There are several variations of the nice guy such as "pleaser," "nonoffender," and "goody-goody."

A judge. This person exaggerates his criticalness. He does not trust anyone and blames whoever he can. In his resentment, he is slow to forgive. Variations of the judge are the "convictor," "vindicator," "blamer," and "know-it-all."

A protector. This person exaggerates his support. He is directly opposite the judge. The protector is oversympathetic, nonjudgmental, and "spoils" others. He will not let the people he is protecting stand up for themselves and grow up. Variations of the protector are the "helper," "mother hen," "martyr," "enabler," and "defender."

The more a pastor/leader understands about behavior, the more he should be able to evaluate "irregulars."

Helping "Irregulars"

The insightful pastor/leader will adapt the following graphic helpful hints into ministering to singles with irregular behavior.

Make personal observations. When a single demonstrates irregular behavior or has become exceptionally manipulative, then seriously respond to the person.

Get close to the individual and build some trust. Though it seems cliché, there is truth in the fact that the irregular does not care how much you know until he knows how much you care.

Help the person in self-evaluation. Dialogue and compare their behavior with others around. When the irregular sees the need for behavioral change, progress will come.

Admit need. The irregular can be gently guided into admitting the answer to questions like, "Is my behavior pleasing God?" This person also needs to realize any offensive behavior to other people.

Resolve problems. Journey with the person toward resolving the personal problems whether behavioral or spiritual.

Accept and help. Educate the church body in accepting and helping the irregular person. The congregation must see even the irregular single as part of the entire body of Christ. A classic example could come from observing how a family treats a handicapped member. They treat the person as a regular person. Society treats them as irregular. The pastor can help to get people to accept this single as a person, not just as irregular.

You can do something about a single who is an absolute frustration in your life. There is no room to cop out. Sometimes the pastor/leader must play "hardball"; he must call sin by its correct name—sin! In other words, exercise church discipline when a member is living in blatant sin.

One type of an irregular single can be a little strange because of lack of capacities and skills. The other type is just plain defiant and deliberate at attention-getting and hurting. If overt defiant behavior is a direct choice of sinful will, then correction must come. The Scripture in Matthew 5 and 18 should be carefully followed.

Do not be afraid to call behavior irregular when it is related to any form of chemical abuse.

Realistic Responses in Counseling "Irregulars"

There are several responses that you may use in dealing with irregulars.

(1) Give and interpret exams. Several counseling tools are available with minimal training required. A licensed counseling/psychological service should be consulted.

(2) Counsel.

(3) Make referrals.

(4) Accept. Some "irregular" singles are not going to change enough to become "regular." We must accept them as they are.

Jim E. Towns, Ph.D.
Professor of Communications
Stephen F. Austin University, Nacogdoches, Texas

Through an extensive ministry with single adults and as a professor on the university campus, Jim has had professional experience in counseling. Three of Jim's books are: *One Is Not A Lonely Number,* Crescendo Press, *Single . . . But Not Alone,* JM Press, and *Solo Flight,* Tyndale House Publishers.

30. HELP THROUGH THE DIVORCE

"Work toward helping both parties accept their full responsibility for the problems which caused the divorce. Many people wish to dump responsibility onto the ex-spouse."

John Splinter

Divorce is recognition of the fact that a marriage has become very ill. The illness is preceded by symptoms, even in cases of infidelity. Very few marriages are truly irreconcilable if given proper support, counseling, prayer, and time to heal. However, in many cases, pastors and friends are not given enough opportunity or time to help effect a healing. This chapter deals with what a pastor or friend may do to be of help throughout the pending divorce process.

By the time divorce is seriously considered, there has usually been a great amount of pain in the marriage. An emotional separation has occurred, sometimes days before, sometimes years before, the actual filing for divorce. Churches have a dilemma to confront: Do they stick to traditional positions and demand that people fit round pegs into square holes, or do they do their best to be as supportive as possible to the couple as they struggle through what may be the most difficult period of their lives?

There are no easy solutions. The issues are frequently as complex as the individuals themselves. What may be right in one situation may be wrong in another. Each situation must be approached individually.

Churches and friends face a challenge: To uphold a standard of biblical and personal values, while at the same time allowing for individuals to fail, and in that time of failure, to be as healing, forgiving, and redeeming as possible. The church must be a place for healing wounds; finding support and prayer; a place wherein divorcing people and their children may find peace, love, redemption, and encouragement.

What can pastors, singles leaders, and friends do to be of assistance throughout this trauma?

Role of the Pastor or Singles Leader
As a person wanting to help, there are some key questions you need to ask yourself before offering help. Some of these questions include: (1) Can you be supportive of divorcing people while at the same time hating divorce? (2) Are you willing to seek reconciliation at high costs? (3) Are you being forced, by your actions or support, to choose sides, or to appear to choose sides? (4) If Jesus Christ were to walk through the divorce with

this couple, how would He offer His support to them?

You as a pastor, have the task of creating a climate of healthy marriages, forgiveness, reconciliation, redemption, love, and healing. Know, however, that forgiveness doesn't solve the problem causing the divorce. It only clears the air, allowing free discussion of the real problems. These problems must be addressed.

Help your people forgive one another. Emotions of vengeance frequently find expression during and after divorce. Children frequently become unwilling victims to parental battles. (Picture a rag doll being used as a weapon to hit an ex-spouse. The child is the rag doll. It's not hard to see who is most hurt by this process.)

If you are able to slow the process of divorce, try to do so. Sometimes separation is a better option, while both parties receive professional counseling. Separation is especially important in cases of physical or sexual abuse. Sometimes a hurting marriage can be saved by simply slowing down the divorce process and having people get help.

From the time prior to emotional separation until well after divorce, one or both parties to the divorce may feel they are losing their sanity. Suicide is frequently thought about by many divorcing people. It can be normal to feel crazy during this time. Acquaint yourself with the grief stages so that you can recognize them when you see them, and help your people work through them as they encounter them.

Work toward helping both parties accept their full responsibility for the problems which caused the divorce. Many people wish to dump responsibility onto the ex-spouse. People will not be ready for a new relationship until they have accepted full responsibility for their part in the last relationship's failure.

Practical Suggestions

Work toward avoidance of war. Try to help maintain an attitude of cooperation on both sides. (Realize that peacemakers are often shot by both warring parties.) If you are able, spend time praying with both parties. Pray for God's healing. Pray for forgiveness. Pray for the children if there are any. Pray for healing. And yes, pray for hope of reconciliation.

Obtain legal counsel. If possible, try to help find competent, Christian attorneys who both value reconciliation and healing if possible, and who will use their professional skills in a biblical way.

Recognize the feelings of the parents of the divorcing couple. Will the parents feel they have failed their children? Will they need counseling or special support during this time?

Go to court. During court hearings or on the day of divorce, ask your people if they want you to be in court with them. They'll tell you if they do. Again, as much as possible, avoid choosing sides. Divorce is never a one-sided issue.

Discourage dating. During divorce, encourage the individuals to avoid dating. Dating during separation or divorce is almost always counterproductive to healing and healthy long-term relationships.

Encourage both individuals to begin forming relationships with new friends and maintaining strong relationships with old friends. Divorcing people frequently isolate themselves. Draw them into the church. Help them realize their need for many close friendships, especially friendships with members of their own sex. Don't let them sit too long in their isolated, emotional puddle, sad and alone. Get them up and moving again.

Help with children. If there are children involved, help the individuals work out a format for ongoing support of the kids. Help them form the strong relationships which they will have to have because of the kids.

Aid in goal-setting. Help both individuals begin to set objectives for their lives. Help them see the consequences as new potentials rather than allowing them to focus on old hurts and old scores to settle.

Role of the Christian Body, the Church

The church should be the place where hurting people go. In too many cases, it is the last place where hurting people feel free to go. Instruction, forgiveness, acceptance, healing, and support should be the primary goals of the church. The church is individual believers together in Christ.

Christians should be encouraged to pray for the divorcing couple. This is the primary tool we as Christians have been given. But prayer alone is not enough. God has given us all many resources which we may offer. Divorcing people frequently face destruction of their former social group systems as friends pull away, either from a sense of not knowing what to do for the couple, or from a sense of failure on the part of the couple. Church people need to draw the divorcing people into fellowship. It is difficult, but necessary.

Will the divorcing couple need help with housing during separation? Will the couple need pots and pans, chairs, tables, silverware, lamps, stove, and refrigerator? Will there be a need for transportation or child care?

Both parties to the divorce will benefit from a solid divorce recovery program. Churches should provide this service both to their members, and also as an evangelistic tool to the larger, broken community.

Will either of the divorcing couple need financial help? While it's not good to create financial dependency, it is important to know that many women going through divorce are left poverty-stricken. Can the church help provide child care while the woman goes to work? Can the church help the woman find employment? Many divorcing women have not used job skills in years, and now must provide for their children.

Divorcing men need other men. Divorcing women need other women. The church can initiate relationships to help fill this gap. Again, many relationships enjoyed during marriage fall away during divorce, which leaves divorcing people very isolated and alone. Divorcing people need to be pursued by Christians. Pursuit should be to love, not lecture.

Without strong pursuit and community within the church, divorcing people are left to a lonely, fast-track, highly sexual subcommunity of empty people. Churches need to have an active ministry that includes separated people, many of whom will come to the church simply for fellowship and encouragement in an atmosphere which is not highly sexually charged.

Churches can help divorcing people by not putting labels on them. Nobody knows better than the separated person that they are going through a divorce. Churches need to avoid such nasty things as gossip and "sharing" secrets about those who are victims of broken marriages.

Churches need to create lending libraries for separating or divorcing people. Subject matter should include: how to understand and handle grief reactions, how to survive during a divorce, how to survive after a divorce, how to be a single parent, how to forgive, how to rekindle a marriage that has been ripped and torn, how to build healthy marriages, how to help children through divorce, and books dealing with second marriages, that is, blended families. (See *Suggested Reading.*)

There are as many variables to divorce as there are divorcing couples. Issues faced include: finances, emotions, fear of the future, sadness over the past, shattered self-identities, thoughts of suicide, anger against ex-spouse, anger against life in general, sadness about the children, sadness about old friends pulling away, fear of forming new social groupings, concerns about setting up new households, physical relocation concerns, feelings of rejection from the Christian community, feelings of personal failure. Churches need to understand that divorce is never the simple thing it may appear to be. Usually it involves weeks and sometimes years of deep emotional pain. The church needs to be the place to which hurting people turn for acceptance, love, healing, forgiveness, and hope for the future.

Finally, churches need to help divorcing people build toward a new future based on things that work, based on Jesus Christ as the center of life. Statistics tell us that there is a 2.5 percent divorce rate among strong, church-attending Christians (*Family Foundations,* by Meier & Meier, Baker Book House).

John Splinter
Associate Pastor; Singles Ministries
Central Presbyterian Church, St. Louis, Missouri

John is the author of the book *Second Chapter,* Baker Books. He has had a healing ministry for many who have experienced divorce.

31. DIVORCE RECOVERY

"Personal recovery is based on the redemptive work of Jesus Christ. It is in the context of a personal relationship with the Lord of the universe that one can regain a balanced perspective on life."

Bob Burns

The purpose of divorce recovery is to help people work through the issues which impact life because of marital disruption. The design is to aid personal recovery from divorce, serving as a bridge between the divorce crisis and life as a single-again adult.

The Biblical Rationale for a Divorce Recovery Program
In our day there are many theological viewpoints concerning separation and divorce. It is easy to examine the theology of divorce and remain isolated from those who experience it. The Bible does not condone such isolation. The Prophet Malachi does state that God hates divorce (2:16). However, God does not say that those shattered by such an experience ought to be treated with the same hatred.

For example, the Old Testament is full of God's concerns and commands for the widow. Yet, a careful study of the Hebrew word for widow (*'almanah*) demonstrates that a forsaken spouse was considered in the same category as the woman who lost her husband through death. Therefore, the compassion of God for the widow was extended to the forsaken (divorced) spouse.

Similarly, God commanded His own wayward spouse (Israel) to repent and return to Him, promising restoration and forgiveness (Jer. 3:12-15). This presented a paradigm for the proper treatment of the spouse who abandoned the marriage covenant.

In summary, we can say that the Old Testament clearly portrays God on the side of marriage. However, when this relationship is broken, He expects His people to take an active role in marital restoration and/or care for the single-again.

In the New Testament we learn that Jesus Christ extended Himself to one who had been divorced (John 4). He led this woman to an understanding of life beyond the disappointment of a broken marriage or a new sexual liaison.

The early church followed a similar pattern of ministry to the discouraged and rejected. In 1 Corinthians 5–6 the Apostle Paul explained that many believers had come out of a variety of lifestyles. Like the woman at the well, these people (who knew they were sinners) grasped the Gospel of grace with eagerness.

The biblical material briefly reviewed demonstrates that God's people are called to be agents of reconciliation in the world (cf. 2 Cor. 5:18). In a day when homes and individuals are being torn apart through divorce, the church must be an active agent in the lives of those who are facing this trauma (1 Tim. 5:16).

The Purpose of a Divorce Recovery Program
The primary purpose of a church-sponsored divorce recovery program is to minister to the needs of the divorced or separated person. Personal recovery is based on the redemptive work of Jesus Christ. It is in the context of a personal relationship with the Lord of the universe that one can regain a balanced perspective on life. But it must be understood that divorcing persons, even those with a relationship with Jesus Christ, can be so emotionally involved in their marital disruption that they are initially unreceptive or unable to apply scriptural truth to their circumstances and needs. Therefore, a divorce recovery program must integrate the truth of the Gospel into a program mix which meets the felt needs of the participants. Such a mix will include crisis intervention and grief management within a framework designed to understand the past, cope with the present, and prepare for the future.

While divorce recovery ministry is designed to minister to the separated or divorced, it also provides the beginning for ongoing ministry to the single-again adult in the sponsoring church. Participants will be attracted to the fellowship which is seen as a place where honest caring is available. Because of this, divorce recovery provides an excellent opportunity for outreach and evangelism. And as the ministry matures it becomes a training ground for leadership development. Similarly, the divorce recovery program can become a natural context for educating the church in divorce-related issues.

The Decision to Sponsor a Divorce Recovery Program
A church must make a strategic decision concerning the investment of its resources. Usually churches desire to do more than their resources will allow them to accomplish. Therefore, the decision to sponsor a divorce recovery program should be carefully considered in the light of the overall purpose and goals of the church. While a decision is being made, the theological and practical ministry position of the pastor(s) and leadership board must also be taken into serious consideration.

If a church is going to sponsor a seminar, they must understand the number of commitments which are involved in this decision. First is the commitment of the leadership board of the church to sponsor the program. In particular, the senior pastor must wholeheartedly affirm the decision. If one part of the congregation desires to have a seminar without the support of the church leadership, they are fighting a losing battle. Enthusiasm from the leadership breeds enthusiasm in the congregation.

A second commitment should be a desire to maintain an ongoing single adult ministry. This ministry provides a framework in which to integrate participants. Without such a ministry the fruits of recovery cannot be gleaned. The church will have sponsored a nice program with no follow-up. Those who attend will feel let down when there is no continued opportunity for response to their experience. The provision for integration of divorced people into the life and ministry of the church is critically important. It must take place if a divorce recovery program is to have a long-lasting and continued influence in the church and community.

The Format and Content of a Divorce Recovery Program

Seminar format. Once a decision has been made to sponsor a divorce recovery program, the *leadership, duration,* and *size* of the seminar must be determined.

The issue of seminar leadership concerns the people who will actually lead and teach the program. At least two options are available to the sponsoring church. One option is to establish contact with a person or organization outside the church who will work with the sponsor in the development and presentation of a program. When using this method the church would administrate the program (with or without the help of the consultant). The contracted resource person(s) would teach, direct content, and guide discussion. The contractor might be a psychologist, counselor, national expert, minister, or paraprofessional in single adult ministries.

There are a number of benefits to bringing in outside support for a seminar. These leaders usually have extensive experience and expertise in divorce-related issues. They can be a great aid in the preparation and presentation of the seminar based on this experience. They also will project a certain level of confidence and positive authority in dealing with potentially volatile issues.

There are disadvantages to bringing in leadership from outside the church and community. The church loses some control over the material and its presentation. There is usually a greater financial cost. And dependence on other resources can create a situation where the sponsoring church fails to foster and develop its own leadership.

The second option for seminar leadership is to develop a program solely out of the resources in the church and the immediate Christian community. This method intimately draws the congregation into the seminar. The time and effort which the members of the congregation and community invest in preparation often pay off in continued ministry for the participants when the seminar is concluded. An "expert" from the outside will always leave the church at the conclusion of the program. When the church uses its own resources, leadership is available long after the end of the program.

Another method of leadership for a seminar could be a combination of these two options: using an outside consultant while training your own leaders.

The second concern regarding format is the duration of divorce recovery ministry. Should the program extend over a period of weeks (time extensive) or take place in one concentrated time frame (time intensive)?

The time extensive method affords more opportunity for content assimilation, relationship development, and personal work in response to the seminar. However, it also allows for greater tardiness and dropout, forgetfulness of information, and gaps in the logical flow which builds concept on concept.

On the other hand, the time intensive method reverses the weaknesses and strengths of the extended program. It lacks an extended opportunity for interpersonal development, but gains in providing a natural flow of information, interaction, and application.

The length of a seminar depends a great deal on the previous decision of the leadership. If the church brings in outside support, a time intensive program is almost required. However, the primary use of church leaders allows for flexibility of program duration.

Again, a combination of short- and long-term programs might be recommended. This could be accomplished through a time intensive program with adequate opportunities in follow-up. A support group ministry may follow a training course.

The final format decision concerns the size of the seminar and the experiences of the participants. A divorce recovery program is more than a lecture series. It requires interaction between the participant and the content, as well as the participants interacting with each other. Therefore, it is not adequate to set up a seminar based solely on a medium- to large-group format. The small group and even one-to-one opportunities must be incorporated into the plans of the seminar.

The number of nondivorced persons should be strictly limited in order that the participants feel the freedom to express themselves with those whom they perceive can understand their circumstances. Separated and divorced persons often have a difficult time sharing their experiences when there are a large number of people in a group who have not experienced marital disruption.

Seminar content. The decision regarding the content of a seminar is somewhat subjective. Every leader and every person who has been separated or divorced feels there are certain critical issues which must be covered. The leaders must decide between the primary and secondary issues, for it is not possible to cover all of the areas of concern.

In the process of deciding what content to cover in a seminar, a few general guidelines must be followed. One is the accuracy of the presentation. It needs to be faithful to the Scriptures and agree with current research and studies. It needs to be thorough, but not overwhelming or

160

scholastic. There need to be practical illustrations and personal applications to make it relevant.

As speakers are chosen and talks prepared, the leaders must interact over the content and viewpoints which will be presented. Is the speaker going to address the issue(s) from a clinical or a supportive/personal basis? Is she/he going to focus primarily on a psychological and emotional model, a biblical/theological model, or an integrational approach? At what point would the coordinator expect a speaker to point out an issue, and when would they expect direct and specific answers? The leaders must be aware of these questions and establish a philosophical direction for the seminar which is affirmed by all of those who present material in the program.

There are a number of topics which should receive primary consideration for presentation in a seminar. A review of numerous programs yields at least four major areas. First is the grief process and its application to divorce. Second is life restructuring, focusing primarily on the dynamics of reentering the single life. Third is emotional issues, with particular emphasis on anger, bitterness, and forgiveness. Finally, there are the biblical/theological issues concerning marriage, divorce, and remarriage. Most people have heard conflicting views on what the Bible states. A church which wants to sensitively minister to the separated and divorced should make its convictions in this area well known.

Other topics, while not necessarily critical, are supportive and helpful in a seminar. These include circumstantial issues, such as, separation and reconciliation; legal and medical (which, of course, would require practitioners in each field); single parenting; personal/emotional issues, such as, depression, anger, self-image, alcoholism, abuse, and developmental dysfunctional problems; sexual issues, such as, personal sexuality, dating, and sexual activity outside of marriage; and interpersonal issues, such as, communication skills, social skills, and friendship development.

Seminar Administration

The basic decisions regarding format and content of a seminar should provide overall direction for the administration of the program. For example a seminar which extends over a six-week period of time might only require light refreshments, while a weekend seminar would need meals provided. Child care is a must.

Some areas of administration which need to be planned are the seminar location and logistics, small groups and follow-up, public relations, food and refreshments, and registration. Each of these needs to be coordinated and prepared prior to the seminar. Costs and scholarships need to be carefully administered.

Conclusion

Should a church sponsor a divorce recovery seminar? From a biblical perspective, the church is required to demonstrate concern for those whose lives have been shattered through marital disruption. This may or may not express itself through the sponsorship of a seminar. A church must consider whether it is prepared to invest the significant resources and leadership necessary for a seminar to be run properly. It must be prepared to sustain the impact of a seminar through follow-up, counseling, and an ongoing support system of ministry to the single-again. For many churches these demands prohibit the use of a divorce recovery seminar as their method of demonstrating concern and compassion. But churches who use this particular program will discover it can be a highly effective method of ministering to this ever-growing segment of our population—the people God has called the church to shepherd.

Bob Burns
Pastor and Associate Director of Fresh Start
Perimeter Church, Stone Mountain, Georgia

Bob is the founder of Fresh Start Seminars, a ministry for divorce recovery. His doctoral studies thesis is "A Fresh Start: A Help Seminar on Divorce Recovery," Westminster Theological Seminary, 1985.

32. HELP FOR SINGLE-PARENT CHILDREN

*"Let the single-parent child tag along with you, help wash
your car, bake cookies, or play with your kids. And you don't
have to do it all alone; get several from your congregation
involved in one-to-one relationships with children of divorce."*

Jim & Barbara Dycus

There are 45 million children in the United States. They bless our lives daily as we come in contact with their enthusiasm, energy, and joy.

Almost one third of these kids are living in one-parent homes. That's about 14 million, with 2 million being added annually to the number. Current predictions are that by 1990, as many as 66 percent of all our nation's children will experience one-parent family life before they reach the age of 18.

How Are They Different from Other Kids?
What do we need to know about these kids? Are they any different than other kids? Is a traditional Sunday School ministry enough for them? Or do they need some specialized ministry that zeroes in on their special needs?

The evidence says that they do! Even the Bible shows the benefit of special ministry to single-parent children.

It appears that both Ishmael, the son of the patriarch Abraham, and Timothy, the spiritual son of the Apostle Paul, were single-parent children. Ishmael grew up to be the leader of a great and mighty nation (see Gen. 21–25). Timothy grew up to be the leader or the pastor of the first-century church in Ephesus where Paul calls him, "You, man of God" (1 Tim. 6:11).

Both men were raised by their mothers. They both had a godly heritage and training. They both had one parent, yet God was absolutely faithful to demonstrate His grace and love to meet their every need as well as to provide them with a future and a hope.

Timothy had some specialized ministry from a man who became his role model and who loved him profusely. This is evident in the way Paul addressed his letters to Timothy. Paul began every letter the same way: "Grace and peace be unto you." Eleven times he uses that salutation. But only in his letters to Timothy does he add: "Grace, mercy, and peace" be unto you. Paul gave Timothy a ministry of mercy which met the special single-parent child needs he had.

Paul teaches us to "see to it that no one misses the grace of God and that no bitter root grows up to cause trouble and defile many" (Heb. 12:15).

In order to follow that advice with single-parent families, we need to understand their special needs.

Emotional needs. The child who loses a parent has an emotional response to that loss. These emotions are normal, but are largely negative responses. They include the following emotions: grief, sense of loss, guilt, rejection, anger, depression, loss of self-esteem, confusion, fear of change.

In order to recover from these negative emotions, the child needs help *identifying* the emotion, *understanding* the emotion, and *learning to make a positive response* in place of the negative one.

Family living needs. A child's security is tied up in the stability of the home. When an event disrupts the stability of the home, the child's security blanket is ripped away.

The stability can be restored, even in a one-parent home! But adaptations to a new form of family life need to be made. These include the following family changes: living with one parent, becoming more independent, accepting more personal responsibility in the management of the home, adapting to financial changes, and learning to effectively communicate with family members.

Ministry must provide tools and practical help in each of these areas.

Relationship needs. Divorce or death creates some problems for a child in his or her ability to establish good relationships. Because the loss has caused a feeling of rejection, the child begins to defend himself against another loss. The walls go up and it becomes more difficult to trust, love, or accept a new relationship.

Single-parent children need help in learning to build positive relationships. And in order to help, we have to first gain their respect and trust! That's why for these children a Sunday School relationship won't be enough. We need to be prepared to offer unconditional acceptance in a megadose, until children take down the walls and let us in.

How Can the Church Help?

It's obvious that we *need* to help. *How* do we do it? The biblical example of Hagar and Ishmael gives us some goals for our design. (See Gen. 21:17-20.)

Recognition of the need for ministry. We begin to help by recognizing the need to help! "God has heard the boy crying" (Gen. 21:17).

To do this we need to decide how we feel about divorce and children of divorce and really understand what the Bible teaches about the family, divorce, and children's needs. Don't forget to dig into forgiveness and God's grace. We need to catch a vision of the need in our local community, and especially our local church.

Unconditional acceptance. "Lift the boy up and take him by the hand" (Gen. 21:18). We have to do some lifting and some hugging to let children in crisis with the walls erected recognize that we accept them. Just as they are—just where they hurt!

We will have to decide where our place is with them. We must decide how much we will have to give. Do this before you begin to minister to them. They can't take another rejection while they hurt.

Develop positive responses to negative situations. "I [God] will make him into a great nation" (Gen. 21:18). We can help the child of divorce begin to make a positive response to his hurt.

Acceptance in place of grief, stability in place of loss, freedom from guilt, love not rejection and anger, worth instead of worthlessness, reality instead of denial, security not fear, forgiveness instead of blame, understanding not confusion, and new relationships to dispel the loneliness. These are the emotional issues that need educational and functional assistance by volunteer and professionals.

Understanding of specific divorce needs. Hagar "gave the boy a drink" (Gen. 21:19). He had a specific need which she was able to meet. We have to deal in specifics with the children of divorce or loss. Discover their needs. Find out from them. This requires long-term relationship-building with child and parent.

Encourage spiritual growth. "God was with the boy as he grew up" (Gen. 21:20). We need to be there too! Paul was there for Timothy. How did Paul help Timothy? He led him to Christ, instructed him, advised him, charged him, praised him, loved him, encouraged him, laid hands on him (moving Timothy into ministry). Paul obviously made the difference in Timothy's life. Today, single-parent children can experience the same difference.

Establishing an Ongoing Ministry to Single-Parent Children

Ongoing is the operative word here! Not some flash in the pan that singles out the child and makes him feel different, but something to which he can belong!

Develop one-on-one relationships. Before the child who hurts will open up and let us in, we have to build a relationship with that child. It helps us both! We get to know this child, his special needs, where he hurts the most, where he'll let us in. The child finds acceptance to dispel his feelings of rejection, love to chase away the worthlessness, and role modeling to lead him into godliness. Here are a few suggestions.

Let the single-parent child tag along with you, help wash your car, bake cookies, or play with your kids. Let the child (children) talk to *you*, instead of you just talking to them. Remove the unnatural, restrictive classroom setting and have some wild and silly fun! You don't have to do it all alone; get several from your congregation involved in one-to-one relationships with children of divorce.

Specialize your ministry to single-parent children. Build a ministry that meets their special needs. Three natural areas of ministry are:

(1) Crisis intervention. This begins with recognizing and dealing with the immediate negative responses to the loss. Help is needed for diffusing anger, mending broken hearts, removing guilt, and helping tear down the walls of hurt.

(2) Recovery assistance. The child must be taught positive biblical responses for the negative. The child must learn how to establish self-worth and independence plus the ability to get on with life.

(3) Life management assistance. Now that the crisis is over and the child has begun recovery, he or she needs to know how to manage life beyond the hurt. He or she must now be taught self-government, how to make good choices, understand God's plan for each family member, and be a part of a program with a plan for spiritual growth (i.e., Sunday School, Awana, family devotions).

Meshing a Children's Program with the Single's Ministry

Ministry to single-parent children can be a vital, exciting part of single's ministry. Single parents need to be in singles ministry, but many of them cannot leave their children to attend. Have them bring the kids! Offer ministry to the kids each time your singles meet.

Here are a few suggestions: Workshops and learning centers for the kids during divorce recovery sessions or fellowship activities for them when you have social activities. Plan a kids' retreat while their parents go with you on the single adult retreat. Encourage your single adults to be one-on-one role models. Let the single adults who are blessed with financial bounty bless the single parents and children without.

Follow the advice Jesus gave in Matthew 18:5-6. "And whoever welcomes a little child like this in My name welcomes Me. But if anyone causes one of these little ones who believe in Me to sin, it would be better for him to have a large millstone hung around his neck and to be drowned in the depth of the sea."

Jim and Barbara Dycus
Jim is Director of Ministry to Single Parent Families
Calvary Assembly of God, Winter Park, Florida
Barbara is a free-lance writer and workshop leader

Jim and Barbara have authored and produced their own curriculum for single-parent children entitled *God Can Heal My Hurts* and *God Can Heal My Owies.*

33. PREMARITAL COUNSELING

*"Let it be understood that the key to premarital counseling
is raising issues for discussion, rather than complete resolution of them."*

Doug Calhoun

When some people hear the word "counseling," an automatic avoidance
response sets in. A pastor can envision long, fruitless hours of talking. Or
a congregation thinks of all the expense to hire a professional. But this
chapter wishes to promote premarital counseling as a possibility for each
and every church and pastor. Because this type of counseling functions in a
preventive fashion, it should be viewed from a positive perspective. A
pastor or a church exercises vision for future health of the church of Jesus
Christ when they prepare couples for committed marriages.

Why Have Premarital Counseling?

Marriage is one of the most important choices a person will make in life.
Virtually every aspect of a person's life is influenced by this decision. How
will God figure into this choice? How integral will the church and the
ongoing work of the kingdom of God be in this consideration? The Scripture calls us to complete submission of our whole lives to God (Rom. 12:1-
2). Jesus leaves little room for speculation about God's expressed involvement in the covenant of marriage (Matt. 19:4-6). Marriage belongs to God
and is a gift from Him to His creatures for their good (Gen. 2:18, 20-25).
It would seem from the attention given to the sanctity of marriage in the
Scripture and to its use as the metaphor for Christ and the church (Eph.
5:25-32) that great care should be used in its nurture and promotion by the
church.

Premarital counseling presents an opportunity for instilling important
attitudes and skills in a couple's relationship. Engagement time is a period
for pattern-setting. The man and woman discover more about each other
every day and possess a high degree of willingness to constructively work
on their relationship. Premarital counseling capitalizes on this eagerness to
facilitate good communication development and realism. The starry-eyed
nature of romantic love can fail to see key issues. Premarital counseling
raises the issues.

A mature counselor brings some truth to the picture by enabling the
couple to grasp that marriage does not solve all their problems or meet all
their needs. Discussion about finances, conflict resolution, in-laws, and

roles generally reveals numerous differences in outlook by the potential mates. In so doing, the counselor opens up a safe arena for dialogue and provides practical skills for the couple to build an even healthier relationship.

Today's culture gives little support to godly and committed marriages, so the church must make a concerted attempt to equip its members. Each marriage is meant to honor God as it demonstrates the true nature of love and the original design for sex (Mark 10:2-9; 1 Cor. 6:12-20; 1 Thes. 4:3-7; Heb. 13:4). Learning obedience and mutual submission in marriage (Eph. 5:21) displays how one lives for God.

Premarital counseling reinforces these truths and strives against the currents that might lead later to divorce. As more and more people wait longer before they become married, the need for loving counsel and forthright discussion increases. People bring more experience (both good and bad) into the relationship and often are more set in their ways. Premarital counseling stands as a time of openness by the couple for biblical instruction and a pivotal period in the development of the priorities of their relationship.

Purposes of Premarital Counseling
In summary, the purposes for premarital counseling are as follows:

1. To initiate or deepen the couple's relationship to Jesus Christ and to the church.

2. To teach and encourage biblical principles of love and communication.

3. To provide objective evaluation of the couple's relational strengths and weaknesses, along with suggestions/resources for improvement.

4. To give personal support and acceptance of the couple as they attempt to follow Christ in their marriage.

Basic Issues to Cover
Let it be understood that the key to premarital counseling is raising issues for discussion, rather than complete resolution of them. Numerous workbooks are available that would assist in discussing the following areas such, as, *The Handbook for Engaged Couples* by Robert and Alice Fryling (IVP) and *Preparing for Christian Marriage* by Joan and Richard Hunt (Abingdon Press).

Biblical basis of marriage and its parameters. The foundation begins in Genesis 1:27; 2:18-25; 3:1-24, highlighting the creational ordinance of marriage and the immediate effects of the Fall on marital relationships and communication.

Family background and in-laws. Each person reflects in some measure their family of origin. Much insight can be gleaned from discovering family histories from each partner and their feelings or reactions to each parent. Identifying strong connections between parents and present behaviors enables the counselor to rightly guide steps of change. Have they visited each other's family yet? What is the parental response to the match? What possible tensions are there in relation to the in-laws?

Communication. Though every area listed is essential, this one serves as the conduit for the development of everything else. Therefore, the counselor cultivates such abilities as patterns of listening, clarifying messages, filtering one's own feelings, speaking out instead of holding it all in, patiently waiting for a slower partner, and speaking the truth in love (honesty with compassion).

Decision-making. How does this couple approach a problem or a decision? Can they calmly work through differing ideas to a resolution? Some individuals need basic training in this, while others simply need assistance in the integration of two different styles.

Conflict resolution. This specifically addresses the couple's ability to argue or fight fairly and to develop a strategy for resolution. This means grappling with methods of expressing anger and giving forgiveness (instead of holding a grudge).

Time, work, and leisure. Explore how each partner views these topics and what opportunities they have had to see differences and work them through. What priorities do they share? How will God's kingdom agenda influence their careers or location?

Money. Statistically, this area leads to a high proportion of marital disagreements and fallings-out. How does each person approach the use of money? How similar are their spending habits? Do they know how to budget? How much do they tithe? Save?

Physical relationship during engagement and in marriage. If sexual intercourse is reserved for marriage according to the Scripture, then the object is to enable the couple to use their engagement to prepare themselves for the best experience of sex in marriage. This changes the issue from how far they can go to how can they assist one another in waiting. Provide them with a chance to talk about their struggles and fears, as well as any past experiences needing forgiveness. Right before the wedding, give explicit information about intercourse and anatomy and allow for questions they might have. Refer to *The Act of Marriage,* Tim and Beverly LeHaye (Zondervan); and *Intended for Pleasure,* Ed and Gaye Wheat (Fleming H. Revell).

Roles in marriage and future plans. With all the concern over equality, where does each one stand? Have they realistically thought out their position and its ramifications? Explore where children fit into their future plans and what family goals they have.

Wedding and honeymoon plans. These two events carry the potential of great joy or conflict. Parents often impact the ceremony a great deal. What does the couple want to show about their Christian faith in their service? Who will be involved? Have they planned enough time and money for a new beginning? Talk with them about the wedding night itself, so they will have prepared themselves for the inauguration of their life together.

Ideas for Premarital Counseling

There are certain essential elements to any premarital counseling approach. Both the counselor and the couple should be in *prayer*, bathing the entire relationship in the care of God and seeking His grace for the couple to grow in love. Next comes the aspect of *instruction and study* on the various issues listed in the previous section. Much of this occurs as the couple reads or talks on their own, but the counselor provides appropriate material. Some helpful books are *The Mystery of Marriage*, Mike Mason (Multnomah Press); *I Married You*, Walter Trobisch (Harper & Row); and *Growing into Love*, Joyce Huggett (IVP). The couple's *discussion times alone* give them an opportunity to interact on the assignments and to specifically tackle tough areas. The *counseling session* serves as an opportunity for them to dialogue with each other and the counselor on issues, and for the counselor to share insights or raise questions. Last comes the avenue of *psychological tests*.[1] These bring the dimension of comparison from a wider resource of couples.

To add to the options, the counselor can look for films and cassette series that will assist him/her. These offer the advantage of tapping into the wisdom of others who have ministered to many couples. Another way to multiply the effectiveness during a course would be interviewing other couples who had been married for 1, 5, or 10 years. The perspective on the stages of growth becomes more apparent with such exposure. A counselor can also draft a doctor or financial consultant to speak to their respective areas of expertise. The leader should always be looking for mature couples who have gifts in the counseling realm and appear to be helping couples in their relationships. Then offer them support to minister this way more effectively.

When it comes to formats, several styles are used. One could meet with a couple for four one-hour sessions over the course of a month or two. This basically includes a get-acquainted session, and then one meeting each on communication, money, and sex in marriage.

The advantages of this program are that it is self-contained and sticks to

---

[1]One of the commonly used tests is the Taylor-Johnson Temperament Analysis Test which is self-scored by a trained counselor. The test is designed primarily to provide an evaluation in visual form showing a person's feelings about himself (or another person) at the time when he answered the questions. It seeks to measure a number of comparatively independent personality variables or behavior tendencies. Testing information can be obtained from Psychological Publications, Inc., 5300 Hollywood Blvd., Los Angeles, CA 90027 (213) 465-4163.

A second test is from PREPARE-ENRICH, Inc., scored by PREPARE-ENRICH but administered by the counselor. PREPARE, for engaged couples, seeks to increase the couple's awareness of their relationship strengths and potential work areas. Twelve different categories are explored. Information can be obtained through PREPARE-ENRICH, Inc., P.O. Box 190, Minneapolis, MN 55440-0190 (612) 231-1661.

170

well-known territory for the counselor. Also the time demands are limited. On the other hand, the couple may not feel they have the chance to delve into anything substantial or develop the vulnerability for addressing personal concerns.

Utilizing some type of group format represents a second option. A Sunday School class for eight weeks or a small group of engaged couples (meeting for a term or for five Saturday mornings, etc.) could discuss a workbook, Bible passages, or a book on marriage. In this way, more people can be involved than in private sessions for the same amount of time invested by the counselor. The church could develop a standard curriculum for all engaged couples, building within the congregation a strong commitment to marriage. But the element of individual attention is harder to achieve with a high degree of openness.

No doubt there are more variations in practice. Keep reading and talking with other pastors/counselors and find something that you can tailor to fit your situation and your own gifts. Though premarital counseling requires time and energy, the rewards of stronger marriages in the church are well worth the effort.

Doug Calhoun
Minister to Young Adults
Park Street Church, Boston, Massachusetts

Doug's ministry in Boston is with the singles and young marrieds of the church. He is responsible for the training and equipping of both single adults and young married couples.

34. REMARRIAGE COUNSELING

"Remarriage should not be an escape from pain—that only draws another person into one's life to help carry the pain that's there. The more unresolved clutter left behind from previous relationships, the more clutter will come home to roost in the new relationship."

John Splinter

According to the March/April 1982 issue of *Solo* magazine, between 1960 and 1978, divorce increased 83 percent for those ages 45-68; for those under age 30, the increase was 296 percent. According to Dr. Armand Nichoff of Harvard Medical School, divorce has increased 700 percent in this century. In the May 12, 1986 issue of *Marriage & Divorce Today Newsletter,* almost 80 percent who divorce remarry within four years. Other studies use even higher figures for overall remarriage after divorce.

Remarriage is an issue with which churches must deal. However, before beginning, there are some critical questions to answer. What is your church's theological position on divorce and remarriage? What is your personal position? Each denomination and each local church will have a slightly different way of dealing with the question, and most will sincerely believe that theirs is the correct biblical position. It is very important to know where you stand personally and biblically before you begin counseling those who are divorced and considering remarriage.

Remarriage Is Not Always the Best Answer
Studies vary, but there is some concurrence that second and subsequent marriages fail at an even greater rate than first-time marriages. Perhaps this is why God placed great weight on making first-time marriages work! (See Matt. 19:4-8.)

One of the most important services churches can offer to people remarrying is to help them understand God's practical plan for marriage and why He gave cautions about treating marriage lightly.

Common Problems
There are many common problems in remarriage. As a counselor you should be acutely aware of them. Here are a few.

Old "tapes" or lifetime methods of relating to others, problem resolution, and ineffective patterns which caused first-time marriages to fail are not left behind. They come along with us into new relationships. We bring with us old messages from the past, messages which have shaped identities, self-esteem, and relational processes. We never really leave our past behind us.

Emotional residue from past marriages almost always becomes a part of second marriages. Unless a person has accepted his responsibility for the first marital failure, and offered and received forgiveness for it, he is not ready for a second marriage. Most people who seek remarriage have not honestly dealt with their own responsibility for the collapse of the first marriage, and thus are prone to pass responsibility on to the new marriage partner for second-marriage problems.

Men frequently remarry women who are significantly younger. This can create potential problems as both continue to mature, but do so at differing rates and stages. The ego of the man is boosted, and the woman is given a sense of security in marrying an older man. It should be understood that divorce frequently causes psychological regression (return to an earlier emotional age). When the man returns to his real age, there can be a very difficult adjustment to manage. The question with which to deal in this situation has to do with understanding the age difference. Of course, it should also be noted that people can be the same age physically and yet be years apart emotionally.

All too frequently, divorcing people jump from one "sinking ship" to another passing "love boat," only to sink again. That is called "rebounding," which is usually disastrous to relationships. Frequently, people don't allow enough time to grieve and heal from old wounds, and to shape their new identities as singles before remarrying. Hence, they take with them far too much emotional baggage as they enter the new relationships. This stresses the new marriage.

Remarriage is frequently sought for the wrong reasons. As a counselor you need to help the couple look at some of these reasons:

- Rebellion against an ex-spouse or parent
- Escape from personal loneliness
- Obtaining a sense of financial security
- Sexual release
- Proving that one is still attractive or desirable
- Finding someone to end one's personal insecurity feelings
- Finding a parent for one's children
- Escaping what one perceives to be a distasteful image of singleness.

Where children are involved, stepparenting usually proves to be a monumental and surprisingly difficult challenge. (The image of the "wicked stepmother" in the story of Cinderella has its roots in the anger of children vs. stepparent. It's a very real problem, and stepfathering can be just as difficult as stepmothering.)

Many remarrying people seek partners who will fit stereotypes rather than partners who will commit to a real relationship.

Key Questions

There are several questions which you may ask remarrying couples to help them wade through some of the potential problems of remarriage.

Healing time. Have you both had sufficient time to heal from past relationships? Have you both had at least 18 months, and preferably two years, after divorce before considering remarriage? There is no substitution for sufficient time to recover after one relational death before plunging into another relationship.

Emotional involvement. Has the divorcing person been emotionally involved with the new marital partner during the time of separation and grieving from the last marriage? If so, the process of grief and growth has probably been slowed or stopped.

Accept responsibility. Has the divorced person worked through the real issues of the last marriage? Has he/she accepted his or her responsibility for the collapse of the last marriage, or was the divorce only the "other person's fault"? The more it remains the other person's responsibility, the more likely it will also be the next person's fault too. One can't work on what the last spouse did to him/her, but on what was done by him/her.

Anger and bitterness. Is the remarrying person still bitter or angry? It is very difficult to carry a load of anger toward a previous marriage and, at the same time, give all the good things needed to a new relationship. We only have so much emotional energy. In which direction will the energy be aimed? How much "emotional residue" will transfer to the new spouse?

Reasons for remarriage. What are the *real* reasons for seeking another marriage? Probe if necessary, to get the remarrying couple to deal with these issues, or other issues which may be the real agenda for the new marriage.

Forgiveness and reconciliation. Has the divorced person taken full steps toward forgiveness and possible reconciliation with his/her ex-spouse before proceeding with the next relationship? Has forgiveness been offered? Sought? Have the emotional clubs been put away? Is there any hope of restoring their first love? As hard as this is, it is important. Remarriage should not be an escape from pain—that only draws another person into one's life to help carry the pain that's there. The more unresolved clutter left behind from previous relationships, the more clutter will come home to roost in the new relationship.

Stepchildren. As a counselor you'll need to help your people deal with such tough questions as: How will the new spouse relate with the children of the previous marriage? What lines of allegiance will be requested? How will the ex-spouse be included in relationships with the children? When couples remarry, especially when there are children involved, the children are connected with the ex-spouse.

God's will. Another question as a counselor: How does God's purpose in your remarrying couple's lives dovetail with their own purposes for life? What does Scripture tell them about their decision to remarry? Have they dealt with God's agenda for handling their past relationships? Their present relationship? In their book *Family Foundations* (Baker), authors Meier and Meier indicate a 2.5 percent divorce rate for strong, church-attending Christians, and a .25 percent rate for believers who pray and read God's Word together in the home. What is the couple's agenda for inviting God into their new relationship? The answer to this question *will* make a difference.

Special Needs of Children
As a counselor you also need to be acutely aware of the special needs brought to remarriage by the children, if there are any. Here are a few thoughts in this regard.

Loyalty. Many children deal with questions of loyalty to the other (now divorced, non-custodial) parent. "Do I need to love Mom better than Dad? Do I need to love Mom's new husband better than I love my blood parent?"

Guilt. Children frequently carry feelings of guilt about their parents' divorce. They need to realize (emotionally) that they are not the reason for the divorce.

Between fighting parents. Children frequently find themselves in a battle between warring divorced parents. Kids are sometimes the "rag dolls" used by fighting parents to hurt each other. As a counselor you need to be aware of this. Look for it. Learn to be a peacemaker.

Authority. Children deal with the issue of authority from a very powerless position. "Do I need to call the new 'parent' Dad or Mom? How hard must I work at being obedient to the new 'parent,' especially when my blood parent (absent) says I don't have to? What lines of authority are now going to operate in this new relationship? What if I am angry toward the new 'parent' and I don't want to obey? What will be my response if he/she tries to punish me?" As a counselor you will need to help kids deal with these issues, and equip parents to deal with them too. A consistent united front is the key for the parents disciplining children.

New routines. New family standards, priorities, objectives, means of support, communication styles, visiting days, and so on will be encountered by the children. You'll need to help parents help their kids understand these.

Favoritism. One very common issue is that of favoritism. "Mom loves me better than you because I'm her kid." This gauntlet may be laid before either a stepsibling, or even before a stepparent.

Provide Support
There are special support needs of "blended families." Here are a few thoughts in this regard:

Provide names of counselors. Have at your fingertips a referral network of good counselors.

Bring families together. Connect "blended families" with one another so they can share common struggles and find out they are not alone.

Make resources available. Churches should have on hand the best possible resources for helping "blended families." There are many good books on the market now. There are tapes, VCR programs, and other tools. Equip your church as a lending library to be of support to these families. (See *Suggested Reading.*)

Address children's special needs. The needs of children of "blended families" should be addressed, giving kids opportunities to deal with their new parents with the support of other kids, and other adults who can encourage and counsel them.

Make them part of church family. Churches need to draw "blended families" into fellowship, service, and leadership. These families need to feel that they are just as much a part of the body of Christ as nondivorced families.

Churches need to position themselves toward dealing with divorce and remarriage. Currently, it is widely known that 50 percent of marriages end in divorce. If 80 percent plus will remarry, this issue must be addressed, and it will not be effectively addressed by simply saying that it should not happen that way. Churches must prioritize ministries to those who do not fit the "mold." Remarriage is a difficult issue to address, but churches must make it a target item for ministry, or risk losing ministry to an increasingly high percentage of families in our country.

John Splinter
Associate Pastor, Singles Ministries
Central Presbyterian Church, St. Louis, Missouri

John has recently finished a book on building healthy marriages and is completing an M.A. degree in Counseling Psychology with an emphasis on ministry to singles.

35. ROLE OF THE SENIOR PASTOR

"The senior pastor is the shepherd who leads his congregation in caring for all the sheep."

Bud Pearson

Every singles ministry in a local church, to be successful, must have the wholehearted support of the senior pastor. The entire congregation will develop feelings and respond to single adults in the same way that the senior pastor does.

The Senior Pastor Sets the Tone for the Singles Ministry
He leads to provide an atmosphere of acceptance. This means an openhearted welcome to all single adults whatever their status.

Often single adults are hurting at a deep level and they need a listening ear and an understanding response where genuine concern is evident. A loving and caring pastor role models this attitude. The senior pastor is the shepherd who leads his congregation in caring for all the sheep.

He leads in welcoming single adults as part of the family of God. Every single adult is either a believer or is potentially a believer. To receive each person as someone loved by God is to fulfill the role God has for us. The family of God needs to be viewed as open to all. For this to be a reality, there can be no second-class citizens because of one's status in life. The Lord Jesus opened up His world to all people, and a congregation can be led to do the same by the senior pastor.

He leads in including single adults in the ministry of the church. Including single adults in the life of the church means opening its doors to their participation at all levels in the ministry of the body of Christ. Every believer needs to fulfill his or her calling, and the church that truly accepts single adults also accepts the responsibility of placing them in meaningful roles in the life of the congregation.

The Senior Pastor Conveys the Concept of the Need for Singles Ministry to the Ruling Body of the Church
The importance of it. He points out the facts of the huge population of single adults and their need for meaningful relationships with others. He makes the ruling body aware of the potential for evangelism and the opportunity of the church to fulfill its role to all people. The Great Commission includes single adults.

The opportunity of it. Single adults are often wounded. Nowhere in society are people equipped to heal hurts like the church is prepared to do. The senior pastor, by being with them, speaking to them, having them in his home, etc., leads the congregation in this ministry of healing.

He leads the church to be the church—reaching out, loving, and sharing Christ with people who are open and ready to listen and receive.

The Senior Pastor Determines the Support Level of Single Adults by the Congregation

By his messages. He speaks to and of them in his messages, letting the congregation know of his love and concern for all the people.

By his support from the pulpit. He promotes them and their programs from the pulpit. This gives credence to their programs and serves to highlight the reality that they are a part of the church.

By publicity. He makes sure that there is space in bulletins, news sheets, and church publications to inform of their programs and events. This not only serves to inform, but to give the congregation an awareness that single adult functions are as important as all other ministries of the church.

The Senior Pastor Makes Sure that Leadership for Single Adult Ministry Is Provided

He sees the vision for single adult ministry and takes the steps necessary to launch it and assure its ongoing ministry. There are several alternatives in leadership.

A full-time singles minister is best, when possible. This assures a more adequate counseling, planning, teaching, and training program for the ministry. Many are now catching the vision for singles ministry and are preparing for it. This assures a bright future for reaching the single adult population and provides many churches with the opportunity to consider their role in it.

Another possible leadership potential is to enlist a married couple who is sensitive to the needs of single adults. This may be a first-time married or remarried couple. With a desire to serve and be used in singles ministry, a couple can fulfill this role very well, as has been demonstrated in many churches.

A high regard must be maintained for the person or persons who lead a singles ministry. They must know and feel that they are a part of the church's ministry, that they are a part of the church's ministry team and be included as such. The senior pastor must lead in giving equal status to the singles leaders so that they and the single adults will know that they are a part of the church in the fullest sense.

The Senior Pastor Must See the Potential for the Ministry of Single Adults in the Church

Singles serve and they serve well. Many single adults have available time. They also want to feel useful. Serving others can be an integral part of the healing process for one who is divorced or widowed. Churches where single adult ministries have been most effective have been those in which single persons have been given opportunities to serve, not only in the functions of the single adults, but in the larger body.

It has been amply demonstrated that, when given the opportunities, single adults are a blessing to the church. Our church reported that 35 percent of its choir members, 40 percent of its teaching staff, 30 percent of its ushers and greeters, and 60 percent of its paraprofessional counselors are single adults.

Perhaps the most significant thing of all is that single adults bring a spirit of acceptance, love, and caring to a church. They have hurt deeply and, through that hurt, have, in the truest way, become wounded healers. The senior pastor will do well to recognize this and desire to be close to the singles in encouraging them in their personal lives and in their service to the Lord. The senior pastor, in a society that includes more than one single person for every married couple, will do well to lead his congregation into a ministry with single adults. He holds the key to the success or failure of the ministry to singles in the church which he pastors.

Bud Pearson
Senior Pastor
Orange Coast Community Church, Orange, California

Bud is a former singles pastor, and now as a senior pastor, he sees the importance of the senior pastor's role in singles ministries. Bud is also an author and conference speaker.

36. PROFILE OF THE SINGLE ADULT MINISTER

> *"When we develop a tenderness toward our singles, all else fades away . . . tiredness, apathy, and ineptness. We begin to see a mission, gain a larger perspective, and a feel challenge to positively minister, once we have learned how to care for people."*
>
> Timm Jackson

His men had just returned from their first assignment. They seemed to talk all at once as they shared excitedly with Him their reports. His plans were to be alone with them for a day . . . a trip to a deserted piece of land . . . a time of rest and lunch . . . a little instruction to help them grow. It was going to be a great day. But the crowds found Him and His "schedule" was tossed aside, for a major miracle was about to occur (Mark 6:30-44).

This little scenario in Christ's life on the day of the feeding of the 5,000 reminds us again of His greatest attribute—His obedience to God. Many of us would choose rather to have a manual of "how-to's"; an easy "problem-solver" we could flip through in search of the perfect approach to "ministry for the moment." However, Christ seems to show us throughout the Gospels that a choice toward obedience needs to precede any direction we could ever take. Let's go back to our opening story.

Here Christ chooses to minister to the masses through teaching and later on, feeding. An inspirational afternoon such as this would never have occurred if Christ had chosen the way of the "calendar book" schedule. Instead, He obeyed God's direction and ministered to thousands, as well as the original focal group, His disciples.

We can learn much from Christ's life. Single adult ministers have been given the seemingly insurmountable task of reaching a specialized group of people with the claims of Christ, so they may in turn affect their world. But the challenge is no greater than what Christ saw on that hot day on the shores of Galilee.

It is easy to look at a world of hurting, stressed-out, lost, or lonely singles and feel helplessly inadequate. One may even think it is ridiculous to consider approaching such a segment of society without years of accumulated credentials, abilities, and tolerances. Yet, Jesus made a difference. We must learn from Him. The following were modeled by Jesus Christ.

Spiritual Preparedness

Be godly (2 Peter 1:5-7). Jesus cherished His personal privacy for those times of spiritual renewal. Direction that comes from moments of personal communion with God gives perfect protection and incredible inspiration.

A Compassionate Spirit

Jesus was "moved with compassion" (Mark 6:34, KJV). When we develop a tenderness toward our singles, all else fades away . . . tiredness, apathy, and ineptness. We begin to see a mission, gain a larger perspective, and feel a challenge to positively minister, once we have learned how to care for people.

Versatility

Throughout His life, Jesus showed tremendous versatility. He lost sleep, overlooked mealtimes, and changed agendas to accommodate people. Programming is useless if it looms as a giant over the needs of people. Give yourself the joy of being able to "break away" from the daily drudgery and get actively involved in the lives of people.

Vision

Jesus saw the crowd as sheep without a shepherd. As we gain a proper perspective of our mission, we too will see our "crowd" as singles who need to be led to the Saviour with life-changing growth. We may also begin to see the needs of each individual as uniquely his own. Singles come from a variety of church backgrounds and life experiences. It is most rewarding to learn how to relate to each one. Also, a ministry to singles becomes a real challenge in dealing with new attenders. Because of their often sensitive situations, they call for a special touch of concern by the minister. If you can develop a "sight" that "feels" the needs of others, you will probably see your ministry become greater than just your church constituency as it encompasses a total community. People will love filling your vision!

Teaching

How discouraged Jesus must have been when His disciples stated *their* solution to the crowd's need for food. Even the fresh return from their preaching trip couldn't change their hearts enough, for they said, "Send the people away." Yet, Jesus chose to patiently teach them, allowing them the opportunity to watch His solution become reality. His response, "You give them something to eat," showed He still wished for the Twelve to inherit His ministry. Don't be afraid to share ownership of the ministry with your single adults. The camaraderie will be greatly worth the effort of patiently discipling others into the inner workings and commitment of ministry. And allow yourself the relief of being accountable to someone for your own spiritual growth. A teacher is a student. You must personally grow as a disciple of Jesus Christ.

Organization for a Purpose

When Jesus was faced with the feeding of the 5,000, He was prepared for it. He divided the mass of people into specifically numbered groups. You too need to plan for your "miracle." Don't just think being "led by the Spirit" will do it all for you. You will be more useful to the people if you have freed yourself from details so you can think about their personal needs. Set an atmosphere for ministry which will lend itself to positive decisions being made for Christ. Organize your life and program of ministry. That shows your love and concern for both.

Speaking out in Support of Your Singles

When Jesus said to the disciples, "You give them something to eat," He was also representing the needs of the humble people to His own men. Don't be afraid to do the same for your singles. Enhance their reputation to your pastor and accept any opportunity to share their stories with the congregation.

Let the church board know of your belief that the singles in your church are among the most important people there. It will help any churchgoer who is on the outside of the singles' world to better understand the validity of an adult singles ministry. It will also comfort your people to know you care enough to verbalize your support to others.

Servanthood

Jesus became the first short-order cook of all time when He fed the 5,000. As Christ, our mission here on this earth should be that we have "not come to be served, but to serve" (Matt. 20:28). Let your people know what a blessing they are to you and how you feel privileged that God allowed you this opportunity to minister and be ministered to. If people start to put you on a pedestal, knock it down! You're not involved in ministry to be a king, but to be a servant. Jesus' choice of a servant's role gives us a great example to follow.

You may still feel inadequate for service as an adult singles minister. Perhaps you have many sentences coming to mind beginning with the word, "But. . . ." The following responses are fallacies regarding the requirements of a capable adult singles minister.

A Person Should Be Unmarried to Best Minister to the Single Adult

False. Though a single can say, "I've been through that too," a married couple can remember their days as singles. A married minister and spouse bring a balance of ministry perspective and life's experiences to both never-marrieds and formerly marrieds. If marriage is a single person's goal, the married minister can help from both sides of the altar, as a former single and now married. The singles can see that the minister chose, with God's direction, to be a part of the single's ministry. Being married does not negate genuine servanthood.

A Minister to Singles Should Have a Seminary Degree

False. This may be helpful, but is not required. Many have not had seminary training. Many seminaries are limited in courses that offer help for singles ministry. Some have come into singles ministry from other careers, feeling a special burden for adult singles. One may have experienced divorce. God can use us with all of our accumulated life experiences. Yet, biblical knowledge is an imperative to be a minister to any people group. If one feels unqualified educationally, seminary is a good consideration, but you may also want to consider other excellent training resources and programs.

Lack of Experience Will Impair My Work with Multiple Staff

False. What will limit you is your lack of love. If you can convince your peers that you feel your ministry is one of the most important ministries of the church, they will learn to respect you. It may take time, but staff relationships can build a foundation of support that will prove invaluable to your mental health. Don't be afraid to share with them your conflicts, dreams, and disappointments. It will make you believable to them and they will become friends that last forever.

I Can't Be a Singles Minister Because I Get Too Burdened by the Counseling

You don't have to suffer from overload. One of the great designs of specialized programs and workshops, such as divorce or grief recovery, is that you can affect many people at once through a group experience. As your people train themselves to become better listeners, the load will decisively change. You may also have professional counselors in your area to whom you can make referrals. The minister should set counseling limits. It cannot be accomplished by one person.

Singles Ministers Need to Have a High Level of Energy

False. No one ever has enough energy. What you need to do is plan ahead. Learn to become versatile. Recruit and train quality, dedicated people to share the programming load with you and you will be amazed at what can be accomplished without your personal attention. Learn to be a good steward of your time and energy. If God wanted you stronger, He would have made you into a superman! Develop wisdom in knowing what you are best at, delegate responsibilities where you are less qualified, and go on from there.

A Person Should Be Highly Creative to Handle Single Adult Programming

False. There are ways to have creative programming without being creative yourself. Look for other people's ideas. Investigate other churches which have had successful programs. Ask your singles for ideas. Don't be afraid to learn from others. And remember, a loving program is much more important than creativity.

Singles ministry is a modern-day parallel to Christ's feeding of the 5,000. Many singles are among the neediest people in society today. Choose to project a personal profile which is in the likeness of our Lord and Saviour. It will carry you toward the reality of fulfilling your portion of the Great Commission.

Timm Jackson
Minister to Single Adults
Tempe, Arizona

Timm has been a singles pastor for the last nine years. He has also served as the Executive Director for the National Association of Single Adult Leaders.

37. OVERVIEW OF THE SINGLES ORGANIZATION

> *"Involving singles in a ministry and organization with a mission also helps each person claim ownership of the ministry. Call something 'your own' and it suddenly becomes very important. It is a special gem to the possessor."*
>
> *Timm Jackson*

Simply said, singles ministry is a ministry of one to one. It is one person drawing from another out of the storehouse and surplus God has given. Organization and structure become most effective when the "one to one" takes precedence. Take a person who is needy, fill that need with a tiny seed of hope from another, and you have begun a fascinating journey—you travel toward reaching God's great goal of making disciples. Whether your group numbers 10, 110, or 1,010, your best first step will be inviting other singles to help you fulfill the Great Commission—one to one. Jesus, in His last days on earth, gave us these special words, "You, then, are to go and make disciples of all the nations and baptize them in the name of the Father and of the Son and of the Holy Spirit. Teach them to observe all that I have commanded you and, remember, I am with you always, even to the end of the world" (Matt. 28:19-20, PH).

Develop a Purpose Statement

Deciding to help individuals effectively reach out to others requires that change will occur. Begin by writing your own philosophy of ministry. Here is an example:

Our singles ministry is in existence to provide a place and a message where modern-day single adults, with or without children, may be attracted to the claims of Christ, both personal and corporate, in a nonjudgmental, nonthreatening, loving, problem-sharing and -solving atmosphere that helps them deal authentically with their needs. The goal is that they will choose to make Jesus Christ not only their Saviour, but their Lord.

A statement of purpose such as this will help clarify and crystallize your focus and approach to ministry. It will also give you a solid base and vehicle for fulfilling the Great Commission and evaluating what is being accomplished. This gives you a *ministry with a mission*. The purpose must be biblical. It must rest and stand on an authoritative foundation.

Develop Personal Involvement

As each person does his part, we discover a simple, yet marvelous and rewarding principle: Give of yourself to others and your own needs will begin to be met. People need to be needed. If a person senses he is important, he has found a definite "comfort zone" in which he will be able to grow. As time goes on, that feeling of support will broaden to the point that the single person will want to relate to more people than those just like himself. Perhaps a woman is 36 and divorced with two teenage children. Initially, she will feel most comfortable with those in like circumstances. If, however, she receives a feeling of personal significance and thus begins to reach out to others from her "comfort," she may soon broaden her "zone" to include other single parents. Perhaps she will begin to relate to an older female who enjoys helping others. Eventually, this single parent will probably find herself happily involved in church activities, such as singing in the choir, or teaching a Sunday School class, or serving on a board or committee. She has found many options in which she can be a part of fulfilling the Great Commission.

Develop Ownership

Involving singles in a ministry and organization with a mission also helps each person claim ownership of the ministry. Call something "your own" and it suddenly becomes very important. It is a special gem to the possessor. It needs protection. It is handled carefully and looked after with love. The more a person claims ownership, the more supportive he will be of your calling and his role of action as a leader and as your coworker.

Singles claiming ownership cause an organization to become efficient. One paid clergy cannot have all the expertise that is needed to lead a well-rounded program. Realizing you are weak in some areas is OK. Let your people use their years of accumulated life experiences for the ministry's benefit. Besides, we all need to learn more. As more people become involved, you will discover a more positive environment is created in which to learn.

Develop a Ministry that Is for Adults

A ministry with a mission to singles must be a *ministry for adults*. Singles have gained much experience with which to reach out to others. They are also in the process of gaining even more valuable experience. The sooner that experience is put to good use, the more effective your ministry will be. Singles are not teenagers, nor are they a secondary adult subgroup.

Develop a Creative Atmosphere

Let your organization be a *ministry that creates*. There will be ingenious people around to help you grow your own ministry, giving you less need for a ready-made format. Use someone else's ideas for a guide to get you started. Once you have developed a plan for programming, a schedule, and a budget, don't be afraid to reevaluate each with your group of leaders. Experiment with ideas. Allow yourself and your leaders the freedom to fail. But always keep your philosophy of ministry in mind and aim toward your goal of fulfilling the Great Commission.

Discover the Needs

Your experiments will have a great chance to succeed if you first consider the needs of your singles. Send out a questionnaire, inquiring about their status. Are they mostly never-married, divorced, or widowed? What is the median age? Are they financially burdened or well-off? Programming should be the response to these needs, as well as other interest points.

Geographic needs may also be taken into account. Does your church reach out far beyond its own city? If so, you may want to occasionally go to the constituency or take into consideration their transportation needs.

Develop a Multifaceted Ministry

The world of single adults holds many different types of people. Because of this, you will also want a *ministry with many facets*. A large, impact-type program with Christian-oriented entertainment is a great draw to introduce the public and local community to your church and your ministry. Seminars will greatly enhance your ministry. These are short-term learning experiences which can either be weekend happenings or weekly series. Singles need to be learning. Parenting, finances, and self-esteem are good topic ideas, as well as divorce recovery and grief workshops, which will probably become a staple of your programming. These times of learning will not only draw people from the community, but will give you a tremendous opportunity to present the Gospel in a positive and relaxed setting.

An ongoing learning experience is also helpful to your organization, such as a Sunday teaching experience with a pastor or lay person who can deal effectively with God's love in a practical response to life's relationships and problems.

You may also want to consider specialty groups. These are often requested by the constituency, due to the comfort zones that they create. For those who feel something in common, you may want to consider groups such as never-marrieds, single parents, or those who are widowed. Age-oriented activities are also conducive to creating a comfort zone among most singles. Specialty relationships such as prayer partners or big buddies or care givers may be considered.

Small group studies, such as talk-it-overs, where people are not tied in with a series but come when they can, are great for many singles groups. The topic can be secular with a Christian orientation that lends comfort to people, no matter what their religious backgrounds may be. A topic such as "laughter" may open people up to what true happiness really is or how

God longs to be a part of our everyday lives and bring joy to us. Bible studies or Christian book studies are also great for small group interaction that can be taken to any geographic location. All of these cause a great camaraderie since each study is subject-oriented and attracts people with common interests. Small-group experiences greatly enhance your base of spiritual ministry.

Sports are valid contributions to a ministry in that they are nonthreatening to the average non-churched single, but offer great opportunities to see the Christian faith in action as people become acquainted with a church campus. A relaxed atmosphere where we can "be ourselves" opens us up to great ministry opportunities.

Retreats and getaways serve a wonderful purpose of taking people away from many of their everyday problems. Here they may seriously consider the claims of Christ and, consequently, make major spiritual commitments. Singles often have limited income for vacations, so this is helpful for their emotional well-being.

Develop Leadership
Last, your organization must be a ministry that develops leadership. You have the opportunity to develop the strongest, most capable leaders a church has ever experienced. Singles have also experienced the extremes of life. They may have had financial difficulty. If problems with children existed they might have stood alone in resolving such problems. If loss and rejection have been a part of their lives, they probably felt it more than those who are married, because of the lack of a "buffer" to comfort them in those moments. Consequently, singles will learn of God's grace and power in a way that marrieds often do not. These experiences are valuable to a church that cares. Give them a chance to become part of the ongoing singles ministry as a part of the church. Let them be a part of its budgeting, its inner workings, its government, and they will show a tremendous commitment. The liaison and input they offer will greatly benefit the whole church as time goes on.

Develop a system of accountability with job outlines, reports, evaluation, and goal-setting. Plans, goals, minutes, and other important information about the organization and ministry should always be in written form for all participants.

Should your leadership staff be large or small in numbers? Make your decision based on what is most comfortable for you, the leader. If you should choose to use a small staff, make sure the other singles still feel a sense of ownership of the ministry. Make every person important, just as they are in God's eyes. Develop good systems of communication and training for your leaders. Remember, recruitment is an ongoing process.

Should you use male or female leadership? Use both because both are so well-equipped to serve and commit to you. However, if you are trying to build up the number of males in your group, feel free to put males up front, on stage, and at the door greeting people. It will immediately demonstrate that guys in the group are important and it will draw more men to the ministry.

Organization and structure are necessary because they are tools with which to achieve a great goal for God's purpose. Focus on the individual . . . and they will in turn focus on one another. Organization and structure will help you keep your eyes realistically on your goals as you effectively fulfill your Great Commission.

Timm Jackson
Minister to Single Adults
Tempe, Arizona

During his seven years at Ward Presbyterian Church, Livonia, Michigan, Timm built one of the nation's largest singles ministries. Timm also served as the Executive Director of the National Association of Single Adult Leaders.

38. RECRUITING AND TRAINING LEADERS

"It is essential that churches or singles groups become the best possible places for training and resources. Equip your leadership with the best possible tools."

John Splinter

Each ministry situation is different. Each has its own "personality." Therefore, it is important to give some thought to the makeup of both the "pool" of leaders from which one will be drawing, and also to the group to which ministry will be offered. Before recruitment begins, a complete evaluation of needs, present ministry, people resources available, and mission statement is most helpful. This is where you begin, realistically and ideally.

After having done a complete analysis of your group and your overall approach to ministry, it is *critically* important to begin *targeting* your ministry. Begin slowly. The best approach is to start with one ministry at a time: one well-researched, well-thought-out ministry. You may only wish to have one ministry for singles, or you may wish to have several approaches to ministry. Ask yourself right from the beginning just what it is that you desire to accomplish.

Not all singles will respond to any one program. What you target will determine who comes, what age they'll be, what their personal backgrounds will be (divorced, never married, etc.), and what level of self-management they possess.

Two common mistakes made by new singles ministries include: one ministry that does not target anything, so it starts up with a solid core group of people, and drops off to less than one half of what it originally started with, and a ministry that targets too many things, tries to grow too quickly, and does not develop the leadership necessary to sustain and grow the ministry, so it dies prematurely from lack of support and leadership.

In targeting, it is very important to tie leadership recruitment to specific needs and specific life experiences. For example, the most empathetic divorce recovery leaders will be the formerly divorced. Sports programs will be best run by people who are keenly interested in the specific sport. Look for people who have direct experience and interest in the area of need you are trying to fill, or else people whom the Lord has blessed with special sensitivities and gifts (see Eph. 4:11-12).

Selection

It is very important to be selective in your request for volunteers. At certain levels of leadership, it is better to handpick those whom you feel will do the best job, rather than to simply ask for volunteers (see Matt. 9:9; Mark 1:17). If you simply ask for volunteers rather than developing a careful training and selection process, you could end up with people with limited skills, experiences, or spiritual gifts that do not match the job outline.

Don't be afraid to ask the people who are most busy already. They're probably the ones best suited for the job. They're highly involved with life. Yet give them the opportunity to change roles, stretch their ministry, or say no.

Exciting people usually create exciting ministry. The inverse is equally true. Create a climate of enthusiasm. Stimulate and motivate your people. Encourage the people with vision and positive energy to lead.

Expectations

It is essential that churches or singles groups become the best possible places for training and resources. Here are some thoughts in that direction.

First, give leadership a job outline or job description. It may be very simple or brief. However, leaders need to know what is expected of them, what they are responsible for, and to whom are they accountable.

Next, give individuals in leadership a vision or objective. For example: "This is the need. These are the gifts I see in you, gifts which can meet this need. This is how the Lord could use you within this ministry. This is what it will take to get the job done. This is where I'd like to see your ministry within the next six months; the next year." It is always important to communicate the vision or the objectives of the ministry or program. (See John 1:42. Christ had a vision for Peter long before Peter could see it.)

Never *under*-ask. Don't be afraid to tell your leaders that their involvement is going to cost them something. It will at least cost their time, prayers, and thought.

Ask for a definite commitment, a specific time period. For example, you may tell a leader that a specific task will take five hours per week, and the duration of the task will be one year.

Give specific task objectives, and use a time frame for completion. For example, "Next week at this time we'll be needing. . . . By next month at this time we'll be at this point, and you'll need to have accomplished thus and so. . . . By four months from now. . . ."

Training

Equip your leadership with the best possible tools. Churches should be the best resource depots—films, books, tape, periodicals, videos if possible, etc. Buy or rent resources as needed, because it is very important to equip leadership for their tasks.

Don't be afraid to ask volunteers to give their own money to purchase resources. If they're committed to a task, they'll probably be willing to participate financially to help see the task accomplished. However, work on developing an adequate budget within the ministry to provide for leadership development, training, and resources.

Involve community resources, such as, professional counselors, program training personnel, community colleges, and the like. There are a host of resources within most communities. Identify and tap them, as they will add much to your ministry to single adults.

Encourage your leadership to visit other churches which have successful singles ministries. Help your leadership attend seminars or training workshops which pertain to the singles ministry, singles needs, singles identity, etc. Develop your own leadership courses, seminars, workshops, or retreats. This is one area of spiritual discipleship.

Send your leadership out to do a task with a vision for the task, prayer support, encouragement, training, and resources to accomplish the task. See to it that you have given the best possible training, done by the best people in any particular field, so your volunteers feel well prepared for their tasks.

Evaluation

As you turn your leaders loose to accomplish their objectives, build in regular "checkpoints." For example, monthly executive leadership meetings are a good idea, in which you meet with leaders who are committee chairpersons only. However, regular contact with most of your key leaders (whether they are chairpersons or not) is a necessary ingredient to maintaining strong leadership teams.

Focus much of your time on building, supporting, and evaluating leadership on a regular basis, rather than spending your time running the various programs on your own. The more programs or ministries you hope to develop, the more important equipping others becomes.

Team Building

Build leadership teams as well as individuals. Get leadership involved in training others to assist them in their objectives, and eventually to take over for them. This gives you the opportunity to recycle the leaders into other ministries.

Ask your leadership to continually be recruiting new leaders to assist them, and encourage your leadership to be on the lookout for new resources which may be of help in building the ministry or program.

Organize your leadership into management/operational committees, with one person acting as chairperson, and each person on the committee being given a specific task, or reason, for being on the committee.

Ask the leadership teams to stay with the program or ministry until they accomplish their objectives, grow the program or ministry past its present

192

size, and replace themselves with leadership of equal or superior potential.

Create an Atmosphere of Choice and Freedom

Help your leadership people understand that it is very important for people to use the gifts which God has given them in ministry (Matt. 25:14-30). Create within your ministry the "ministry-identity" of creating leadership, rather than the identity of coming to the church to be just "nurtured."

Give freedom to your leadership teams once they're created. Let them own the ministry (see John 17). Don't feel a need to immediately rescue them if they flounder. Let them struggle and grow to set their ship back aright. Keep encouraging them toward the ministry objective. Keep equipping them. But let them own it.

Rotate your leadership, moving people from subcommittee up to vice-chair, to chair, and then out to new challenges. This process will take time. Be patient.

Allow leadership teams to chart new directions as they see the vision for ministry. Create an atmosphere which encourages input from the bottom up. Active democracy encourages active participation.

Additional Leadership Principles

Need dictates ministry. If a program or ministry is dead, leave it for a new program. If there's a need, it will succeed, and God will raise up leaders to meet the need.

Hungry people make poor shoppers (and leaders). People who are too close to acute trauma should be avoided for leadership positions until they stabilize. Chronically traumatized people need to own responsibility for their own traumas before being given leadership responsibility.

Use married people too. Married people can be as effective in leadership to singles as singles can be, but select couples as carefully as single leaders.

Turnover. Singles ministries are often transdenominational and highly transient. Expect an annual turnover as high as 50 percent.

Integration. Singles leadership should be integrated into the church, and onto church boards. Work toward developing integration into the church body. Many times singles are seen as outside the church and they feel it.

Growing leadership. Grow your ministry leadership team by accepting individuals as they are when they come to you, and taking them to the next step in their own spiritual growth, whatever that step may be.

Avoid burning out your best leaders. One or two responsibilities are plenty for most.

John Splinter
Associate Pastor; Singles Ministries
Central Presbyterian Church, St. Louis, Missouri

The strength of John's single adult ministry has been the building of strong leadership teams. He has also had an extensive ministry helping other churches organize and develop single adult ministries.

39. DEFINING PURPOSE, GOALS, AND PLANS

"A total ministry should be planned as soon as possible, but developed in stages. Establishing and directing a ministry to adult singles is a very complex and challenging undertaking, due to the many issues that adult singles face."

Dennis Franck

Imagine a ship setting out to sea without a course, or a plane taking off without any specific destination. It would be potentially disastrous. So it would be for a ministry without a distinct purpose, clear goals, and definite plans. Any ministry needs to have these elements, and ministry to adult singles is no different.

Purpose
Purpose can be defined as an aim, an intention, a reason for existence. The purpose for ministry to adult singles can be simply stated as: *to develop healthy Christian singles.* People desire and need to be whole spiritually, socially, emotionally, and educationally. Ministry should strive to attain the purpose of assisting individuals in building healthy, whole lives in every sense of the word. Three ways for achieving this are suggested.

Provide an Accepting Ministry
An atmosphere of unconditional love and acceptance needs to be portrayed and sensed at all times. People need to feel acceptance without condemnation. The example of Jesus in John 4 with the woman at the well shows Jesus accepting, forgiving, loving, and ministering to a woman who was divorced five times and now living with a man. He did not judge or condemn her.

This attitude needs to be genuinely displayed and sincerely sensed in ministry to adult singles. This is desperately important because of the varied backgrounds of the people you will be ministering to. Some may come in the midst of a divorce or separation from their spouses. Some may have lost their spouses through death. Others may have never married. Some may be currently living with persons of the opposite sex. There may be individuals who are involved in homosexual relationships. Drug addicts and alcoholics may attend the group. Single parents who have lost their mates through divorce or death, or who have never married may come. People who are socially handicapped, mentally handicapped, and physically handicapped may appear. In addition to this, individuals from every church background and theological persuasion may come. Many of these people's situations present issues which are of major controversy and consequence. However, *all* of these people *desire* and *deserve* our unconditional love and acceptance. Without it, it is doubtful they will return.

Provide a Whole Ministry

To foster the purpose of wholeness, ministry to adult singles needs to develop four elements: the spiritual, the social, the emotional, and the educational. Each element is a key part of the total ministry and will play a vital role in contributing to the development of people's lives.

A spiritual atmosphere and thrust should be foundational. When this is present, the group will be known for its biblical basis and Christian emphasis. The Christian emphasis can be portrayed in every aspect of the ministry (music, prayer, classes, retreats, etc.).

Since adult singles desire fulfilling relationships, various types of social activities and opportunities for fellowship can be offered. Their needs of support, friendship, learning, relating, dating, and mating will begin to be fulfilled from within the social network provided by the ministry.

The need for individual emotional growth can be met through counseling with the minister/leader, or through counseling with other adult singles. Many times people are their own best counselors due to the knowledge gained from similar experiences.

Educational growth is needed in the areas of managing money, raising children as a single parent, preparing for a permanent relationship, determining identity, understanding sexuality, and others. These issues are often discussed in one-to-one relationships but could also have instruction in class settings.

Provide a Growing Ministry

A third means of contributing to individual wholeness is to provide opportunities for personal growth through discipleship and involvement in the ministry. As leadership people and support people are developed, a personal sense of contribution and importance is felt by those involved. Personal joy is derived from assisting in a ministry that is providing help and healing to people.

Involving many individuals also eliminates burnout of a few and brings a feeling of ownership. "This ministry does not belong to the leader; it is ours! We are responsible for its success or failure."

A natural consequence of personal growth is group growth. As people assume responsibility for the ministry, the group will begin to grow spiritually, numerically, financially, etc. The reality of people helping people will influence and foster corporate growth. As individuals grow, the ministry will grow.

Goals

Goals can be defined as set objectives which achieve a purpose. Goals need to be determined which, when met, contribute to the enhancement and achievement of the ministry's purposes.

Who Are We Targeting

Either at the onset of the ministry or sometime in its early stages, a decision will need to be made concerning *who* is going to be targeted. Will you be providing a ministry mainly for those in *your church*? Will you endeavor to reach the *unchurched*? Will you accept adult singles from *other churches*? Some will probably come from hearing about your efforts to provide for this huge segment of society. It should be made clear that you are not trying to "get people out of their churches and into yours," but that you are only providing for a need that may not be met somewhere else.

What Needs Are to Be Met?

Another issue which needs to be considered concerns the type(s) of adult singles you are trying to reach. The term "adult single" includes individuals 18 years and up. If the decision is made to plan for the younger adult ages 18-30, it will mean ministering mainly to the never-married person. If the goal is to attract mainly the adult between 30 and 55, it will mean ministering primarily to the divorced person.

Within each of these age-groups, however, all three types of adult singles are present. There are people in their 40s, 50s, and 60s who have never married. There are those in their 20s and 30s who are divorced and widowed. Even more complicated is the fact that, within all age-groupings, there are people who are currently separated from their spouses. There are also single parents who are single either by divorce, death of a spouse, or who have never married but happen to have children by adoption, circumstance, or design. (These mainly fall into the 20-50 age bracket.)

Many of the needs and struggles of the adult single are similar, regardless of the reason for singleness. Five basic categories include:

1. Spiritual—to know God through a personal, vital, growing relationship with Jesus Christ.
2. Relational—to learn to relate to people of all ages in casual and/or intimate relationships with the same and opposite sex.
3. Emotional—to maintain emotional stability in a complex world.
4. Directional—to find direction in the many areas of life.
5. Financial—to learn to effectively manage money.

These basic needs should be clearly identified and established as goals set for the ministry.

Plans

It has been said that "those who fail to plan, plan to fail." I believe this is true. Definite plans achieve specific goals which fulfill clear purposes. A *total ministry should be planned* as soon as possible, *but developed in stages.* Establishing and directing a ministry to adult singles is a very complex and challenging undertaking, due to the many issues that adult singles face. An effective, need-fulfilling ministry does not happen overnight. It takes time to develop. Be patient and allow time for it. Several things must be considered in the planning process.

Leadership. People to assume various leadership roles will need to be found, appointed, trained, and motivated. Are potential leaders currently present or must there be a waiting period? Consider what kind of person is needed for the position. This may be determined largely by the type of activity (Bible study, social, retreat, publicity, etc.).

Time frame. Consider the timing in planning for the ministry. Is there currently verbal and moral support or must it be developed? Is the need for this particular segment of ministry present already, or is the intention to begin it first and expect those who will benefit from it to come? When is it possible to begin?

Finances. Is there currently enough money for this ministry, or will it have to be raised? How will it be raised, and by when? Has the church or sponsoring organization budgeted for it? If not, what would it take to get them to? Or, will the ministry be self-supporting?

Facilities. A ministry to adult singles can be developed one of two ways— inside the church building/campus, or outside the church building/campus. Since there is not an overabundance of these ministries in most areas of the country, location is a very important factor. There are several advantages and disadvantages either way you choose.

In the church—advantages.
- Meeting room(s) at no cost.
- Availability of storage space.
- Visibility to the church body—the sponsoring church begins to sense and understand the purposes of the ministry.
- Spiritual image and thrust is easy to maintain.

In the church—disadvantages.
- Attracts lesser percent of the unchurched—many people are reluctant to step into a church because of stereotyped ideas and images.
- Misunderstanding of purpose from leaders of other churches—other churches may think you are proselyting, or fear that people may leave their churches and become part of yours, even if the ministry does not meet on a regular church day.
- Possible scheduling conflicts.

Out of the church—advantages.
- Attracts a higher percent of unchurched people.
- Attracts a higher percent of other-church people whose churches have no ministry to adult singles.
- Community witness—the city/community may eventually receive the impression of a city-wide ministry and a genuine caring for people.

- Parking space (depending on scheduling).

Out of the church—disadvantages.
- Finding a suitable room(s)—it may be difficult to find a room. Things to consider may include location, image of the establishment, seating arrangements, availability of refreshments (purchase or bring in), location of restrooms, and other items depending on preference and need.
- Storage availability—many times props and materials may need to be taken out of the building after each meeting.
- Lack of church leadership support—church leadership may not be secure enough to allow a ministry out of the church. The sponsoring church may not benefit numerically and financially.
- Possible scheduling conflicts.
- Image of the ministry—both churched and unchurched people may have false images and stereotyped ideas of the group. These may include: "A Dating Club," "A Losers Group," "A Swingers Group," "A Spiritual Clique," "A Lonelies Group," and others.

Curriculum/materials. Five to 10 years ago, resource and teaching material was difficult to find for developing a ministry to adult singles. It may still not be as easy to find as many other types of materials (youth, children, etc.). However, more writers are responding to the ever-growing need for resources.

When seeking resource material, be sure to obtain material that is *geared to adults.* Some people mistakenly assume that the word single refers mainly to the young adult, ages 18-24 (the college-age person). These people can indeed be single. However, a very high percentage of adult singles are between the ages of 25 and 75 and are single due to a divorce, death of a spouse, or never marrying. These people's needs and interests are distinctly those of adults, and most of the time differ from those of college-age adults. Using material that is mainly geared to the college-age person would reach only a small percentage of America's single adults.

It would be wise to ask leaders of other single adult ministries what materials they use. It is always helpful to obtain a good recommendation before purchasing and/or using a particular book, tape, etc. For practical ideas on resource material consult the *Suggested Reading* at the end of this book. But again, the needs are adult, not just single.

Evaluation

In the final analysis, two questions must be answered. Evaluation is imperative to discover whether or not goals have been met and the purpose fulfilled. The two questions are: Is there *effective ministry to* people? and, Is there *effective ministry for* people?

For the answer to the first question, look closely at what is happening in the *individual lives* of people. Are lives being changed and people being made whole? Is there an attitude of enthusiasm among the people? Are there continually first-time visitors attending? Are individuals being treated warmly, respectfully, and with genuine hospitality? Are the current programs really meeting the definite needs of the people? These are the types of things which should be evaluated to determine the effectiveness of *ministry to people*.

For the answer to the second question, look closely at what is happening *in the group*. Are there many kinds of involvement opportunities, both for leadership people and support people? Are people really ministering to each other by giving encouragement, prayer, counseling, and support? Is there a genuine feeling that this ministry belongs to the people and not the pastor/leader? These are the types of things which should be evaluated to determine the effectiveness of *ministry for people*.

Dennis Franck
Singles Pastor
Bethel Church, San Jose, California

Dennis has served as a singles pastor in the local church since 1979. He has led workshops, written several magazine articles on ministry goals, and is a member of the executive board of the National Association of Single Adult Leaders.

40. BUILDING COMMUNITY IN A SINGLES MINISTRY

"People need each other and need the support that belonging to a community gives . . . which comes from involvement, not passive observance."

Jim Smoke

The average singles group in America turns over its population from 40 to 60 percent every six months. Knowing that makes it rather difficult to think and plan for long-term community building. The people who seem to stay longest in any singles group are usually the leaders. Because they are in leadership together, they tend to form a very tight community of support and caring for one another. The struggle to form community beyond the leadership team is a difficult one that most leaders struggle with. The answer to the age-old question of what draws people together is as wide and varied as the weather patterns across the country. One thing does remain constant: people need each other and need the support that belonging to a community gives. The following are a few key principles that have been learned and demonstrated among many singles ministries in recent years.

Community Does Not Happen by Legislation
You cannot *make* people become important to one another in a loving and caring fashion. Building community is a process that takes an endless amount of time. There is little or no sense of community in the forming of a new group of singles. People cannot belong to one another until they really know one another. Using group dynamics and group gymnastics does not make a community.

The Leadership Must Model What They Want the Followers to Become
Jesus' final commands to the disciples contained the admonition to "love each other." In the best of times, that is seldom easy. In tough times, it can be virtually impossible. The tenor of any ministry is set by the leadership. If there is dissension in leadership, you can be sure there will be tension in the ranks. Since leadership is usually "up front," their community patterns with one another are highly visible. I have had people tell me they wanted to be in leadership only because they were envious of the

spirit of community the leaders had with one another.

Building Community Is a Teaching Process
Community should come from a biblical base with the model of Jesus and His relationship with the disciples in the Gospels (Luke 22:7-14; John 13:1-17; Acts 4:32-35; Phile. 14; Heb. 10:24-25; 1 Peter 5:2). You always teach your people what you want them to do and be. Then you model your teaching. It is easy to become fragmented in a singles ministry because there is little or no emphasis on community. Sports teams spend as much time building community as perfecting their athletic skills. That is why when one team member gets in a scuffle with an opposing player, the bench usually empties as the rest of the team comes to the rescue.

Building Community Is Based in Teaching People How to Build Healthy Relationships
Many people lack relational skills or have been hurt so deeply that they fear any form of relationship. You cannot build community with everyone by walking on eggshells. Life is about relationships. Building them involves risks. There are no guarantees.

Good Communities Last because They Become Based in Solid Friendships
I still meet yearly for a dinner with about 40 of my old singles ministry leaders from the early '70s. And we will continue to do that each year because we were and still remain a community. Common needs, interests, dreams, and struggles brought us together. Those same things held us together and the ties strengthened over the years.

People Only Support What They Help Create
A sense of belonging comes from a sense of ownership. People need a good reason to attend, join, participate. Yes, I know there will always be a crowd content to just be sideline spectators. They are everywhere in life and they usually run from responsibility. Leave them alone with their reasons and concentrate on those who want to be involved. Community comes from involvement, not from passive observance. Whenever you can, give your people a reason to be at your events and programs. Make sure the reason goes beyond just filling the seats.

Fellow Strugglers Build Solid Community
There is a dynamic of a shared experience or shared struggle that draws people closer to each other. It needs little explanation. It just happens. It is true in Alcoholics Anonymous and it is true in divorce recovery work. When strugglers experience healing and wholeness, they give it back to others who need it, and the bonds of community through caring become even stronger.

Building a community is a slow and often torturous process but the finished product is worth the process!

Building Community Does Not Mean Having One Big Happy Family

In a singles ministry, it means having one common objective and having many happy families. There is more of a mystery concerning what draws people into different communities than there is a simple explanation. The important thing is that they find a place to belong. We all search for that place or places where we know we belong, feel comfortable, fit in. We are never hesitant to go where we feel secure and accepted. A sense of belonging seldom happens overnight. We need to test the waters to see where we belong best.

Joining a Community Can Become a Tremendous Struggle for Some

One of the dynamics of any singles group is that many of the people attending it have lost their former communities and have little or no sense of belonging anywhere as they pass through your door. They need to hear someone say, "There's a place for you here. You will be loved and accepted and you will find a home." Many single adults are in transition, experiencing a difficult time. They often wander from group to group, looking for a safe place to pitch their tents and camp for a while. Any group of singles could be described as containing those who have lost community, those in search of a new community, those who have found a new community, and those fearful they will be nomads from community for the rest of their lives.

Jim Smoke
President of Growing Free
Tempe, Arizona

Jim has often been called the "Father of single adult ministry in America." As a pioneer, author, speaker, and former singles pastor, Jim knows the importance of building community in a singles ministry.

41. BIBLE STUDY

*"It cannot be assumed that adult students will naturally
and correctly apply biblical principles to life situations. We
must help them."*

David Weidlich

The Bible, Our Textbook

Single adults desire security, fulfillment, healthy relationships, and help
raising children. These are important needs, and adults want more than
just opinions when it comes to providing solutions.

An old cliché says, "Consider the source." A person may be quite
capable of teaching truth using science, psychology, and philosophy as
sources. But how can people know what that person is teaching is true? A
lot is based on the trustworthiness of the source.

The Bible claims complete trustworthiness for itself. It was written by
God who is, after all, the Author of all truth. When correctly interpreted
and applied, the truth of Scripture is a powerful and profitable tool (2 Tim.
2:15; 3:16).

You cannot have that confidence if you are teaching the latest discoveries reported in a journal written by men or women. What you're teaching
may prove to be helpful. Or, time and further discoveries may prove that
you were unhelpful. However, if you are accurately conveying the truths
of the Bible, you can't go wrong!

Christians are given the responsibility of teaching others about God and
His expectations of people. Jesus left His disciples with the words, "Go
and make disciples of all nations" (Matt. 28:19). Jesus' followers were
called *mathetai*, "disciples." The word means "learners" or "pupils." So
the process of disciple-making is the process of producing learners or
pupils of Christ. If people are expected to be learners, there must be
teachers.

A ministry to single adults must include biblical teaching. A church does
well to be concerned about singles, but if they aren't offering biblical
solutions to life's problems, they're not training disciples. Therefore, the
Bible is our number one textbook in training and nurturing single adult
disciples.

Learning is considered tedious to many because the goal of many teachers—in and out of the church—is merely to transfer ideas from the teacher to the student. Certainly, that's part of it, but the Christian's goal in
ministry is to make disciples mature in Christ (Col. 1:25, 28-29).

With that in mind, it can be seen that Christian teachers must teach certain facts from God's Word and life's situations, but they must encourage and motivate their students to apply and practice those ideas in real life. Not only is that the right thing to do; it's what people need the most.

Jesus the Master Teacher

In discussing how best to teach the Bible, it should not be forgotten that Jesus was Himself a Bible Teacher. And what an effective one!

The most influential teachers are those who not only communicate facts well, but also communicate love and concern. Jesus certainly did. Who wouldn't listen to a teacher who said, "I am the Good Shepherd . . . and I lay down My life for My sheep"? (John 10:14-15) It's easily proven that students learn much more effectively when the teacher communicates genuine concern and warmth.

Jesus not only taught a righteous lifestyle. He lived it! His integrity of life taught what mere words could not. He modeled what He taught. His attitude and last words on the cross, "Father forgive them," added immeasurable impact to His teaching of love for one's enemies. Teachers must be models of the actions and attitudes they teach.

Jesus' teaching style involved constant interaction with His pupils. They were free to interrupt or ask questions. Often He asked them questions to guide them toward truth. He taught from the Scriptures (Luke 4:17-27). He employed parables, discussions, and natural, everyday situations and events (Matt. 13:34-35). He motivated the disciples to think and discover for themselves. This produced confusion at times, like when He left them so they could ponder the meaning of a parable or "hard saying." But in the long run, He was more effective than if He had only dispensed factual data to His disciples. They *discovered* God's good Word for themselves.

Principles for Effective Teaching

The example of Jesus and the insights of modern educators can be used to draw several principles about effective teaching.

Pray. Continually seek God's guidance as you prepare and teach. Ask the Holy Spirit to guide you and your group into the truth (Eph. 1:17-18).

Let go of the reins. Too often teachers continue bottle-feeding their students long after their students are able to feed themselves. Give up your desire to have control. People are more motivated to learn when they share in ownership of the learning experience.

Be a facilitator. Teachers need to see themselves less as dispensers of knowledge and more as facilitators who point fellow-learners to the truth (Christ). The teacher is still an important part of the learning process. But the role is different. He or she is a guide, consultant, and resource person. Remember, singles are adults. Adults learn best through personal discovery during the journey.

Accept the role of motivator. Show *why* people need to learn something. This can be done by asking questions that arouse felt-needs. Or use a case study that parallels their experience followed by the question, "What would you do in this situation?" Use questions to open their minds to new possibilities, not to lead learners into parroting expected answers.

Encourage participation in learning. Let students dialogue in an atmosphere of freedom and acceptance. Give them ownership of the learning experience by allowing them to formulate their own thoughts and goals. You might ask, "What is it that you want from this study?" Also, encourage them to evaluate the learning experience from time to time.

Design a pattern of learning experiences using a variety of techniques and materials. Include small group discussion, role plays, readings, lectures, interviews, drama, music and art activities, research activities, tests, and writing assignments. Create learning activities, not learning passivities.

Always emphasize application. It cannot be assumed that adult students will naturally and correctly apply biblical principles to life situations. We must help them. For example, ask, "How does Paul's discussion of humility apply to your relationship with your ex-spouse?" Or, "Name one thing you will do this week that shows humility." Use assignments to encourage the integration of new attitudes and skills in life situations. Remember, assignments are best carried out when learners participate in designing them. A group may want to assign themselves to memorize a verse or carry out a service project.

Evaluate and encourage. Learn from your teaching experiences and improve your teaching skills. Also help learners feel a sense of progress toward goals by reviewing and affirming their achievements. Divide learning into distinguishable segments and, at the end of one, celebrate!

Forms of Bible Study

God's creativity in making people is limitless. We're all different, and all groups of people are different. But there are several general forms that teaching may take that seem to apply to all people in all cultures and situations.

Large group study. In this form, communication is necessarily more one-way, though not exclusively. Recognize the diversity of your group and gear your studies to be broader in application. The larger the group, the less commitment you can expect. For this reason, make each session a self-contained unit to include even those who haven't attended before. While doing a series, keep it short; 3-4 sessions is a reasonable length.

Topical lessons work well in a large group context because you are better able to meet the felt-needs of those participating. However, Bible book studies should not be ignored. Many people won't come unless they can see right away that there's something in it for them. So address a subject that a wide variety of singles would be interested in—like relationships, sex, career success, single parenting, money management, etc. Start with these felt-needs and then present a biblical perspective on these issues. For simplicity and impact stick with one appropriate passage of

Scripture as your main text and apply it faithfully to the issue at hand.

Small groups. This form provides for more flexibility. Groups can be more homogeneous; that is, made up of people who have many things in common. This way, you can meet specific needs. For example, you may have a group for career women, one for never-marrieds, one for single parents, one for new Christians, one for people who are not (yet) Christians, and one for any combination of people. People are generally attracted to people who are like themselves and they will make a stronger commitment to the group.

The success of a small group is largely dependent on its leader(s). The best leader is one who will take the role of a pastor/shepherd to care for needs of the individuals in the group. He or she must maintain a balance of control and freedom. Group members must own the group but the leader must hold individuals accountable to the group and to their goals.

Small groups provide for more flexibility in studying. In a group of dedicated people you have a good context for an in-depth inductive Bible study. Or with a group of single-parents you can study what the Scriptures say about parenting. So the application can be more specific according to the more common needs of the group.

Cramming. Another effective form of Bible study is called "cramming." Of course, cramming isn't highly recommended in academic circles, but if it weren't for this method, many college students wouldn't learn anything.

The same principles can be transferred to informal education by holding conferences, seminars, and retreats. People are more likely to commit to a one-time experience for a long period of time than to an equal amount of time stretched out over several weeks or months. These "cramming" sessions are good opportunities for intense study with application to specific needs. For example, you might hold a seminar on money management where scriptural attitudes and principles are studied, or a weekend retreat where 1 Corinthians is taught as it relates especially to singles in sexual morality, relationships, marriage, spiritual gifts, and more.

The task of Bible study is not an easy one. Sadly, many teachers are content to go for the quick rewards of serving up popular, but ultimately unsatisfying spiritual food. Jesus has called us to make disciples and this can only be done by teaching them about God and His expectations of us and then motivating them to respond through faith and obedience.

Go and make disciples. "And surely I will be with you always" (Matt. 28:20).

David Weidlich
Director of Singles Ministries
Fair Oaks Presbyterian Church, Fair Oaks, California

Dave's ministry in California and formerly in Colorado, has had a strong emphasis on discipleship and Bible study. As an extension of his ministry in Bible study, Dave has written five leader's guides for curriculum courses for Victor Books.

42. DEVELOPING SMALL GROUPS

"In starting a small group, it is important to recognize the needs of people within the group and make the group's purposes very clear. The support, fellowship, and interaction provided by such a group will serve to meet many needs in the lives of single adults."

Jeff McNicol

The development of small groups is not a new phenomenon peculiar to recent years. However, the realization that small groups are a crucial aspect of vital, dynamic, growing ministries is. Churches and other organizations are focusing on groups with fewer participants and have experienced great benefits as a result. This approach is particularly effective in singles ministry.

What Is a Small Group?
Numerically. It is quite difficult to suggest a specific size which is optimal for each and every single adult small group, due to the fact that no two are alike. Yet there is a range in which small groups function most effectively. This range is approximately 4 to 12 participants. More than 12 will tend to stifle interaction, causing the group to become dominated by just a few.
Functionally. If one were to reduce all the functional benefits of small groups to a single word, it would be *interaction.* Nearly all of the other positive elements are an outgrowth of the interaction possible in small groups. Not only does it encourage personal interaction between members of the group, fostering relationship-building, it also aids in increasing personal ownership of the group. The more an individual participates and contributes, the more he will feel as though it is his group—because it is! Once he considers it "his" group, his commitment and desire to make it successful increases significantly.

The Need for Small Groups
Interrelationally. The relational interaction of the small group for singles is important because this may be the only source of support for some. Each of us has certain needs in our lives, and it helps to know that others are aware of our hurts. A group of caring individuals can listen to those needs and provide comfort on that basis alone. Secondly, a small gathering of singles can provide a tremendous support for one another. Beyond being a place to share needs, there is the potential of a deep camaraderie that

can develop between all the members of the singles small group. I have experienced a great warmth and love from the singles I work with, and have also seen group members involved in a significant caring ministry among one another emotionally, physically, financially, and spiritually. A support structure such as this takes time and an investment of ourselves in the lives of others, but the results can be life-changing and well worth the effort.

Functionally. Small groups are a very effective vehicle through which the following activities may be accomplished. First of all, 4 to 12 people is an excellent size for a Bible study. A larger group is plagued by its numbers and essentially becomes a teacher/listener environment, failing to encourage discussion. With the smaller group, however, it is feasible that all those present can take part. Second, there is the opportunity of prayer for one another. Prayer on behalf of all the others in the group is possible because of the reduced group size. One additional exciting aspect of the smaller group is that personal follow-up can be done with relative ease. After praying for someone, give that person a call and let him know you are thinking of him. Chances are that your concern alone will provide comfort.

The Leadership of Small Groups

Developing leadership. Leadership is not something a person is born with; rather, leaders are trained and taught. Learning to be a leader is not much different than learning any other skill; with practice and perseverance, it can be developed. For this very reason, potential future leaders must be given opportunities to "try their wings" and serve in leadership. Sharing the leadership is an absolute necessity in singles ministry. Due to the high turnover, unless we are nourishing leadership replacements, we will be left without small group leaders.

Choosing a leader. How do we go about recognizing a potential small group leader? We must begin with prayer. If God wants us to have a singles ministry, He will provide the necessary personnel. We, however, must be in a position to recognize God's provision. Praying for the Lord's guidance is the first step. There are also certain characteristics which suggest leadership qualities. One such quality is vision. One who does not have a good idea of where the small group is headed and what its purpose is will probably not lead well. However, vision can be caught by the potential leader. Additional leadership qualities include a love for God, spiritual maturity, affinity for others, pleasant personality (not necessarily outgoing), diligence, and a willingness to be a team player.

Leader's role as facilitator. Within the small group setting, it is preferential to think of the central figure as the facilitator. It has been stressed that interaction is the major function of small groups. If a leader operates as a dictator, that interaction will not take place and the small group may as well be a large group. If the leader is a facilitator, however, he will only enhance the group, teaching others to lead in the process.

Modeling leadership. The leader must model leadership to others. There are a few specific principles to be kept in mind. First of all, it is crucial to invest time and effort into potential future leaders. Essentially it is a discipleship process whereby one leader trains another, who trains another, etc. (2 Tim. 2:2). Second, when modeling leadership, it is important to demonstrate a teachable attitude. No one of us has all the answers, and to pretend we do will only diminish our credibility in the eyes of others. Remain open to the ideas of others.

How to Implement and Sustain Small Groups

Getting started. The best place to start is with prayer, seeking God's direction for the small group(s) you are planning to initiate. When the time comes to determine who the group members will be, take time and care to assure a grouping of people sharing common interests or backgrounds. Some extra effort in this area will certainly be time well spent in the long run. Within the given parameters, determine what you feel would be the most effective number of participants for your specific situation, and stick to it. Once the group reaches the maximum number, start a second group. If numerical growth is a goal, two groups of 6 have a greater growth potential than one group of 12 simply because a group already at its maximum number will not tend to be "growth-minded." The final key in starting is to recognize the needs of the people within the group and make the group's purposes very clear. Hidden agendas will only serve to frustrate a group focusing on a separate purpose.

The small group meeting. Along the same lines as clarifying purposes is goal-setting. As with any ministry or organization, goals give direction. A small group will tend to flounder if members do not have a clear understanding of the goals. During the actual small group meeting, there are two overriding procedures or approaches in presenting material, namely the use of constants or variables. Constants are necessary to give the group continuity from week to week. It gives group members focal points to recognize and keeps the meetings from becoming disjointed. On the other hand, the meetings also need variables. Without variables, the group will become dull and boring. There needs to be a balance, and it is the leader's responsibility to maintain that balance.

Moving forward. The small group should never be satisfied with the status quo. There must always be a sense of direction plus a feeling of achieving goals and moving ahead. Group vision and ownership will help to accomplish this. The leader and group must share and ultimately agree on a purpose and plan for the group. This in turn will develop ownership, and the group will move forward with a common focus. Another hint in this area is to ask for and expect involvement. A small group needs commitment from its members. If someone wishes to be in a group, you have the right to expect some level of involvement in due time.

Termination of small groups. In a chapter on developing small groups, you might be surprised to find a discussion on terminating the small group. However, it is an important, often overlooked necessity in many groups. No gathering of people is guaranteed to be successful forever and ever. Even the most efficient small group can reach the point where its goal has been reached and effectiveness has run out. This is nothing to be ashamed of, but for the sake of all involved, do not be afraid to admit it and dissolve the group.

Potential Dangers for Small Groups

Individual domination. The strength of the small group is found in the interaction it can generate. The dominator may not be the "official" group leader. Therefore, when one individual dominates the discussion, it will be a setback to the group.

Lack of focus on goals. Without clearly focused goals and purpose, the group will lack meaningful direction. Continually be emphasizing the group's goals as it meets together.

Superficial relationships. There is a measure of vulnerability involved with being in a small group. It is, however, that risk of showing others who you are inside as a person that transports the group from superficial relations to a more meaningful involvement in one another's lives.

Forced transparency. Due to the risk and vulnerability involved with sharing oneself, we must be careful not to force it. Nobody shares their innermost feelings with someone he has just met. A level of trust and acceptance must be attained before intimacy will emerge.

Growing beyond a small group. Once a group gets too large, it can no longer be effective as a small group. Too many members will kill the group. Determine your boundaries and, when you reach the maximum, form a new group.

Cliques. All cliques are not bad. The formation of a small group in and of itself is a clique. However, if different cliques form within the small group, it could be devastating. Inner cliques could create an atmosphere where open, honest, vulnerable interaction cannot take place.

Dead groups. Many small groups reach the place where they cease being effective. To force the group to continue will only frustrate those involved. Let dying groups die, and allow their members to move on.

Small groups are a significant means through which ministry to singles can take place, The support, fellowship, and interaction provided by such a group will serve to meet many needs in the lives of single adults.

Jeff McNicol
Pastor of Associate Ministries
First Baptist Church, Rochester, Minnesota

Along with directing the singles ministry, Jeff has spoken at numerous leadership retreats and coordinated singles small group ministries.

210

43. DISCIPLESHIP FOR DEPTH

"Discipleship helps us see our real roles in light of God's plan, and that we are forgiven only by the grace of God, having no price to pay, just thanks to give."

Timm Jackson

Discipleship Is God's Idea

God's clear biblical imperative to us is to "make disciples" (Matt. 28:19). That is our role as leaders. That is God's design for ministry in people's lives. Our programming and organization goals should be the making of disciples.

The word "disciple" comes from the Greek, meaning "learner, student, adherent." It must first be recognized that there is a lot more to being a student than just being in a classroom with a textbook and a teacher up front. Matthew points out that the first element in discipleship is going (v. 19). In other words, evangelism. Discipleship begins with winning "students" to *the* Teacher, Jesus Christ. The other elements involve: identification of the student, teaching, obedience, and a relationship (vv. 19-20). It is all of these elements that are part of the discipleship process and growth experience.

Indeed, discipleship is a process. It takes time. It requires perseverance and a plan for growth. If not, shallowness is the result and growth is limited. It is the same for a builder, farmer, soldier, and athlete. For each to grow, there must be a design, a goal, a training period, and testing ground for the one in training.

Discipleship Involves a Relationship

The key to any learning situation is often the students' relationship with the teacher. Students looking back over their academic years of training will often remember a teacher or professor far beyond the subject matter or a particular text. Students often quote their "profs." Seldom do they remember what they, the students, wrote in a particular test, assignment, or term paper.

Therefore, it is imperative to build solid teachers (disciplers) in your singles ministry. It is the discipler who will "go" to win the heartbeat and capture the desire of the learner to learn about spiritual things. He/she must be well equipped and ready to go in-depth with disciples. It has often been said, "Spiritual truths are caught, not taught." For that to be true, the discipler must be skilled and trained in the disseminating of spiritual imperatives so that the adherents can catch what God has for them.

Of course, the key relationship is with the great Teacher and the true Discipler, Jesus Christ. It is a relationship with the God of the universe that changes lives and creates growth in the lives of disciples. And so it is a relationship with two of God's children, the discipler and the disciple (both of whom are disciples to Christ) and the person of Jesus Christ.

Discipleship Design

There are many plans and programs for leading disciples into a closer walk with Jesus Christ. The Navigators, Campus Crusade, InterVarsity, Scripture Press, David C. Cook, and Moody Press all have excellent materials available to help guide the learning process.

However, if there is to be a deep growing experience in the process with the discipler and the disciple(s) then there are a few keys that go beyond a "curriculum" or program of "filling-in-the-blanks." One key is a loving, caring, and compassionate relationship with all involved that motivates and stimulates each one to a deeper walk with Christ. Another key is recognizing that singles are adults and they learn best by the "discovery method." That means that singles need to explore, experiment, and be guided in their observations of God, His Word, and His plan for living. Other keys include: singles setting their own spiritual goals, study of God's Word, prayer, Bible memory, worship, service, and reproducing their lives in Christ in the lives of others. The process is long, yet exciting.

Discipleship Brings Great Benefits

The process and relationship with the discipler and disciple is never an end in itself. There are many marvelous benefits as believers grow in their personal relationship with their Creator.

As I see it, promoting true discipleship in a single adult ministry will benefit four major areas.

It will benefit your singles. The average single adult lives a life of extremes. He may experience financial ease or difficulty; he may be sad or happy; he may be overworked or bored with life. But these experiences are usually felt to the extreme. There is no buffer, no marriage partner to ease the load, listen, or even laugh with about the predicament—he is in an open field with no one to guard him from the pain or stress, and no one to share his joy or success.

Discipleship becomes another extreme, where God will bless in a special way. And why not? It could be that, because of what a single has experienced, full force, that the commitment will also be extreme.

It will benefit your leaders. When a person learns the importance of his continual growth and development of his relationship with God, and makes that the first priority, his area of responsibility in the ministry will take on a new life perspective. *He will become more productive.* Connecting with God and another caring individual through discipleship breeds a disciplined lifestyle. It is only natural that this will carry over into the more mundane areas of life, as well as the responsibilities of single adult ministry. *He will not suffer burnout as easily.* Discipleship helps us see our real roles in light of God's plan, and that we are forgiven only by the grace of God, having no price to pay, just thanks to give. Church tasks can be a part of those thankful actions. Also, sharing with another person helps us see that ownership of anything, even a church program, is an unnecessary ego-booster. In fact, involving others actually makes it more enjoyable. Friends who share a common love for a task make for great discipleship friends. They may also be great replacements for us later on, and it will be easier for us to give up our church positions because that person has shared with us the commitment to and burden for that ministry involvement.

It will benefit your church. Because the single adult has experienced so much in life, the church should take advantage of his expertise. Your church probably longs to fulfill the Great Commission in its local area, but if the single adult population has not been invited to share in the process, probably not much has been accomplished. Let your singles "invade" or "pervade" your church as strong, committed, joyful servants of God, and the change will be electric! On the average, two thirds to three quarters of the first-timers in your church are probably single. That gives you a small indication of the frontier that is before you as a church. Your singles can make a difference!

It will benefit the singles pastor. For those pastors who have ever felt "cemented to the pedestal," there is good news for you. Discipleship will destroy all facades. Just remember that this is not a time to be just a teacher. Jesus Christ is the true Teacher . . . you need to be a friend! Be learners together with your discipleship friend. Learn how to receive because you have nothing to give outside of Christ. That's called humility, and all of us need a regular dosage. It's your time to be with your fellow strugglers, your fellow learners. Give yourself a chance to be fed spiritually by someone besides yourself. This is a perfect chance for you to discipline yourself to become accountable to someone else. Remember, "It is not good for the man to be alone" (Gen. 2:18).

Discipleship Means Coming Together

There are many choices and options for coming together. I prefer a designated time together with one individual at a time. I like knowing that one particular person gets my total attention for at least one hour a week and that we both know we are looking toward an ending date when we can celebrate the strides we have taken together. Weekly assignments can be chapters of Scripture reading, a Bible study guide with questions to answer, memorization, and some type of practical action to put recently learned knowledge to good use. Materials can be as simple as a Bible, concordance, an empty notebook, and a pen. Whatever you do, make sure the individual you choose to "come along" with you and share your walk is a person who understands the beauty and urgency of having a continuing personal relationship with Jesus Christ. If he also desires to be more adequately equipped for a self-disciplined life and longs for personal growth, you will have a productive discipleship experience.

We are living in a world with a short attention span. Everything can change in a moment, from the red light on the corner, to the channel on the TV set, from the frozen microwaveable dinner, to the daily newspaper headlines. One thing, however, never changes, and that is God's love for us (Rom. 8:35-39; Heb. 13:8). He put that love into action long ago when He said, "It is not good for the man to be alone." You will want to take this opportunity of discipleship to link yourself to the two most-needed assets in your life—your connections with God and fellowman.

Timm Jackson
Minister to Single Adults
Tempe, Arizona

In Timm's ministry as a single adult minister for the last nine years, a major focus has been an emphasis on spiritual discipleship and Christian maturity.

44. EVANGELISM FOR EXPANSION

"When single Christians realize that the power of the Holy Spirit is available to them to be His witnesses, that this message of Good News has been entrusted to them, and that people are hungry to know Christ—they get motivated!"

Georgia Coates

Often I've been asked, "What evangelistic program can we put on that will win lots of singles to Christ and build vision and faith in our members?" After much thought and searching the Scriptures, I've come up with an answer. Sharing Christ on a one-to-one basis is the most effective method that I have seen and is the "program" I practice and teach to singles groups. The result? Changed lives and a growing ministry.

I am convinced that there are many singles who don't yet know Christ personally but would accept Him if they were given the opportunity to understand the Gospel. If we as leaders are not sharing Christ often and praying for opportunities, then how will we help those whom we are to lead?

"How Can I Be Born Again?"
There really are single adults who ask that question. Whenever I travel I pray that God will give me a chance to share Christ with those I meet in airports and on planes. On one trip, as I sat down in my pre-assigned seat on a flight from San Francisco to San Diego, I noticed that the woman in her 30s next to me had a book on her lap which I recognized to be a self-help-type book put out by a cultic "self-actualization" group. Even as a "trained, professional Christian" my first response was *fear* as I immediately assumed that she was an "expert" in these things and was ready to talk circles around my presentation of the Gospel. But, *expecting* her to be the "divine appointment" that I had just prayed for, I took a deep breath and jumped in. As it turned out, she had been "searching for God for about four years" and just that morning she had been told by a close friend that he was disappointed that she was not as "spiritual" as he had hoped. He said that he was "trying to become spiritual" and had hoped she would help him.

As our conversation developed, I shared my testimony and then the *Four Spiritual Laws* booklet from Campus Crusade for Christ, and she accepted Christ as her personal Saviour. She kept telling me that she couldn't wait to share the *Four Spiritual Laws* with her friend. Then she said that she wished she had understood these things during the previous "lonely" single years. She told me that she had literally gone around to friends and colleagues at times, asking them how she could get to know God or be "born again" and they couldn't tell her. Finally, she had brought along the book lying on her lap, which was a gift from a friend and which she hadn't even begun to read. She was hoping that she might find some answers on this weekend trip for her friend and herself.

When her ride didn't show up at the airport, we had even more time to talk as I took her to my home for dinner and finally to her destination much later. Excited, she thanked me over and over and left, this time, with a Bible in her hand!

The Urban Single: An Untouched Jungle

There are about 170 million unchurched people in the U.S. according to Church Growth research. If we consider that singles make up 48 percent of the adult population, then this would mean that there are over 81 million unchurched singles!

In 1984, there were 4 million singles living in the metropolitan area of New York City. Media services, and product manufacturers target this segment as their key market. Each weekend, a *National Review* study showed, 35,000 singles will each spend tens and hundreds of dollars each on entertainment alone in the metro area.

California is the third most-unchurched state in the nation. About 170,000 unchurched singles are living within a 20-minute drive of most Los Angeles suburbs. If a church could reach only one tenth of these people, it would need additional sanctuary seating for 17,000 and parking for at least 15,000 more cars! Within a 50-minute radius of Los Angeles there are about 4 million unchurched (or 1,920,000 unchurched singles) and 100 different ethnic groups. In the L.A. public school system 106 different languages are spoken. Most of these ethnics would never come to a Christian church, and the vast majority, if they came, would not even understand what was going on.

Minneapolis/St. Paul, in 1983, estimated that 59 percent of their adult population was single. At that time they had 150 various organizations for singles—from Singles' Yoga to Single Republicans! The "harvest is plentiful," the methods abundant, but the workers are few!

Equipped to Share Christ

When single Christians realize that the power of the Holy Spirit is available to them to be His witnesses (Acts 1:8), that this message of Good News has been entrusted to them, and that people are hungry to know Christ— they get *motivated!* I have personally seen this happen and have seen a group of singles take their eyes off themselves and begin sharing Christ on a daily basis. Singles in the church need to be encouraged and should be trained to effectively share their faith in Christ.

What they need is training in:

(1) telling *my story*—my personal testimony (which isn't the Gospel but illustrates its power)

(2) telling *their story*—determining how the Gospel relates to the person to whom we are witnessing, and

(3) telling *His story*—the Gospel of Jesus Christ, being His birth, death, resurrection, and ascension, that we can know Christ, experience forgiveness of sin, and the guarantee of eternal life (tools like the *Four Spiritual Laws* are very helpful).

Rebecca Manley Pippert once made a very astute observation: "Jesus always seemed to be doing two things: asking questions and telling stories. Christians always seem to be doing two other things: giving answers and 'preaching.'" Asking questions, even personal ones, is a great way to start and develop a conversation. *Telling our own story* (which everyone can become comfortable doing) is a personal way to develop our listener's interest in Christ. Most people find it hard to argue with personal experience, especially when it is briefly told with sincerity and compassion.

A Historically Proven Method

Scriptural examples of witnessing opportunities usually contain these three elements in some order. In addition, most singles interviewed claimed to have received Christ as a result of the personal witness of another.

- "A roommate shared Christ with me. . . . He spent time answering my questions."
- "I became a Christian through the influence of various friends. Finally one friend gave me the 'bridge illustration' (the Navigators' plan of salvation).
- "A student teacher told the students in my biology class about his recent conversion to a life of faith in Christ. The more he spoke, the more I understood how this related to me. I asked him what I should pray for and what I should expect. I prayed to receive Him and received in my turbulent heart a peace that I could not understand."
- "I accepted Christ and started attending church with a young woman whom I met on a business call."

The beauty of the Gospel is that it relates to each person where he is, if in a point of desperate need and searching or at a time of joy and success (see 1 Cor. 9:19-23).

Matching Methods to Your Market

The level of activity, intensity, diversity, and career orientation effectively insulates singles from traditional methods of outreach employed by the evangelical church. They don't often watch television (let alone "religious" programs). They are too busy to read bulk mail. They are never home. They don't have much contact with the community and its churches. Evangelistic events and crusades do not usually touch their felt needs. Professional singles' values differ widely from the average evangelical and his middle-American or rural orientation. How can singles be reached? What bridges can be used to touch their culture?

Building Bridges to Your Church Door
Appropriate evangelistic events. Try evangelistic dinner parties aimed at affinity groups, such as, teachers, executives, engineers, and women.
Felt-need seminars and courses. Hold seminars based on scriptural principles on self-improvement, time management, and divorce recovery.
Establish relationships where singles are. Go to health clubs, community or political activities, etc.
Neighborhood or condo complex "party with a purpose" or evangelistic Bible study.
"Bring a non-Christian" social activities.

Hard Questions to Answer before They Come to Our Door!
Have you considered what you would do if a person who has formally practiced a lifestyle you abhor decides to visit your singles group? Among others in this category, we must consider the homosexual, the single who has tested positive for the HTLV-III Antibody virus which leads to AIDS, or the pregnant, unwed mother. These are the unchurched too, and God will bring them to Himself in the midst of their predicament or sin. Will you accept them as forgiven and help them deal with the remaining consequences of their past? This decision needs to be made now, not when they are standing on your doorstep.

Fellow Strugglers
Those who would seek to win other singles to Christ ought not consider themselves as those who have "arrived" but "fellow strugglers." Paul's advice to the early church, after naming the most despicable traits of those (singles?) in Corinth was, "And that is what some of your were" (1 Cor. 6:9-11). We sometimes roll our eyes when we hear of the actions, attitudes, or struggles of others, but God would cause us to withhold our judgment and proceed in love. Too much is at stake!

Georgia Coates
Founder and Director of Christian Singles United
San Diego Evangelical Association, San Diego, California

For the last 17 years, Georgia has been on the "cutting edge" of evangelistic ministries. Her ministry is primarily focused on reaching the nonchurched single with the Gospel.

45. A BALANCED MINISTRY

*"A well-balanced ministry is reached when spiritual
growth and relational development (community building) are
both happening in some way at every function of the
group."*

Chris Eaton

Balance is as important to a ministry as it is to a high-wire walker. Even
just a slight shift to one side or the other may create a disastrous imbalance. Therefore, the leadership of a singles ministry should think *balance*
every step of the way. Unfortunately, too many ministries do not start
thinking about balance until a fall has occurred and, at that point, the
damage may be irreparable.

Balance Defined
It is important to begin by defining what is meant by balance in a ministry.
One reason balance sometimes escapes the planners of a ministry is that it
seems an element too vague to incorporate into the planning. Therefore, it
is wise to begin with a rather simple working definition:

> Balance in a ministry is attained when both the social and the spiritual
> needs of the participants are met *in such a way that the two are
> viewed as inseparable.*

The ideal ministry situation is when both the social and the spiritual
needs are treated as interdependent. This philosophy is especially important in a single adult ministry, where the social need is so much more
apparent. The mistake often made is to view these needs as separate
entities in the planning of the ministry. For example, a spiritual time is
planned once a week and a social time is planned once a month. There is a
"fun" time and a "serious" time. Yet in the Scriptures the two go hand in
hand. Certainly relationships play a vital part in a person's relationship with
God (for example, examine all the "one another" verses in the Scriptures).

A well-balanced ministry is reached when spiritual growth and relational
development (community building) are both happening in some way at
every function of the group. Now of course there will be times when there
is more social than spiritual, and vice versa, but it needs to be balanced out
in the end. Just as it would be ridiculous for the high-wire walker to
continually lean in one direction, so also is it foolish for a leader to allow a

ministry to continually lean in one direction.

Importance of Balance

The importance of balance to a ministry can be understood by looking at the results of both proper balance and improper balance.

Individual growth. Participants will be growing in their spirituality. They will not just be learning material, rather they will be developing a "cutting edge" relationship with Jesus Christ. Learning is always more effective in the context of a community. In a community people are challenged not only to learn, but are stimulated to put that learning into practice.

Group growth. When there's proper balance in a group, there will be more of an interest in visitors. An interest not only in their spiritual state, but also in their relational situation. Obviously when there's an interest in the visitors, a larger percentage of them will return to the group. To be quite honest, the reason why some single adult ministries stagnate is simply that there is nothing worth coming back to. When balance is evident there will be something for most everyone. Healthy growth will usually be a good indicator of proper balance.

The results of improper balance can be seen in one of two extremes. *Group "too" spiritual.* Primary focus is inward. The emphasis is only on the spiritual dimension. *Motto: Study!* The characteristics of this group (signs to look for) are:

(1) Social sought elsewhere. The need is still there and has to be met. A program may be great on Sunday morning, but chances are the single adults are not staying home Saturday night studying their Sunday School curriculum!

(2) Boredom within the group.

(3) Poor evangelistic/outreach attitude. Christians are commissioned to carry the Good News to the world they live in. However, when the concern of a group is only on their own spiritual growth, their concern for the needs of those around them can drop off.

(4) Low visitor return.

Group "too" social. Primary focus is outward. The emphasis is only on the social. *Motto: Party!* The characteristics of this group are:

(1) Little spiritual growth in individuals.

(2) Lack of a solid foundation in the group.

(3) Complaining in the ranks when personal needs are not met.

(4) Low visitor return. There's no community being developed when the spiritual is ignored. It is purely superficial.

In summary, both situations fail to insure longevity for the group. Chances are either type of group will die a slow, stagnating death.

Hindrances to Balance

There are certain hindrances to maintaining a balanced ministry. Imbalance is not something a leader decides one day to have. Instead it is usually a gradual slide to one side or the other—a slide that may at times go unnoticed until too late!

Ways a single adult ministry may slide out of balance:

Demands of people. It is quite obvious that what people demand may not be all they need. Therefore, it is important for the leadership to keep the demands in the proper perspective.

Expectations of people. Meeting everyone's expectations can be as unhealthy as meeting everyone's demands.

Preoccupation with numbers. This causes a leader to go for the "big" number events in programming. The problem is that often less glamorous needs go without being met. Another problem is that the ministry ends up only "tickling" the single adults' ears and not challenging them to grow.

What has been done in the past. Especially if the past includes a ministry way out of balance. The mentality will need to be gradually changed.

Staff pressures/board pressures.

Lack of creativity. The "rut" mentality of ministry results in doing the same thing year after year. Leaders fail to come up with innovative ideas.

When the leadership allows these to control or influence the direction of the group they run a high risk of imbalance. Any one of these or a combination of several may cause a gradual shifting of weight and eventually a fall off the high wire for the ministry.

Maintaining a Balanced Ministry

Leader. Balance begins with a balanced leader. It is an essential element to having a balanced ministry! The leader should be an example of balance in his personal life. Participants should see both the spiritual and social needs of the leader being met in an integrated manner. How well does the leader balance the spiritual and social in his life?

A leader must not be so quick to lay the blame for the imbalance of the group on the people involved, the church board, or certain circumstances. Often the imbalance may simply be a reflection of the leader's own imbalance!

Group. As with anything else, attitude is of key importance to a group desiring balance. Maintaining these attitudes will play a major role in maintaining a balanced ministry.

Understanding. Leaders should understand that people are not exclusively spiritual or social.

Sensitivity. A leader must be sensitive to the changing needs within the group and in the world around the group. Without sensitivity a leader may try to do the same things over and over again even when the program or idea has outlived its usefulness.

Adaptability. Be willing to adapt a program or method to a certain situation or need. Have a structure that is able to shift in one direction if there seems to be some imbalance.

Flexibility. The leader must avoid rigidity in the approach to people and ministry.

Risk-taking. Be willing to try new ideas, new methods, new strategies. A leader who desires a balanced ministry will be a leader who is willing to take some risks in that ministry!

A balanced ministry is a necessity for effective, long-term ministry in the single adult community. Therefore, the leadership needs to pause from time to time and get a feel for whether or not the ministry is balanced. The high-wire artist contemplates each step because often his life is on the line. In ministry, leaders need to be equally thorough in thinking through each organizational step because the lives of so many single adults, both in the church, and perhaps more importantly outside the church, are dependent on those balanced steps.

Chris Eaton
Executive Director, Single Purpose Ministries
St. Petersburg, Florida

As a singles ministry leader with many churches, conference coordinator, director of short-term missions ministries, and as a board member of the National Association of Single Adult Leaders, Chris has learned well the importance of achieving balance in ministry.

PROGRAMS
FOR SINGLES
▪▪▪▪▪▪▪▪▪▪▪▪▪▪

46. RETREATS

"Prayer is the underlying force which causes the retreat to be a success. Prayer should take place not only before the retreat, but also during the retreat. It is exciting to sense God's presence and direction as the whole group prays together for God's blessing."

Dennis Franck

One of the highlights of the year for adults involved in a singles ministry is the retreat. A retreat is a time for "getting away from it all," a time for refreshing the mind and spirit, a time for renewal of purpose, a time for rekindling of enthusiasm, a period of time set aside for learning, relating, and growing.

Targeting a Purpose
There are several different types of retreats which could be planned. Each type may require differences in format, organization, teaching material, etc. Depending on group size, a decision may need to be made to target one particular type of adult single. For instance, the retreat may be planned to meet the needs and interests of one group, or a combination of needs.

The purpose(s) of the retreat need to be determined far in advance to ensure direction, organization, and proper planning of every area. The retreat setting easily lends itself to a variety of purposes. Some of these include:

Spiritual growth. Teaching sessions and activities could be planned specifically to influence and affect spiritual growth in individual lives.

Practical instruction. Specific topics could be addressed in-depth at the retreat. Issues relating to the single life as well as other needed areas of growth could provide excellent topics for teaching.

Personal fellowship. Adult singles do not have a mate with whom they can laugh, cry, pray, make decisions, ask opinions, share, and grow. It is important that they experience genuine, healthy relationships and fellowship. The retreat provides an atmosphere conducive to the interacting of minds and hearts in a concentrated, intimate setting.

Ministry. Because ministry to adult singles is new to many parts of the country, the majority of churches do not plan retreats for singles. If the retreat is publicized correctly, many people will come whose churches do not have a local ministry to singles.

Encourage development of new ministries. Another possible purpose of a retreat could be to help inspire people to begin a ministry to adult singles. After attending this event, people not having a local singles ministry become extremely excited about the possibility of beginning one. A workshop entitled "Beginning a Singles Ministry" could even be offered at the retreat to help others know how to begin.

Training leaders. Leadership people need training, motivation, fellowship, and a sense of team spirit. A retreat is an excellent setting to establish these basic components of the leadership core.

The purpose of the retreat could be any one, or a combination, of these. It is important that the purpose(s) be clearly and adequately identified so that people may have an understanding of what to expect. The retreat leader should not try to meet too many different needs. It is possible to aim at too many and hit none.

Location/Facilities

Make the location of the retreat close enough to home so that parents could return in case of an emergency with children, but far enough from home so that people are not distracted by work associates, friends, and children whose general interests and demands may tempt them to run home for insignificant things. A distance of one to three hours may be ideal to contributing to a "getaway" experience.

Several different types of facilities could be considered.

Motels/hotels. These usually offer comfortable sleeping rooms and meeting rooms equipped with tables, chairs, P.A. system, and visual aids. Many motels/hotels also have restaurants, food services, and some recreational facilities. Price may be somewhat of a concern; however, negotiation of prices is many times possible with the motel staff. The motel/hotel provides a neutral atmosphere which may attract some who would not attend if the retreat were held in a church.

Retreat center. These can be found in many parts of the country. Benefits of the retreat centers are similar to the motel/hotel with the possible further benefit of additional recreational opportunities.

Camp. The camp setting provides usually a "rougher," more casual setting and may be less expensive than a motel/hotel or retreat center.

Church. A church building/campus might also be considered. The church usually offers a closer location and would be less expensive, if not free in regard to meeting room expense. Unless the church has a gymnasium, recreational facilities may be limited and might need to be found elsewhere. Sleeping and shower facilities must be considered (remember singles are adults, not teenagers).

Depending on the style of retreat desired and the preferences and interests of those expected to come, one facility may be more appealing than another. Whatever type is chosen, many items will probably prove to be basic needs. Among them are: sleeping rooms, restroom facilities, meeting rooms equipped with tables and chairs, P.A. system and microphones, piano, overhead projector, chalkboard, meal facilities, recreational facilities, and more.

Involving People

Planning the retreat involves a great deal of effort on the part of many people. Planning should begin 6 to 12 months in advance to ensure selection of the speaker(s) and adequate time for organization.

The first and most important person to secure is the retreat coordinator. This person should be someone who is spiritually mature, organizationally competent, and one whose leadership abilities are respected and proven. His/her responsibilities will demand that he/she be visible and able to spend many hours in working to ensure a successful retreat in every way. The retreat coordinator will need to recruit support leadership to coordinate various aspects of the retreat. These people would direct such ministries as:

- Publicity
- Registration
- Emcee
- Transportation
- Music
- Drama

- Devotions
- Recreation
- Sound/taping
- Photography
- Book table
- Housing

These individuals play a vital role in making the retreat effective, and by utilizing them, a sense of responsibility, importance, and ownership of the ministry is felt.

Selecting the Speaker(s)

Selecting the speaker(s) is a very important task. He/she will affect the lives of many individuals as a result of the time spent together. It is important to look for certain qualifications in his/her life which will provide direction for productive ministry and spiritual growth. Questions to consider are:

- Does the potential speaker have an understanding of the needs of all types of adult singles? (college, career, never-married, divorced, widowed, single parent) If the retreat is open to adults of all ages, a speaker will need to be familiar with these.
- Does the potential speaker have an understanding of the local church? Most people attending the retreat will be involved in a local church. The life, ministries, problems, and opportunities of the church need to be understood for him/her to relate effectively.
- Does the potential speaker possess good communication skills? Is he/she able to hold people's attention? Is material presented in a logical, thoughtful manner? Is there good eye contact with the listeners?
- Does the potential speaker have a good knowledge of the topic(s) to be covered? Definite interest and teaching experience is needful. Will the speaker present biblical truth?

- Does the potential speaker have a vital, growing relationship with Christ? A person cannot give anything that he/she does not possess. To give lasting spiritual significance to people's lives, the speaker must have a personal relationship with Christ.

It would be very helpful and even necessary to obtain this type of information from other individuals who have heard the person speak. Recommendations are usually trustworthy, if you know the source. Other means of becoming acquainted with a particular person include books and/or articles he/she has written. In some instances there may be a problem in even obtaining names of potential speakers. If this is the case, contact others who are currently involved in single adult ministry for suggestions.

Selecting the Topics
Know the needs of your target group of singles for the retreat. If adult singles of all ages are invited to the retreat, ask the main speaker(s) to use a holistic approach in teaching. By doing so, needs and interests of people of all ages and all single statuses will be touched on, thereby, ministering to everyone.

Be mindful also of the unique needs that people may have from the various singles ministries represented at the retreat. Examine these too before deciding on the topic(s).

Scheduling
The length of the retreat can be varied. Several formats have been used in the past:
- One day
- One day and one night
- Two days and one night
- Two days and two nights
- Longer

It is even possible to plan a four- or five-day retreat/camp experience. For many groups, however, a weekend retreat usually serves the purpose well. Since most adults work weekdays, beginning Friday evening and concluding Sunday noon is a very workable schedule. (See sample schedule.) Whatever length is decided on, make certain that it is agreeable to the speaker(s).

A variety of components could be included in any retreat; however, there are several basics that should be considered important:

- Main sessions
- Recreation
- Refreshment breaks
- Elective classes
- Special events
- Free time
- Devotional times
- Meals
- Rest

These nine components seem to surface as major parts of a retreat. Balancing them would be a task that the retreat coordinator and speaker(s) should decide on.

Special events can be used effectively and become a highlight of the time spent together. There are numerous ideas that can be utilized depending on preference, availability, and cost. Ideas may include:

- Film
- Concert
- Tour
- Drama group
- Comedy group
- Shopping
- Talent show
- Amusement park
- Athletics

These, as well as other ideas, would be good for bringing a balance to the teaching, listening, concentration times that are part of a successful retreat.

Publicity

Publicity for the retreat needs to begin three to five months in advance. This would allow adequate time for planning and coordination. Announcements about the retreat should begin two to three months in advance to allow for building enthusiasm, momentum, saving money toward the cost, and planning for possible child care. If the retreat is sponsored by a church or group within the church, two major areas of publicity should be considered.

In-house publicity including:

- Brochures
- Posters
- Announcements
- Skits
- Slides
- Pictures

Out-of-house publicity including:

- Brochures—other churches/groups, etc.
- Posters—other churches/groups, laundromats, shopping centers, apartment buildings
- Letters—other churches/groups, organizations
- Radio—public service announcements
- Newspaper—public service announcements
- Cable TV—public service announcements

All advertising should be as specific and clear as possible. The who-what-when-where-why-how needs to be told. Remember, the person who knows absolutely nothing about the retreat needs to be adequately informed and enthused.

The General Sessions

The general sessions are the times when everyone comes together for teaching from the main speaker(s). These meetings are the principle times of communication and inspiration to the whole group, and consequently, need to be planned and coordinated well. There are many different items which could be included in the general session. I would like to suggest five major components that I feel are "musts" to include, and several other components that could be considered "mights" to include.

Musts.

(1) Music. Music of some sort should be playing before the session begins as people are coming in. Taped background music seems to

work very well. It can establish a mood or atmosphere for the session and help achieve a sense of excitement, relaxation, inspiration, etc.

(2) Icebreaker. An icebreaker is a short, action-type activity designed to help people become acquainted. As they participate they will feel comfortable with each other and will be more receptive and responsive to what is to follow.

(3) Announcements. There will inevitably be several informational items which will need to be conveyed to the group (schedule times and changes, meal information, etc.). These should be given during the general sessions.

(4) Prayer. Prayer is the underlying force which causes the retreat to be a success. Prayer should take place not only before the retreat, but also during the retreat. It is exciting to sense God's presence and direction as the whole group prays together for God's blessing.

(5) Speaker. Plenty of time should be allowed for the speaker. He/she is the main part of the general session and needs to be given adequate time to present his/her material.

Mights.

(1) Group singing. This is an effective addition to any retreat. Singing helps to relax and inspire people as well as center attention on God and spiritual matters. The words to each song should be displayed for all to see. An overhead projector and transparencies work well.

(2) Special music. Endeavor to utilize the musical talent of several people who sing or play instruments. This gives people a chance to participate, and brings a personal sense of contribution as well as blessing to the group.

(3) Drama. Drama is also a very good addition to the retreat. It could be used for emphasizing a particular point in the speaker's teaching, presenting an announcement, or just for entertainment.

(4) Testimony. An individual sharing personal information about his/her life is an effective tool for inspiring, motivating, and challenging others. A testimony also helps to solidify faith and direction in the life of the one who shares.

(5) Book review. Short book reviews pertaining to the speaker's topic(s) help to further inform and inspire. Check with the speaker for any books he/she may have written as well as names of other books that would relate.

Additional Ideas

Scholarship money. Some will not be able to afford a retreat. A fund should be set up to assist these people. Offerings, donations, and fund-raising activities are three ways of raising money. It's good to have the person being helped financially pay part of the cost if at all possible. This personal investment is important for self-esteem and encourages value for the time and effort of the retreat.

Child care. Most single parents may not be able to come to the retreat because of either not being able to find child care, or not being able to afford it. Helping to provide child care through announcements in the church bulletin and the pulpit not only assists the single parent, but also brings understanding of single parents' needs to people in the church because of personal involvement.

Evaluation form. A comprehensive evaluation sheet allows people to respond to the many facets of the retreat, and gives the leadership input into the retreat's strengths and weaknesses for future planning.

Taping. It is helpful to tape the general and workshop sessions for those who would want to purchase these tapes. Many who cannot attend may also wish to purchase them. A small profit could also be made to help finance the retreat.

The retreat experience can bring fun, learning, new friends, direction, and much more to people's lives! It is an effective tool for developing the individual as well as the group. The retreat is usually a highlight of the year for those who attend. The knowledge learned, inspiration received, and friendships formed leave lasting impressions and produce meaningful fruit in people's lives.

Dennis Franck
Singles Pastor
Bethel Church, San Jose, California

Dennis has served as a singles pastor in the local church since 1979. He has led workshops, written several magazine articles on ministry goals, and is a member of the executive board of the National Association of Single Adult Leaders.

47. THE SINGLES CONFERENCE

"The content of the conference should be biblical, otherwise it will accomplish no more than what the community adult education program provides."

Doug Fagerstrom

A singles conference is single people coming together from a variety of backgrounds to be stimulated to personal growth through a common short-term, high-intensity Christian experience. The singles conference is often a life-changing experience for the conferee. That fact must be remembered when considering to have a conference and during the planning of the conference. Indeed, God uses short-term teaching and training experiences to draw us closer to Himself and to motivate us to make significant decisions in our lives.

The Purpose
As in any and every ministry, there must be a purpose. The singles conference is no exception. The purpose should clearly answer the question, "Why are we having this conference and what specific needs of singles will be met?" The answer must be very clear to the leadership designing the conference. There must be a unity and single-mindedness toward meeting the purpose statement. The purpose statement could fall into one of these categories: discipleship or spiritual growth; evangelism; leadership or ministry training; divorce recovery or inner healing; building of relationships.

The Theme
It is from the purpose statement that a theme for the conference should be developed. For example, if the purpose is to help singles grow in their personal devotional life, then the theme could be, "Building a Better Body"—A Conference for Spiritually Growing Single Adults. The purpose is rather specific—to target a particular need. The theme should be broad enough to give freedom within the structure and program of the conference to meet the need with variety and creative means of ministry.

The Target Audience
The next question is, "Who are and where are all the people we can reach with this conference?" The initial need to have the conference was probably born out of the specific needs of a few singles in the sponsoring group.

They represent a large number of singles with the same need in your community. Are there more in your church? Are there singles with that need in other churches? Where are the singles with that need in the community?

It is important to understand that not all singles will want to come to your conference. The reason is because of felt need. If the greatest need is for fellowship, then the conference should be on relationships and be very relational. If there are many divorced singles in your area, then a Divorce Recovery Conference might be the best. However, the key is to target the conference toward the group of people who have that need. Consider the people and where they are before planning. List all their characteristics before you line up a place and a speaker. You may discover that the target group cannot financially afford to cover the cost of "your favorite speaker" or cannot spend the time that you idealized for a three-night, or weekend conference. Know your people first. Now you can think about plans.

Conference Staff

The conference staff is the first and most important element in designing and developing the conference. A wise leader will begin by taking a few potential conference planners and leaders to a singles conference that has been planned by someone else. It is there that a vision is born and the dream turns into reality. The concepts become transferable and much is learned.

The singles leader must then recruit a team of people who have a vision for meeting the purpose statement and can formulate as well as expedite a strategy to implement the conference. The strategy asks, "How can we make this conference a reality in the lives of a certain (maximum potential) number of singles?" Who, what, where, why, when, and how much must be asked by the leaders. The team must begin by starting at the need and owning the conference from that point of beginning.

Ideally, the team should represent the felt need and the target group. Some members should also have administrative skills to design a plan. Some should be willing to work very hard in recruiting others. The "expanded" conference ministry team (people your staff will recruit) is a key to reaching many more people. The more people who are involved with some task for the conference, the more groups of people outside of the group will learn about the conference. The conference team should probably include all or a combination of the following staff members:

General Coordinator (makes sure the staff members do their jobs)

Conference Administrator (recruits all of the behind-the-scenes personnel including people to be workshop leaders, handle food service, taping, child care, resources, etc.)

Program Coordinator (recruits speakers, musicians, and emcee, and designs the conference schedule)

Facilities Coordinator (secures the needed facilities and physical ameni-
ties [overheads, tables, chairs, etc.] and works closely with custodial
crews for setup and teardown)

Registration Coordinator (recruits people to do the conference registration, ushering, signage, and ministry table)

Publicity Coordinator (recruits a team of people to publicize to the target
audience)

Prayer Coordinator (designs a plan and recruits many people to pray for
the needs of the conference)

Follow-up Coordinator (designs a plan and recruits members of the
sponsoring ministry to keep contact with conferees after the
conference)

Finally, beyond leaders "owning" the conference is allowing leaders
freedom to design and develop their own areas of responsibility. If you
have a registrar, encourage that person to design the registration card,
recruit other people to help, and plan the registration event. Remember
your team members are adults and also know that reporting back to the
conference leader is part of the responsibility. Recruit them with both
aspects in mind.

Conference Personnel
These are the people who will make the actual conference come alive.
These people are the most visible and are responsible to be at the conference itself. The conference staff plan the conference, the conference personnel carry out the plan at the conference. In some cases the two teams
can overlap where gifts and abilities apply.

The personnel team will often include:
Conference Keynote Speaker
Emcee
Workshop/Seminar Leaders
Musician(s) and Entertainers
Registration Personnel
Hosts and Hostesses
Food Service Staff
Small Group Leaders
Book/Record/Resource Table
Ministry Booth Representative
Information Host/ess
Child Care Coordinator
Sound/Taping/Lighting Coordinator
Counselors
Decoration Coordinator

The conference personnel team must own the conference just like the
conference staff. They all must know and clearly understand the purpose
and theme. They are responsible to build the spirit of the conference and

to work for the common good. The food service should not run the conference, nor is the keynote speaker the whole conference.

The Conference Speaker
The speaker must be carefully chosen. Dennis Franck has given some excellent guidelines in choosing a speaker in chapter 46 of this book.

It is also helpful to have one person assigned to host the speaker. That person should be available to meet the program and personal needs of the speaker.

The conference leaders and the single ministry leaders of your group should concentrate their time and relationships with conferees. The speaker will leave after the conference, but the conferees will still be in your community in need of ministry.

It might be good to plan a time for leadership to meet with the keynote speaker at another time outside of the conference program. This can be a special growth time for your leaders and a way to say thank you to them.

Content of the Conference
The keynote speaker should be able to address the general theme of the conference from a biblical base. He/she lays the foundation for the entire growth experience. The keynote speaker stimulates, motivates, asks key questions, and challenges the conferees to make some kind of a decision for God, for themselves, and others.

The workshops, seminars, and other small-group experiences are places to learn and discuss specific areas of life that fall under the general theme. They should not be minikeynote sessions. Interaction is imperative.

Again, the content of the conference should be biblical, otherwise it will accomplish no more than what the community adult education program provides. Lives must be changed, not just altered. Finally, the conference should challenge the conferee to evoke a response to either know Christ personally or make a life-changing decision.

The Promoter and the Registrar
To the promoter: You can have the best and most well-known speaker come to your conference, but if the community has no idea who your speaker is and when he is coming, the attempt is futile.

To the registrar: You and your people are the first impression and contact that the conferees will have with your conference. If you do not handle their needs with care and gentleness, the entire conference can be a very negative experience.

The quality, sincerity, atmosphere, and spirit of a conference is caught when the conferees see their first brochure and enter the front doors of the conference. What will their impressions be? What will you give them and show them? Will they see a quality conference with a quality brochure that says, "We care enough about you to put in the extra effort," or will people see that this is a disorganized effort that was just thrown together for "who knows what reason"?

Atmosphere is created by the conference staff; it does not just happen. Will singles be prepared to receive the message that you have to meet the stated purpose? Or are they there for a totally different (misunderstood) reason?

The Many "Extras"
Now that you have your purpose, staff, personnel, and atmosphere created, the following details will help make a conference work and flow a little bit smoother. Remember, it is often the little things that make the big difference.

- Facilities: They should be known and accessible to your conferees. Be sure you have the freedom to do in the facility what you need to.
- Schedule: Plan the schedule tight. But plan time for relationship-building. Keep to the schedule that you set.
- Communicate: People want to know what is going on. Print schedules and maps. Let your conferees know that you know what is going on. Always have someone at the registration/information table.
- Costs: People will pay for what they receive. However, be sensitive to what your target group can afford. Conferences should not be planned as fund-raisers. That is a weak purpose statement.
- Hospitality: Have a hospitality room or area where conferees can come to relax, meet the staff, meet other singles, etc. Too many come alone and are left to wander the halls looking for someone to talk to, sometimes unsuccessfully.
- Name tags: Everyone should have one!
- Food: Keep the menu light, but use quality as the standard. Buffets and box lunches work well. Allow time for people to eat and enjoy the fellowship around the tables.
- Dates: Be careful not to "stack" conferences with other events. Don't give people so many choices during the conference month that they cannot afford the conference or they choose other events instead. If your purpose statement is strong, then you can be single-minded about the conference.

Single conferences can be used of God to change lives. Decisions will be made. Friendships will be found. God's truths for everyday living will be discovered.

Doug Fagerstrom
Co-Pastor of the Dalton Baptist Church
Muskegon, Michigan

Doug has had full-time experience in single adult ministries since 1979. As a singles pastor, ministry consultant, conference and retreat speaker, he has ministered with his wife Donna to the many needs of single adults.

48. COMMUNITY AND FOREIGN OUTREACH MINISTRY PROJECTS

*"The excitement of leaving the familiar setting and travel-
ing, often to a deprived Third World culture, can be a life-
changing experience."*

Carolyn Koons

Service and Outreach: A Well-Rounded Program

Service and outreach projects for single adults often are last priority items
on the agenda of goals and future programs in most single adult ministries.
Solid teaching, counseling individuals struggling through the pains of a loss
due to divorce or death, attempting to build community through fellowship
and worship, and developing new leadership are continually needed and
demanded in singles ministry. Programs developed around each of these
goals are geared to "reach in" to help, to heal, give new insight and bring
wholeness to singles. In order to have a well-rounded singles ministry,
singles need to be encouraged to "reach out" and help others, whether
that means helping other singles in the group, reaching out to others in the
church or community, or moving beyond our borders into other countries
to share their faith and love. These opportunities not only create a well-
rounded, healthy singles program, but a healthier single.

Outreach and service helps singles get a balance and perspective on
their own lives as they share in the joy of healing by reaching out to
others. When one is hurting the most, it can be the best time for service.
Looking outward and seeing a bigger, needier world deepens our walk
with God.

Which Project Shall We Choose?

There is no set formula as to which service project you should choose.
You can reach out as close as helping and serving others in your own
singles group or church. The community surrounding the church is dotted
with dozens of needy and exciting ministry potentials. Or there is the
opportunity to venture outside the state or across the border of the United
States for outreach.

A singles group should begin locally, choosing one community service
project. Service can be either a one-time project, such as special holiday
projects for the elderly, poor, or handicapped, or long-term projects, such

A Well-Rounded Single Adult Ministries Program

TEACHING
- SUNDAY A.M.
- BIBLE STUDIES
- SPECIAL SEMINARS
- RETREATS
- DISCIPLESHIP

COMMUNITY
- SOCIALS—FELLOWSHIP
- BIG EVENTS
- SMALL GROUPS
- RETREATS
- RECREATION—SPORTS
- FOOD—COFFEE BREAKS

WORSHIP
- MUSIC
- BODY LIFE
- CHURCH
- BIBLE STUDIES
- AFTERGLOWS
- RETREATS

COUNSELING
- PERSONAL
- TEACHING
- SPECIAL SEMINARS

LEADERSHIP TRAINING
- LEADERSHIP TEAM
- TRAINING
- DISCIPLESHIP

EVANGELISM
- SOCIALS
- RECREATION—SPORTS
- FRIDAY NIGHTS
- HOSPITALITY—VISITATION
- WORKSHOPS
  (DIVORCE RECOVERY
  SINGLE PARENTING
  SELF-ESTEEM)
- EVANGELISM TRAINING

OUTREACH & SERVICE
- PERSONAL &
  COMMUNITY
- BIG BROTHER—
  BIG SISTER
- BIG GRAMS & GRAMPS
- MEXICO, HAITI, ETC.
- INNER CITY
- HOSPITALS
- HANDICAPPED
- INNER CITY PROJECTS
- ORPHANAGES

"IN" REACH

"OUT" REACH

Single Adult Ministry

CHRISTIAN MATURITY

Eph. 4:11-16

Ephesians 3:8

Acts 8:4

as, weekly or monthly Big Brother/Big Sister programs, hospital projects, or convalescent homes. As these ministries are experienced, the challenge can expand to an outreach trip for a couple of days, even up to a couple of weeks, across the border into Mexico, Haiti, or the Dominican Republic, to name a few. The list is unlimited and the needs of the world are big. No dream or vision is too great. If you are not ready to take on the project yourself or sense that the singles group is too small, join with two or three other churches in a combined effort of ministry.

In Southern California a group of seven churches combined their efforts during Memorial Day holidays with 135 single adults venturing into Ensenada, Mexico for three days of exciting ministries in orphanages and villages. Three years later the excitement and momentum attracted other singles, and the group grew to 650 single adults from 25 different singles ministries for the Memorial Day Ensenada Outreach program. The three-day outreach project had such an impact in the lives of those who participated that most of the participating singles groups have expanded this once-a-year project into monthly trips into Mexico, or monthly local community projects.

Reaching out changes lives within, and will bring vitality, energy, and commitment to a growing singles ministry.

Planning, Motivation, and Training

The key to a successful and effective outreach ministry is thoroughly planning the specific service project, motivating the group, and training the team for ministry. Talk it up, advertise, plan well, and have singles who have participated in past projects share their testimonies during various meetings. Build an excitement and passion toward ministry and service.

Training is vital for the success of the service or outreach project. The training program needs to prepare team members for each aspect of the ministry project. This may require a meeting per week for several weeks in advance, or a number of all-day sessions. Plan carefully each aspect of the project, develop a leadership team, and let them coordinate the various committees responsible for aspects of the project. Let the singles be the leaders.

Develop an application form for the service project that will help eliminate certain individuals who are not ready for the project or who are wanting to participate for the wrong reasons. The application process should also help you discover new leadership and hidden talents. Identifying and utilizing these can enhance the project outcome.

Community Service Projects

Community projects are found everywhere, with endless opportunities. The following are a few ideas of current projects being worked on by singles groups, and resources for starting your own project.

Handicapped children. Hospitals are eager to have groups work with the handicapped, taking them on field trips, helping them with their training. One church planned a Zoo Day, and took busloads of handicapped children to a special day at the zoo.

Orphanages.

Convalescent homes.

Homes for abused children.

Big Brother/Big Sister programs.

Welfare Department programs. Check your local Welfare Department, a place where there are usually an abundance of programs and projects that need volunteers.

Hospitals.

Inner city/urban plunge projects. Check several agencies for a listing and description of projects and needs.

Latchkey projects. This is a valuable program for children and teens that can be conducted throughout several neighborhoods or at the church.

Juvenile facilities.

Mentally retarded adult homes.

New becomers (divorce recovery) dinners. Monthly or quarterly.

Foreign Projects

Foreign projects usually require a major trip. The excitement of leaving the familiar setting and traveling, often to a deprived Third World culture, can be a life-changing experience. Contact missionary organizations, missionaries of your church, or another singles group who has been on an outreach trip for project ideas. Know what kind of project your group wants to undertake, and remember to plan carefully, train well, and minister.

Projects will vary according to the needs of the culture and missionary organization, so the key is flexibility. Some project ideas include:

Orphanages. Deliver food and clothing; clean up; children's programs; recreation and crafts; adopt an orphan.

Building. Building projects are in abundance but the key is finding a contact person attached with the project who will get the project ready and have the supplies available.

Food or clothing distribution. This can generate a lot of enthusiasm. Work closely with the missionaries or sponsoring organization.

Evangelism. Conduct children's programs which consist of Bible stories, crafts, games, and recreation; women's ministries; teen projects; church planting projects; evening church or mission services with music, drama, testimonies, and more.

Getting singles involved with reaching out to others is one of the major keys to developing a healthy single adult ministry.

Carolyn Koons
Executive Director for the Institute for Outreach Ministries
Azusa Pacific University, Azusa, California

Through the Institute for Outreach, Carolyn has taken over 70,000 people on foreign and domestic mission trips over the past 27 years. Carolyn is a busy college administrator, mother, and singles ministry speaker.

49. INTEGRATING SINGLES INTO THE LIFE OF THE CHURCH

*"Many singles are totally uninformed about activities going
on in the life of the church and can easily remain that way. It
is not that they don't care; they don't know!"*

Mary Graves

Single Adults Want to Be the Church Too
"One of the most important concepts to catch in the single adult ministry is
the idea that the church is composed of both two-adult family units and
one-adult family units. Too often, by default, it is assumed that the church
is the married adults and that when the singles get married and have
homes, then they too can be the church. We need to stretch our vision of
the church to include the single adult."

Such is the perceptive counsel of Britton Wood in his book *Single Adults
Want to Be the Church Too* (Broadman). The proof that a church has this
kind of vision is not in the number of programs offered for singles, but in
the number of singles involved in all the programs of the church. Approximately one half of the adult work force in this country is single. What
percentage of the church work force is single? A successful singles ministry helps the church realize that single adults are not just one part of the
church to be ministered to (like the youth). They make up an important
part of the ministry team, and the church must recognize their part in the
body (Rom. 12:4-5).

One single adult leader claimed that if you took all the singles out of his
church it would be paralyzed. This is the vision. That is what it looks like
when singles ministry comes to full maturity. It isn't just providing a place
where singles can learn and grow with other singles; it is connecting them
to the larger body of Christ. As Bill Flanagan (Newport Beach, Calif.) put
it, "Integrating single adults into the life of your church is an absolutely
fundamental principle for doing ministry."

The Attitude of Your Church toward Single Adults
When Highland Park Presbyterian Church in Dallas hired a singles pastor,
it was spelled out in the job description that this person was to bridge the
gap between singles and marrieds and, by a consciousness-raising on both
sides, to bring singles into the center of the church's life. But when a large
community church in southern California hired a singles pastor, there was
no such intention. This pastor was to take care of single people and their

needs and keep them "out there" as a separate department, a specialized area of ministry, apart from the whole life of the church, almost like a satellite church—what you might call a "leper colony" mentality. Whether articulated or not, every church has an attitude toward singles and singles ministry, and that attitude is lodged in the leaders of the church. The task of integrating singles into the life of the church begins and ends with their vision. All the creative program planning in the world cannot overstep the boundaries set by the ruling bodies in each church. And that includes the boundaries set by the singles leader.

There seem to be two basic images of singles ministry: singles as a separate colony or as a necessary part of the whole. The first task is to determine the premise that prevails in your church and in the singles leader. If the "separate colony" image prevails, then consciousness-raising will have to happen in the leadership first before integration is even a possibility.

Single Adults as a Problem or an Asset

In conversations about people it is hard to find the word "single" without also hearing words like lonely, divorced, depressed, swinging, sleeping around, etc. Most single adults don't like the title of "single" because of negative connotations. So with that kind of press, it is not surprising that many churches hold singles at arm's length, unable to ignore them and unwilling to draw them in. They are often perceived as people with problems whose lot is contagious; people who demand much more than they can give; people whose only hope and solution is to get married.

But more and more churches are discovering that single adults are not a problem to be solved but a gifted work force to be employed for the work of Christ's church. Singles often ask the honest questions and come up with new solutions; they break out of the conventional and/or make the conventional more practical. Singles are an asset to the church not because they have more time and money (a mythical stereotype which is simply untrue) but because they bring a new and fresh perspective that allows God to do the "new thing" that needs doing. Perhaps it's a program for latchkey children, or a support group for abused women, or an adopt-a-grandparent brunch, or a breakfast club for men, or a "Run for Missions," or a Christian concert for the whole church—all of these are ideas which have been spawned and developed by single members who are discovering that they are the church.

The Attitude of Single Adults toward Your Church

Between the "why" and the "how" of integrating singles into the church lies one huge assumption that should be addressed: it is necessary to have a church that singles want to go to. Several critical factors will make your church a place where single people want to be involved.

The worship service must be enthusiastic, not lifeless. The preaching must be inclusive of the experiences single adults are facing. The church must express an openness to the wounded—especially to the divorced. Sunday Schools must address the needs of single parent homes with a sensitivity to custody arrangements. The church must have a desire to do outreach and a willingness to bring in some "different people" (i.e., those with non-Christian backgrounds).

There are many subtle ways that the church can say to singles, "You do not belong here." The leadership, program, and language of a church can say very loudly, "This is a family church," and singles will be left out. Singles will go where they aren't put on hold until they are married. They will go where they are recognized and counted. And that's where they will want to get involved.

Cultivate in Your Singles a Desire to Serve

Single adults must first have a desire and willingness to serve before they will move into areas of ministry in the church. This grows out of discipleship; it results from people being nurtured and trained to think of themselves as belonging to Jesus Christ, His family, being His servants.

This happens at an academic and experiential level in Bible studies (e.g., studying the "one another" passages in Scripture), in leadership training (e.g., studying Jesus the Servant), and in one-on-one discipling. Teach about Jesus washing the disciples' feet and then follow that with your own foot-washing. Talk about serving the needy and then follow that with a volunteer assignment to work at the local soup kitchen. Affirm that it is more blessed to give than to receive and then live out that truth with a mission trip to Haiti. With this training and exposure singles will already be thinking ministry and looking for ways to do more.

Orient Your Singles to the Church

Many singles are totally uninformed about activities going on in the life of the church and can easily remain that way. It is not that they don't care; they don't know!

At a deeper level singles need to know where they can serve in the church. It is important to note that different commitment levels are required for the various volunteer opportunities. Low-level commitments might include ushering, greeting, or serving coffee, whereas high-level would include teaching Sunday School or singing in the choir. Look for the commitment level suited for the different singles in your church.

Singles seem to respond well to commitment responsibilities where high demands of energy and attention are required for a short period of time (the task force model). Planning a one-day conference on "Intimacy" or a New Year's Eve party for the whole church family—these tasks have a beginning and an end and much visible reward for invested labor. Other opportunities in this category might include teaching Sunday School just for the summer or organizing a mission trip.

High-level commitments require training and equipping and much en-couragement. Perhaps the first high-level commitment for your singles is church membership. Every church has its own requirements, some more rigorous than others. But whatever the requirements, the commitment involves consciously making one particular church their church home. All other major commitments to the church spring from that. Let your singles know when new members' classes are and what is required for church membership. Encourage your key singles leaders to be members (many churches require leaders to be members). Move your singles into training events and experiences that will prepare them for greater levels of service in the church (e.g., training classes for Sunday School teachers or lay counseling).

Orient Your Church to the Singles
It's not only the singles that are uninformed about the life of the church; often church members are totally uninformed about their singles. Once again, it is not necessarily because they don't care; they don't know!

Single adults and your singles ministry can be made more visible to the whole church in a variety of ways. Starting with the obvious means of publicity, use your church newsletter, featuring articles on the activities of your single adults (e.g., specific acts of service by an individual or report-ing on group events). Find a way to get your singles on every bulletin board or publicity piece in your church. The more pictures the better.

Search for ways to be creative. The singles at Calvary Community Church in Thousand Oaks, California have an annual Single's Day at their church which features a big jamboree with a pastor's dunk booth, a chili cook-off, live music, a car bash, and all kinds of fun for the whole church family. It is effective for the singles to sponsor events for the whole church, even simply a reception after church with good food and catchy displays of the things that your single adults are doing.

These events do not always have to be overtly advertising in nature.

Another area of promotion is among your staff and church leaders. The singles leader should keep them aware of the gifted people available and encourage them to invest these leaders in their own ministries. This means that you must be willing to let go of these leaders to let them serve elsewhere.

It is also up to the singles leader to help the church leaders know what's going on in the lives of your single adults. Keep them informed about your program. Give them a copy of your newsletter and the minutes from your leadership meetings.

In the body of Christ we are one family with one Father and "He made known to us the mystery of His will . . . to bring all things in heaven and on earth together." It is in that union that we will attain "to the whole measure of the fullness of Christ," when we are "joined and held together" and each part of the body is working properly and "builds itself up in love"

246

(Eph. 1:9-10; 4:13, 16). That is the vision. That is what it looks like when singles ministry comes to full maturity.

Mary Graves
Associate Pastor—Minister with Singles
Solana Beach Presbyterian Church, Solana Beach, California

Mary has experienced the ministry of integrating singles into her church over the last four years as a full-time pastor with the majority of her responsibilities focused on single adults.

50. GROWING A SINGLES MINISTRY

*"God has not just called us to build strong programs; He
has called us to build people who have strong ministries."*

Rich Hurst

"You've got to keep them busy!" This statement was made by the
senior pastor of a large metropolitan church when asked how to grow a
single adult ministry. He was of the opinion that a church must offer
something every night of the week or singles will go somewhere else to
have their needs met.

For the Right Motives
When you decide you want a growing single adult ministry, you must start
by asking yourself *why*. It is easy to find yourself feeling like you have to
grow because of some outside pressure. Paul, speaking to the church at
Philippi, said, "Do nothing out of selfish ambition" (Phil. 2:3). There is
such a temptation to do a ministry like single adult ministry for the wrong
reasons. When you do, the results can be failing or unhealthy ministries.

Before we look at how to grow a single adult ministry it is important to
ask ourselves the reasons not to grow a single adult ministry. One tendency is to try to "keep up with the Joneses," but that cannot be our goal or
motivation. We grow single adult ministries to meet needs and to develop
a ministry that helps bring about wholeness in each individual's life. We
must always check our motives.

**Do Not Grow the Single Adult Ministry because It Is the Thing to
Do**
There is always the temptation to try to stay current with the latest in
ministry. Staying current has nothing to do with being the church God
wants you to be. God never called us to be trendy; He called us to be
faithful. Trying to grow a single adult ministry based on popularity is the
wrong reason and can often hurt all involved once it is no longer trendy.

**Don't Grow the Single Adult Ministry because Other Churches
Are Growing**
The reason others have growing single adult ministries is that they had
people who had a heart to see that ministry develop. In Nehemiah 1, we
see that Nehemiah became heartbroken when he heard about the conditions of his home city. The Scripture says he wept and mourned for days.

Out of that broken heart came a desire to help his people restore the walls of Jerusalem. Out of a broken heart came a desire to do something. This is the same way healthy ministries are grown; they develop from leadership that has a heart for single adults and wants to do something.

When I moved from one city to another several years ago I received a call from a local pastor in the new city asking me to come and talk with him. As I sat in his office he asked me questions about myself and my move, but after a while he got around to his real interest. He said, "I understand you had a very successful singles ministry before you moved here." I replied I had, to which he responded, "We would like to have you help us start one." He told me there were several single adult ministries in the area and that he felt they should also have one. I wish now I had asked him why. We began small, but within six months we had grown to large numbers on Sunday nights. Since this was a church with a Sunday morning attendance of 350, we became a threat to the membership and to the pastor. It became apparent over the next two years that the pastor had only wanted a single adult ministry because he saw that others had one. It was costly for him, for me, and for the ministry that we had not counted the costs before starting. From that experience I learned you must never start a single adult ministry out of competition but from a heartfelt desire to meet needs.

Don't Grow a Single Adult Ministry because There Are Single Adults in Your Church

Need does not always dictate the call to do a ministry. Just because there are single adults in your church does not mean God wants you to have a single adult ministry. There are many churches across this country that are growing fine without formal single adult ministries. If the singles themselves don't feel the need to change the way the church is meeting needs, then your church is probably doing its job.

On the other hand, do not ignore a genuine need in your church. Several years ago the church I attend began to hear murmurings from the single adults that they needed a singles pastor. Not much was done until they did a survey and discovered that over half of their 3,000 members were single! They began at once to look for someone who had a heart for single adult ministry.

Don't Start a Single Adult Ministry to Keep the Single Adults Busy

It's easy to assume, like the pastor mentioned in this chapter, that you must have a ministry that will keep single adults busy or they will go to another church or to bars. Single adults do not need to be kept busy; most single adults are busy enough! Instead, they need to be encouraged and trained to be all God has planned for them. They need to be free to become all that they have ever dreamed, and if we keep them so busy that they can't discover this dream, then we have shortchanged them.

With the Right Purpose
If you choose to grow a single adult ministry you are making one of the most exciting choices of your ministry life. Growing a single adult ministry is one of the calls of our changing society. It will stretch you and cause you to grow in your personal life, and will bring about new life in your church as well.

I want you to understand what can happen when you do decide to grow a single adult ministry. Frank Tillapaugh of Bear Valley Baptist in Denver says, "No target-group ministry holds more potential for the church today than does this one. We have found a special ministry to them has greatly helped our Christian singles grow spiritually and become fully integrated into the church. We have also found that non-Christian singles tend to be responsive to a ministry that is not out to exploit them. The evangelical church has the greatest product in the world to attract today's single—we have the Gospel. Our challenge is to find a way to bring together the ministry of the church and [the] single."

John Westfall of University Presbyterian in Seattle says, "The question is not what kind of single adult ministry do we want to have, but what kind of single adults do we want to send out into the world? I believe our goal is not to have a strong single adult ministry but to train single adults to have strong ministry." If our goal is just to have a program, then we are defeated from the beginning. Though it may work for a while, in the end, it will be the program that is important to you and not the people. God has not just called us to build strong programs; He has called us to build people who have strong ministries. There is a real but subtle temptation to allow the few to get better at being ministers while the majority become better at watching.

In the church, our first priority should be making sure each member sees him or herself as a minister. This is especially true for single adults because, somewhere along the road, single adults have been given the message that life begins at marriage. Having a healthy ministry will depend on each single getting the message that you believe God has a dream for his/her life.

By Training Leaders
In growing a healthy ministry it is important how we spend our time. As a pastor and a leader, I see my main responsibility to train others to be leaders. For example, I limit the time I spend counseling and participating in meetings with those people who are not in leadership. I spend a lot of time with those who are or will someday be in leadership and, in turn, it is their ministry to meet with others.

We must operate purposefully to grow a healthy single adult ministry. By purposefully I mean that you plan and choose those in whom you will invest. Paul wrote, "You shine like stars in the universe as you hold out the Word of life—in order that I may boast on the day of Christ that I did not run or labor for nothing" (Phil. 2:15-16). It is your role in growing a single adult ministry to train leaders. This means you must commit to invest in individuals, not crowds. It is so easy to find yourself spending time investing in crowds or doing things that will bring out the crowd. Usually you do this at the expense of the individual. You must make it a priority to train leaders and, though everyone is a minister, not everyone is a leader. Invest your time in leaders and you will grow a meaningful and vibrantly alive ministry.

Through Certain "Crossroads"

When growing a single adult ministry there will be normal crossroads along the way. Here are five which you will encounter.

Why do we exist? It is very important to answer this question before you do anything else. The best way to find the answer is to have a group of single adults get together for a "dream session." A dream session is a time when you list the needs in your church and community as they relate to single adults. Needs can be both felt and unfelt. For example, a felt need is to grow spiritually, and an unfelt need might be to become more emotionally supported by the church. To acknowledge that there is a need does not mean you have to meet it. This is a time to list needs with no expectation as to meeting them.

Who will lead? It is always hard to pick leaders. When you look at the ministry of Jesus you see that even He had ups and downs in the area of His leadership team. His disciples had times of utter confusion and of not getting along. There were times of positioning to be first, and then times of betrayal and denial.

It is simply not easy to choose leaders, but there are several guidelines that will help you to have a growing single adult ministry. First, choose people you know and have had a chance to watch for a while. There is always a temptation to choose the people that look good or the ones that seem to have it all together, only to discover they were not ready to be leaders. This is usually a very disappointing experience both for you and for them. Instead, choose people you know to be faithful, responsible, and positive in outlook. Nothing will kill a group quicker than a negative leader. In addition, leaders need to be relational with each other and must understand how to relate to others in a caring, responsible way.

If you find yourself short on leadership, begin to pray (Matt. 9:35-38). In the first singles group I attended, the singles pastor, Jerry Donaldson, along with the senior pastor, began to pray for more male leadership; there were plenty of women available for leadership but Jerry wanted a balance. Within several months there were enough men and women to move forward.

Ask your leaders for a commitment, and make it reasonable. Remember, we are building people and not programs, so new people need a chance to try their gifts.

What should we do? Pray! A growing single adult ministry begins by taking time to start with a small group of committed people who are willing to pray. Mike Regele, a former singles pastor in California, decided with a group of people to start a singles ministry. They were only a small group, so at first they met together once a week to pray together about when to start this ministry. After a few months there were 25 people, and so Mike suggested it was time to start the ministry. The rest of the group did not feel the time had arrived so they prayed for another six months. At the end of this time there were over 100 people coming together weekly, and everyone agreed it was time to "begin." Never underestimate the power of prayer in growing a single adult ministry.

What should we do when people fail? People will fail in any ministry, and single adult ministry is no exception. The one difference is that single adults are likely to be more open and honest about failure. Failure is never the final word in peoples' lives; it is often the beginning of newness.

What happens when things begin to change? Change is an everyday word in single adult ministry. We must learn that status quo should not be a way of life in a growing single adult ministry. We will encounter the need to change on a regular basis; we never exactly arrive or have a complete program.

There are three stages of ministry: (1) moving ahead, (2) maintenance, or (3) meltdown. The healthy and growing single adult ministry will always be defined with an attitude of moving ahead and welcoming change.

All the world is asking for answers: single adults have a lot of them and are looking for a place to give and serve. When you make a choice to have a growing single adult ministry you are making a choice that will change the whole direction of your life, your church's ministry, and the lives of 50 percent of the people in your community. You will make a difference when you grow a single adult ministry.

A growing and healthy single adult ministry will produce unbelievable results in your church and community. As the ministry begins to meet needs it will dispel the stereotypes that some people may have that singles are irresponsible and socially unaware. In our church the Sunday School classes are heavily staffed by single adults. Because the church is located in an urban setting, the singles have begun a street ministry. There are groups of single adults who bake bread monthly for food distribution centers, and others who meet downtown for lunchtime Bible studies.

Growing a healthy single adult ministry will change you, your church, and the community you live in. When you have a well-balanced ministry it sends a message that you want to care and participate in your community. There are plenty of disinterested churches all around the country, but I have yet to see a church with a growing single adult ministry that is not making an impact on its community.

Rich Hurst
Director of Singles
University Presbyterian Church, Seattle, Washington

Rich has been in the singles ministry since 1980. He has been on the board of the National Association of Single Adult Leaders, a singles conference speaker, and the Vice-President for Christian Focus.

51. MINISTRY TO SINGLE ADULTS IN THE SMALL CHURCH

> *"The goal needs to be to win singles to a personal faith in Christ and help them with their spiritual walk through ministries that all can share in creating."*
>
> Jim Smoke

While programs in large churches get even larger, small churches struggle to keep their existing programs functioning. The nagging question in single adult ministries seems to be, "Can a small church have a successful singles ministry?" Fifteen years of ministry in the single adult field prompt me to answer with a resounding yes! But the reality is that a ministry to singles in a small church will be different than in a larger church.

One of the relational "givens" in a singles ministry is that single people go where other single people are. The more singles you have, the more seem to come to meet the existing group. Since many singles are looking for relationships, they will attend the larger groups in order to broaden their relational base. That may or may not be the right reason to attend a singles group but it is a reality. Not many get excited about traveling across town to attend a singles group with 11 members. How does the 11-member group stay well and grow to 12? How does the 11-member group offer quality programs and ministries that will cause their group to grow? Here are some keys to these questions from observing small, growing ministries across America.

Think Outreach
Many singles groups limit their growth by the number of potential members within the walls of their churches. They feel their task lies solely in getting every available single body in their church into their group and then living happily ever after as they plod their way through endless potlucks, parties, Bible studies, and retreats. Within shouting distance of most churches there is a vast, unreached population of singles who would happily reach out to a church group rather than a bar group if they only knew the singles groups existed and what they had to offer. Singles groups in most churches are the best-kept secret in the community. If you only have 11 singles, target the ministry toward the needs of the unchurched to reach singles for Christ in your community.

Think Interchurch

One of the toughest things we face in church life is that most every church wants to be an entity all wrapped up in itself. Many areas of singles ministry become virtual impossibilities for the small church. But when small churches join together, any dream can be realized. A retreat, a singles conference, a Friday night singles rally, or a missions trip can all be better accomplished when churches unite. I know that the impasse often lies in the pastor who is fearful his singles will leave and go to another church if churches cooperate. If a single has a strong tie to his home church and has received personal ministry, that will seldom happen.

Think Community Network

In some areas, smaller churches have united to form a city-wide singles network with each church having representation on the council. Large events are planned by the network where all share equally in leadership and responsibility. Problems are openly shared and resolutions sought. The goal needs to be to win singles to a personal faith in Christ and help them with their spiritual walk through ministries that all can share in creating.

Think Through Your Own Church's Distinctives

People go to different churches for different reasons. What is there about your church that would make singles want to become a part of its life? The reason for a single being in a church singles group should reach far beyond the group itself and into what that particular church is all about. Learn to highlight your church when building your group. Churches have their own unique personalities. The entryway to your church may be through the singles group but your singles should not hit a wall after they walk in!

Think Ministry

Most singles groups think PROGRAM AND CALENDAR. They feel their job is to fill all the open dates in any month with activities. It is true that we all need things to do but, more than that, we all need to be spiritually ministered to by the things we attend. MINISTRY COMES FROM KNOWING THE NEEDS OF YOUR PEOPLE. Plan the things you do with a purpose. Ask yourself why you are doing what you are doing.

Think Team, Think Leadership

The question in a small church is usually, "Who are the leaders and who are the followers?" The lingering singles malady across America seems to be lack of good leaders. This is always true and this will never end. Leaders must be challenged, built into a team, and allowed to lead. People seldom go where they have no vested leadership interest. Leaders should be selected, not elected. If your group is so small that all you have is leaders, train them and then go find some followers. You have to have both kinds of people to have a group. People only support what they help create.

Think Lay Leadership
In a small church, you will never have the luxury of a full-time singles pastor. That type of role will need to be filled by some lay person who does other things to make a living, but has a heart for singles ministries. I have met hundreds of those special people across America, and they are doing a great job. Somebody must be in charge of the ministry or it will fail. God calls people to those responsibilities. Leaders lead.

Think about the Things You Can Offer Your Own Group
There is a time to come together with other singles groups and a time to do things with your own group. Community is seldom built in a crowd unless there is a shipwreck that draws people together. The Sunday morning singles class is a must in every church. Sunday night afterglows are important fellowship times. Weekly prayer, share, and care groups can be real times of closeness in your small church ministry. Occasional retreats with just your own people are important to growing close. Learn to do what you need to do for just your own people. Learn what you need to invite others to share in.

And finally—don't worry about what others are doing. Ministry takes place in the heart and is never evaluated numerically. Whether you have 6 or 600 makes no difference in God's measurement scale. What you put into the hearts of the 6 or 600 does!

Jim Smoke
President of Growing Free
Tempe, Arizona

Jim is the author of six bestselling books targeted at the needs of adult singles. Jim's speaking ministry brings him to churches both large and small across our nation.

52. MINISTRY TO SINGLE ADULTS IN THE LARGE CHURCH

"Single adults need to see themselves and be seen with the church as a whole, not only as a target group that needs a special outreach ministry."

Bill Flanagan

Church planners and demographers who are analyzing the development of the church in the last years of this century see a continuing growth in the number of large congregations. At the same time, the need for fellowship and intimacy in a neighborhood context will also bring an increase in the number of smaller churches. In the middle will be the congregations of medium size (200-600), which may suffer by the growth of churches that are both larger as well as smaller. This is an important development for single adult ministry in that it is difficult to develop a full-orbed singles program in a small parish. Not every congregation will have a single adult ministry, but every church needs to minister to single adults.

Studies of larger congregations reveal that churches that have well-established singles ministries have one or more of the following ingredients present.

- A vacuum in the community creating a large felt need into which the church as a whole and the singles ministry in particular could move rapidly.
- A strong leader with a clear vision, focused goals, and plans of what needs to be done.
- The use of solid ministry skills, good management techniques, and excellent support leadership.

The following are some principles and guidelines that need to be understood in order to develop an ongoing ministry in the total program of a large multiple-staff congregation.

Know Why You Exist

In the midst of large numbers and personal diversity, it is fundamental to know why you exist. A clear statement of the ministry's purpose and its goals is crucial in order not to get sidetracked into peripheral issues. A constant reference point as to *who* you are and *what* you are about saves a lot of energy and time as the ministry matures.

Understand Differences

It is important to understand the differences between single adults as a group and the rest of the church. Singles tend to be fickle and mobile. They like large groups with lots of relational possibilities and yet, at the same time, small groups where there is relational intimacy and close fellowship. Single adult ministries have a greater turnover than the church as a whole. It is axiomatic in most singles fellowships that the turnover is 50 percent every six months. This necessitates rapid growth just to stay even. Single adult ministries must be set up and organized to grow, or very quickly they will die. Also, females tend to outnumber males, particularly in groups where the average age is over 30. Due to this, ongoing programs of welcoming newcomers and developing leaders are crucial not just for growth but for your continued existence.

Realize the Ecumenical Spirit

Single adult ministries are always ecumenical in spirit. Even in denominational churches, a singles ministry is a smorgasbord of humanity and a melting pot of various denominations, traditions, and sectarian backgrounds. Teaching and structure that does not recognize this is bound to get in trouble and have to overcome some severe difficulties.

Invite Smaller Churches to Activities

Large church ministries are wise to invite and include in their special activities adults who are involved in smaller congregations in the community without expecting them to sever their roots. Many adults have strong emotional ties to a smaller church where their children may be involved, and find it difficult to sever those ties. Yet, they also have needs that may be met by a singles ministry in a larger church. For a season, at least, it is possible for an adult, as long as the geographical and scheduling conflicts can be worked out, to relate to the programs of two churches. Time tends to take care of any tensions and pressures that are created.

Integrate Singles into Church Life

The integration of singles into the whole life of the church is important for the ongoing nature of the ministry. The singles pastor, or professional leader, needs to be patient and persistent to get single adults to join the larger life of the church. Over a period of time most single adults who are not there just for superficial reasons will be ready and willing to do this.

Make Use of Church Facilities

It is important to use the church plant or campus for most of the main events of the singles ministry. Single adults need to gather in the church facilities both to feel included and accepted by the larger church as well as to feel a part of its life and fellowship. Churches that use off-campus facilities for main events very soon have the problem of the single adult ministry feeling totally independent and disconnected from the body of believers. It is also significant for the senior pastor and other staff to participate, at times, in the singles ministry.

Divide into Age Groups

Singles groups in large churches need to be broken down into age-groups rather than the status of the participants' singleness. In other words, it's not a good idea to organize groups for divorced, never-marrieds, or widows, but rather to divide singles in terms of their ages, usually within about a 15-year span, denoting the age-limits of each group. This is often easier to project and plan than it is to actually make happen. The attempt to put single adults of all ages into one fellowship to form an ongoing program is not realistic. It is important that each of these various groups have its own name, identity, leadership team, and place to meet as well as a calendar for its events and activities week to week.

Understand the True Meaning of Family

Most large congregations that develop a singles ministry need to come to a new understanding of the term "family." Many married adults understand their congregation as a "family church," which whether consciously or unconsciously does not include single people. In beginning a singles ministry, churches consciously need to decide whether they will be inclusive or exclusive. Many congregations have not had their consciousness raised or are unaware of the singles phenomena in America in the past few decades that has brought the number of single people in this country to almost the same as those who are married. This involves a great effort to overcome stereotypes. The singles pastor, or professional leader, should be invited to speak to the various couples groups in the church to raise their vision and overcome the stereotypes and myths of singles that are in the church. The married portion of the congregation needs to understand clearly that singleness is not a disease for which the only known cure is marriage. There are many myths to be shattered in order for a congregation to become sensitive, informed, and whole.

Maintain Communication between Staff Members

It is important to maintain the communication and unity of purpose within the pastoral or program staff. It is an excellent model for churches with large staffs to have single adults as a part of the staff in proportion to the singles in the congregation. This leadership team needs to have a clear understanding together of what each department and area of ministry is doing, and be able to pull together in a common unity of purpose. A large congregational program staff is no place for lone rangers, solo artists, or the building of exclusive, autonomous little churches within the larger one.

The Importance of the Senior Pastor

Team unity is primarily built by the head of staff, or senior pastor. It is the responsibility of that person to be the primary interpreter of the singles ministry to the church at large. The singles pastor needs the total support and consistent encouragement of the senior pastor.

Singles Are a Part of the Church

Single adults need to see themselves and be seen with the church as a whole, not only as a target group that needs a special outreach ministry. Rather than simply viewing singles as people who "need our help," churches need to understand how much they have to benefit and receive from single adults. Single people can teach the larger congregation much about coping with living alone, handling pain, living without a spouse, and turning loneliness into an opportunity for focusing on one's own inner strength. A congregation needs to be ready not only to minister *to* singles, but to celebrate ministry *from* singles. They have something very valuable to offer the whole body of Christ.

Vision and Strategy for the Community

A single adult ministry in a congregational setting needs to have a vision and strategy to reach the broader community. The size and influence of a large congregation is a valuable asset in developing programs of community outreach that are significant and measurable. It is important that the ministry is seen not just as an aspect of the church's program, but rather as a service to the community. If your singles group is meeting the felt needs in a quality way, advertising such programs and special events through the local media will attract people who normally wouldn't darken the church's doorway. Single adult ministry assists a congregation in getting into the marketplace in a way that many churches never really experience.

Prepare for Additional Ministries

A growing program needs to prepare for additional ministries. It is also an axiom that the more a congregation does and the more ministries it develops to meet felt needs, the more needs will be felt. The more you do, the more you realize you need to do. A door opening to a new ministry opportunity will usually open three or four related doors to other possibilities to meet the needs of people. A divorce recovery ministry will raise the issue of working with remarried couples, single parents, and teenage youth of divorcing parents. It will also raise questions about the quality of your premarital counseling and opportunities for marriage enrichment. A single adult ministry will have profound influence on both the children's and youth ministries as a whole in the church. Single adults ultimately filter into every aspect of the church's life and work.

Generally, as the doors open, there will be people there with the vision, energy, and commitment to assist the staff in providing for such opportunities. Workshops, small groups, classes, and special seminars will present themselves in great diversity. Program people are constantly faced with the pressures of time and priority as to which needs are greatest and how to respond to them. All of this leads to a visionary church that is constantly following the leading of Jesus Christ into new avenues of evangelism, outreach, caring, and mission.

Bill Flanagan
Minister with Single Adults
St. Andrew's Presbyterian Church, Newport Beach, California

Bill has served in two large churches (over 3,000 members each) since 1971. He has conducted divorce recovery workshops for over 5,000 singles and has authored the book *The Ministry of Divorce Recovery*, NSL.

FINAL
WORDS TO
LEADERSHIP
ı ı ı ı ı ı ı ı ı ı ı ı ı ı ı

53. ROLE OF THE SINGLES MINISTER IN THE CHURCH

"It is up to the singles minister to redefine and update congregational understanding of the word family as well as the word single."

Jim Smoke

The role of today's singles minister is not an easy one. He or she must be involved in interpreting and communicating an often unknown, misinterpreted, and, in some places, controversial ministry in the local church.

The reality of a single adult ministry is that it will not exist and thrive unless the senior pastor endorses, church board approves, the body encourages, and the finance committee budgets money to insure its implementation. The singles minister is a key to gaining these endorsements. There are several things a singles minister can do once a church starts a single adult ministry.

Present Ministry to Congregation

It is the responsibility of the singles minister to present the ministry and those who work with it to the congregation. This is not a "once-a-year, let's cheer for our singles" event. It is weaving information and blessing from the singles ministry into the fabric of daily church life. If this is not done, the ministry will be largely misunderstood and filed under "not important" in the annals of church life.

Define Family

It is the responsibility of the singles minister to help redefine the word "family" in a broad sense so as to include single parents and children. Too many single, parents are hammered into the ground each week when they are treated as "less than family" by church interpretation. The word family, as once defined in American life, now only represents about one half of our population. It is up to the singles minister to redefine and update congregational understanding of the word family as well as the word single.

Be Available

It is the responsibility of the singles minister to be actively available to the singles of the church. Beyond speaking to them, it is always special to just be physically present in their homes, workplaces, and at their functions.

Simply sitting behind a desk will disintegrate the ministry. The shepherd must actively meet the sheep's needs of nourishment and healing. Most mature singles ministers are able to cover a lot of ground in a week without camping in any one place. Human presence means to the adult single, "You are important."

Interpret Ministry
It is the responsibility of the singles minister to interpret single adult ministry to the rest of the church staff and the church boards if necessary. Because a single adult ministry deals with divorced people, a church staff should have a solid understanding of what this means in other ministry areas, such as, youth and Christian education. It could also have implications theologically, and this needs to be talked out and understood on staff levels. The remarriage issue looms large in this respect as well. Some churches will marry the divorced, others will not. There is even a division on some church staffs. This can cause great disharmony on a staff if not properly and biblically addressed.

Inform Community
It is the responsibility of the singles minister to let the community at large know that his/her church welcomes singles and will minister lovingly and positively to their many needs.

Stop Discrimination
It is the responsibility of the singles minister to make sure that singles of all ages and stations of singleness are not discriminated against in positions of church leadership. Prejudice is a subtle thing and often masquerades as godliness. If singles cannot serve in your church because of their divorces, it is unlikely they will come to your singles group. If an unmarried 35-year-old single cannot serve on a church board because he or she is not married, we are saying, "We love you, but. . . ."

I realize that churches have had policies on many things long before singles arrived in quantity on the scene. Some policies need to be reexamined and some need to be changed.

Have Correct Motives
It is the responsibility of the singles minister to not start a singles ministry because he/she was put in the position to do it. He must support its inception as a ministry born of need in our time that will continue on in the church even if the leadership changes. It is too easy to approve a ministry, then ignore it until it evaporates and the voices promoting it disappear.

Research to Understand Ministry
It is the responsibility of the singles minister to do research, reading, interviews, and homework in the area of singleness to understand the

ministry directed toward singles. Taking the time to talk with singles can in itself be a learning experience. Visiting another singles ministry or a divorce recovery seminar can give a new understanding and vision to singles ministry and hurting people. Four years of Bible college or three years of seminary cannot be enough training and preparation.

Share Vision and Burden

It is the responsibility of the singles minister to share with the senior pastor the vision and burden for a singles ministry. Most senior pastors I know have very full agendas. It takes time to get behind a new vision. Most ministers are willing to be lovingly brought along in any new dream. It is only when they are pushed and shoved into something that they look for a side exit. Present your vision and burden honestly to your senior pastor and pray about it. Remember, the ministry is the Lord's, not the singles pastor's or the senior pastor's!

Jim Smoke
President of Growing Free
Tempe, Arizona

As a national singles speaker and author, Jim is ministering to singles pastors all the time. Jim served as a singles pastor at the Hollywood Presbyterian Church and founded the singles ministry at the Crystal Cathedral in 1974.

54. ETHICS FOR SINGLE ADULT LEADERS

"Single adult leaders must not attempt to diagnose, treat, or advise on problems beyond the recognized boundaries of their competence."

Harold Ivan Smith

The Emergence of a Profession

What does it mean to be a single adult leader, particularly a professional? Clearly the definition of "professional" is open to discussion, perhaps debate. F.E. Bullett has defined it as "a field of human endeavor with a well-defined body of knowledge, containing basic principles common to all application and techniques unique to the field, with practitioners skilled and experienced in applying these techniques, dedicated to the public interest" ("Why Certification?" *Certification Registration Information*, 1981 [Washington, D.C.: Research Report of the American Production and Inventory Control Society], p. 5).

W.E. Sheer suggests that a profession has eight essential characteristics: (1) a code of ethics; (2) an organized and accepted body of knowledge; (3) specialized skills; (4) minimum educational requirements for membership; (5) certification of proficiency before a member can achieve professional status; (6) an orderly process in the fulfillment of responsibilities; (7) opportunities for the promulgation and interchange of ideas among its members; and (8) requirements for acceptance of the disciplines of the profession, realizing that the price of failure or malpractice is being "out" of the profession ("Is Personnel Management a Profession?" *Personnel Journal*, 43 [1984], pp. 225-261).

In establishing a new vocation—single adult leader—it will take time and effort to formulate a commonly held set of perceptions on the recognized practice of the profession.

The first shared battleground is the need for this profession. Many pastors and church leaders presume that this movement contradicts or impairs the church's traditional commitment to the nuclear family. Mary Ann Mayo observed, "This subtle discrimination is part of an unconscious ideology so ingrained that [married leaders] don't even recognize it as a biased view" (*Parents' Guide to Sex Education* [Grand Rapids: Zondervan, 1986], p. 203).

Indeed, many churches have no problem ministering to young never-married singles or to those who are widowed. Some congregations choose to ignore the divorced or those who are unmarried by choice.

There are 64 million single adults who need the church. By the time some churches decide to minister with them, choices, patterns, and experiences may have hampered the redemptive lifestyle to which Jesus calls *all* single adults.

Expectations of Single Adults

A single adult leader must realize that single adults view leadership with certain expectations.

1. Single adults have a right to learn the extent of their ignorance and misinformation.
2. Single adults have a right to expect the Christian community to replace misinformation with facts.
3. Single adults may have uncomfortable questions they have a right to ask and a right to expect biblically sound answers/responses.
4. Single adults, when adequately enlightened, will be more moral than when they are un- or underinformed.
5. Single adults, even when faced with impossible circumstances, can be victorious through faith in Christ.

Competence of Single Adult Leaders

How does one become a single adult leader/minister? Two routes have emerged: one, a staff professional, often with a background in youth ministry or Christian education, takes a personal interest in single adults and gradually assumes formal responsibility, either full time or part time, until "someone can be found."

The volunteer leader, the second route, is common because of budget considerations. In other settings, single adult ministry has been "forced" on a most reluctant (and often already overworked) staff minister or leader with the instruction, "Do something with those single adults!"

In light of such a selection process, to say nothing of the "whosoever may . . ." approach in other churches, how are we to develop competence in leadership?

The American Association of Marriage and Family Therapy offers some guidance. Single adult leaders must be "dedicated to maintaining high standards of competence, recognizing appropriate limitations to [our] competence and services and using consultation and referral to/from other professionals." Realistically, in working with single adults, one finds every sort of mental, social, and theological disability. In some settings, simplistic solutions border on quackery, though disguised in religious jargon. "Take three Scriptures and you'll feel better in the morning."

What about those fellowships that offer immediate "deliverance" to persons wandering through the emotional wilderness of singleness? What about single adults yearning to be whole and healed? Have we not encountered theological/psychological abuse, even if well intended?

A tougher issue is the psychological needs of the leader. Do you wish to be a messiah? The deliverer? Have you developed a network of referral resources to which you can confidently and appropriately make referrals? Single adult leaders must not attempt to diagnose, treat, or advise on problems beyond the recognized boundaries of their competence.

Integrity for Single Adult Leaders

Paul warned Timothy, "Do your best to present yourself to God as one approved, a workman who does not need to be ashamed and who correctly handles the Word of truth" (2 Tim. 2:15), and "Watch your life and doctrine closely" (1 Tim. 4:16). Dr. James Brown offered four reasons why people don't initiate counseling with a single adult minister/leader—all of which strike at the heart of integrity:

- "I don't trust him/her!"
- "He/she is unable to handle my inner secrets and sins."
- "I am afraid to reveal my 'dirty little sins' to a minister."
- "I am really afraid he/she will reject me when he/she hears how I really am" ("The Need for Confidentiality," *Luther Rice Journal* [Spring 1984] pp. 14-19).

A single adult minister must guard his/her integrity.

Confidentiality for Single Adult Leaders

The single adult leader must respect the rights and reputations of single adults who participate in their programs/ministries. In the helping professions, confidentiality is a significant concern. Any individual who counsels with a single adult leader/minister has a right to expect that his/her privacy will be respected. However, a single adult leader serves in a church and community that wants to be informed about certain acts and intentions. That inevitably creates tension in the church and group.

Today, ethics is becoming a hot legal issue. The single adult leader is privy to much more information about the lives of single adults than many other professionals. You can expect more legal involvement in questions of practicing ministry and leadership in a church setting. Two major precedent-setting cases involved single adults: *Nally vs. McArthur,* and *Quinn vs. Elders of the Church of Christ of Collinsville* (Oklahoma).

Other cases create conflict between the single adult leader and other church leaders. Suppose your pastor or deacons want information about a certain counseling case, i.e., an adultery that leads to a divorce. Suppose there are "third parties" involved who happen to be key church leaders. Through your counseling (or through rumor), you discover the relationship. What do you do with that data?

One single adult minister discovered that his senior minister was sexually involved with a single adult in the singles group. If he confronted the senior pastor with the allegation, he had to be certain that the woman's accusations were factual and exact because word would get out in the singles group that he had violated confidence. His effectiveness would be jeopardized, perhaps destroyed.

The single adult minister, in this case, chose not to confront, but tried to persuade the woman to terminate the affair. That suggestion, however, angered the senior pastor. Eventually, the counselee "shared" the story with another single adult in the group who, in turn, quickly made the relationship common knowledge throughout the church. The senior pastor resigned.

Still, some single adults believe that the single adult minister blew the whistle and breached confidentiality.

Frequently, in working with the separated or divorced, the single adult minister/leader gains information that is troublesome. Moreover, in a church setting, he is to minister to all concerned. Therefore, a single adult minister/leader must be slow to take sides, or to jump to conclusions, particularly in emotion-laden issues such as incest, homosexuality, child custody, date rape, or child abuse.

Divorce stimulates curiosity, especially in small groups or congregations, particularly when things "don't add up." Moreover, there can be a significant difference between the public reasons for a divorce and the *real* motivations.

You must remember that in the foe-adversary nature of many divorces, events can be staged or taken out of context. You should carefully weigh active participation in any litigation.

Again, Dr. James Brown, a Christian psychologist, raises four assumptions on confidentiality. (1) Without assurance of confidentiality, many single adults will *not* seek help for their problems or their secret sins; (2) without confidentiality, many single adults will delay their entry into counseling for fear of being exposed; (3) without assurance of confidentiality, many single adults will be reluctant to divulge essential information during the course of counseling; and (4) without confidentiality, many single adults who have needs for counseling will end up terminating their counseling prematurely and not receive the help that they so desperately need and that you can give.

Brown concluded, "We must take our promises [stated or implied] seriously when dealing with the injured, tortured souls of God's people. If you truly wish people to seek out your wisdom and guidance, then you must learn to listen *and* to keep their faith by maintaining confidentiality" ("The Need for Confidentiality").

Simply, a single adult minister/leader must be cautious in sharing in prayer groups, committees, or private conversations, material which is confidential or unsubstantiated. If the cat's out of the bag, it doesn't matter how "spiritual" the setting in which it escaped.

Finally, confidentiality raises a significant question in lay leadership selection and development. Suppose a committee nominates a person for leadership. However, in counseling, that individual has confessed to a struggle with an issue that would cloud or compromise his leadership. What are you to do to guard both the integrity of the group and yet maintain confidentiality? What is your responsibility should that person move to another group? Is your problem "solved"?

One single adult minister asked a man to leave his group for "hitting-up" sexually on female members. Imagine his surprise when he received a newsletter from another single adult group and found this individual actively involved in a position of leadership.

Simply, the problem is not new in single adult ministry. Paul warned about those "who worm their way into homes [groups] and gain control over weak-willed women [and men], who are loaded down with sins and are swayed by all kinds of evil desires" (2 Tim. 3:6). The vulnerable, fragile emotions of single adults must be protected, particularly within the body of believers.

Conclusion

Paul offered good advice with the words in Titus, "In *everything* set them an example by doing what is good. In your teaching [counseling] show integrity, seriousness, and soundness of speech that cannot be condemned" (2:7, italics added). Every single adult leader needs a desk copy of *Clergy Malpractice* by Malony, Needham, and Southard as a guidebook for referral.

Paul warned, "Give the enemy *no opportunity for slander*" (1 Tim. 5:14, italics added). That is still sound advice for those who wish to provide leadership with America's fastest-growing subculture. Ethics is not an option but a vital ingredient in serving single adults.

Harold Ivan Smith
Executive Director of Tear-Catchers
Kansas City, Missouri

As a lecturer and singles ministry speaker, Harold has demonstrated a great concern for leadership development. He was General Director of Single Adult Ministries for the Church of the Nazarene, 1979-1981, and a charter member of NSL.

55. THE IMPORTANCE OF PRAYER

"When we quietly lift the needs of single people before God's throne, their hurts become our hurts, their burdens rest on our hearts too. And through the ministry of prayer, a love and compassion develops where there was none before."

Mary Graves

Prayer: The Ground out of Which All Ministries Rise

"If My people, who are called by My name, will humble themselves and pray and seek My face and turn from their wicked ways, then will I hear from heaven and will forgive their sin and will heal their land" (2 Chron. 7:14).

We end this *Singles Ministry Handbook* at the very place where all ministry begins: prayer. Paul Cho, pastor of the world's largest and fastest-growing church (12,000 converts per month), traces the success of that Korean ministry to its beginnings in prayer. The Christians in Korea have learned how to live their lives in prayer and, because of that, a revival is happening in that country.

The late Keith Green, who made contemporary Christian music big in the '70s, addressed a concert crowd of college-age Christians in Chico, California with this question, "How many of you would like to see a revival happen in Chico?" to which the crowd cheered their enthusiastic approval. Then he asked, "How many of you are praying for it?" Silence.

The single adult population of America hungers for the healing and wholeness that Christ brings; they are a revival waiting to happen. "No one can schedule a revival," says Dr. Cho, "but . . . when prayer ascends from a few earnest hearts, then history teaches it is time for the tide of revival to sweep in once more" (*Prayer: Key to Revival,* Paul Y. Cho).

Singles could easily be considered an "unreached people" that need to be reached, touched, and revived with the grace of God given in Jesus Christ. We can do our best to make that happen but no one can program a response to God's grace. A handbook can give information but only the Spirit of God can bring faith. A handbook can put flesh and bones to the whole idea of singles ministry but only the Spirit of God can give life to it. And prayer helps breathe that Spirit of life and faith into our ministries.

This book depends on people kneeling before God in prayer before its ideas and suggestions can come to life. So we conclude with prayer—more than a suggestion, more than one ingredient for success—the necessary beginning place of ministry. God commands our prayers (Luke 18:1) and

He has made His work contingent on them. "The command to pray is a reminder that we cannot live without God's power, love, and guidance" (*The Practice of Prayer,* David Allen Hubbard, InterVarsity). It is also a reminder of what can happen when we do pray, for all things are possible with God.

Obstacles to Prayer

"Prayer is a problem," says Hubbard in the opening line of his guidebook on prayer. Christian leaders can teach it, advocate it, believe in it, and yet national surveys show that very few Christians spend much time doing it, including those Christian leaders. Why is it a problem? Because there seem to be so many good reasons not to pray.

In light of the sovereignty of God, prayer can seem a bit presumptuous. If God knows our every need before we even utter it, and if God rules over all things in power, and nothing falls outside of His control, why pray? To miss a prayertime here and there doesn't feel all that tragic because God is still on His throne doing business as usual.

With our tendency to champion "human potential" it is easy for us to let work become a substitute for prayer. After all, God does expect us to do our best; and we must not use prayer as an excuse to dump on God the work that needs to be done by us; and "God helps those who help themselves." So, fueled with that kind of logic, we busy ourselves with the tasks of ministry and end up with no time or energy to pray.

Richard Foster in *Celebration of Discipline* (Harper and Row) claims that "in contemporary society our adversary majors in three things: noise, hurry, and crowds. If he can keep us engaged in 'muchness' and 'manyness,' he will rest satisfied." Here we catch a glimpse of the average singles leader who always has more needs to address than any one person could attend to, who continuously struggles with the demands of being present and being prepared, who majors in muchness and manyness and barely has time for personal hygiene much less moments of quiet before God. And in this "tyranny of the urgent" the popular conclusion is that the less urgent thing is prayer. Only the father of lies could convince us that that is true.

There may be a myriad of other obstacles that trip up the prayer life of eager singles leaders. Perhaps God's silence at a critical time of need provided convincing proof that prayer is ineffective. Perhaps our sin and pride have convinced us that we cannot pray right, and so we don't try. Many times, in many ways, and for many reasons, we just don't feel like praying.

But prayer is too important to depend on our feelings. According to Jesus, by far the most important thing about praying is to keep at it. Prayer is a response, it is an answering speech and presence to what God has said and done, and the call to pray transcends our own ability and desire to do it.

"When prayer does not come easily to us, we should still make the effort to pray, whether we 'feel like it or not.' It is salutary to cultivate the habit of prayer. I concur with the counsel given in Georges Bernanos' *Diary of a Country Priest*: 'If you can't pray—at least say your prayers!' " (Donald Bloesch, *The Struggle of Prayer*, Harper and Row)

Prayer in Your Singles Ministry

Prayer can be built into your ministry: as an activity that engages you, your leaders, and your singles. And there are several sides to the treasures that time in prayer will bring. First we will explore the treasures and then we will look at intentional ways of grabbing those treasures and making prayer a priority in your singles ministry.

The treasures. Singles ministry brings an overwhelming variety of life situations under one umbrella, and often an overwhelming assortment of needs. As one singles leaders described it, "There are more problems per square inch than anywhere else in the church." If the church is a hospital for sinners, then singles ministry is the intensive care unit. Not all singles are hurting, but the hurts that singles bring are critical and often beyond human healing. Singles ministry can be overwhelming.

But with all the promise of a treasure hunt, Scripture declares that "the prayer of a righteous man is powerful and effective" (James 5:16). Indeed, we already affirmed that at the outset with the words of the Chronicler. Prayer brings forgiveness of sin and healing to our land and far greater things than we could possibly ask or think. There are unnamed treasures in store for the men and women poised in a posture of prayer. And no problem is too overwhelming for our God.

"Prayer is our Declaration of Dependence on God," says Hubbard. We are humbled by our own neediness and lifted up by the only One who is able to save. That is a treasure and a necessary assurance for anyone who hopes to do singles ministry.

Another jewel from the treasure chest of prayer is compassion. To pray for others is to affirm our concern for them. There are many singles in the category of "unlovely" and "socially inept" people who are not easy to care for. But when we quietly lift the names and needs of these people before God's throne, their hurts become our hurts, their burdens rest on our hearts too. And through the ministry of prayer, a love and compassion develops where there was none before.

One more gem from the wealth of prayer's treasures is intimacy. As one seminary professor said, "If you want to get to know someone, pray together." Prayer brings an honesty and openness that can only occur before the throne of God. It brings a bonding, a spiritual unity, that cannot be manufactured by human engineering and cannot be easily severed by human weakness. Singles have a hunger for honesty. Singles do not want to be alone, and many are starved for intimacy. Prayer speaks to their deepest longings and brings them to the only One who can fulfill all of their needs.

Where to start. As far as building prayer into your ministry, the most appropriate place to begin is with the leader and the utter necessity of a predictable, consistent, structured time in daily prayer. Many end up praying for the needs of their singles as they happen to come to mind. Instead of that random method, try putting the various people and programs on a weekly calendar. For example, on Monday you might pray for divorce recovery and the people giving leadership there (by name); Tuesday pray for single parents—and on through the week, making sure that all your key people and need areas are covered regularly in prayer.

Then look at the day's schedule—the counseling appointments, the leadership meetings, the programmed events—and lift them, one by one, to the Lord, expressing your greatest fear and asking for your wildest dream. And look back with a thankful heart. Praise God for what He is doing, for the lives that are being touched, and the prayers that have been answered.

But you are not the only one called to pray. Cultivate prayer as a priority agenda item for your leaders. In your leadership meeting, pray not only at the beginning and end (popularly known as the "Oreo prayer"), but make a major time commitment to a prayertime together. Teach on the necessity, the urgency, and the power of prayer—and then pray. One minister takes his leaders through the singles mailing list, praying regularly for each one by name. Other leaders are gathered together before the programmed event to pray for it. Program prayer into your leadership training.

And program it into your singles gatherings. The fear is that prayertimes will exclude the non-Christians at your outreach events. But some have found that prayer for the whole group at the end can be very nonthreatening and offer great love and support to everyone there. Perhaps some of your small groups can do explorations into the topic and activity of prayer. What a great way to build closeness and disciples at the same time!

"If My people, who are called by My name, will humble themselves and pray," then they will see ministry happen, they will see lives transformed, they will experience the reviving and saving power of God in and through Jesus Christ. Talking about prayer, writing about prayer, reading about prayer accomplishes nothing unless it causes God's people to pray.

Mary Graves
Associate Pastor—Minister with Singles
Solana Beach Presbyterian Church, Solana Beach, California

As a conference speaker, pastor to singles, and as a single adult, Mary says, "I am one who is both a teacher and eager learner in the school of prayer."

APPENDIX A

A ROUND-TABLE DISCUSSION WITH SINGLE ADULTS

"Church leadership has access to information of all kinds about the singles they are reaching. But what of the singles themselves? What do they feel about the church? Are we living up to our responsibility to meet the singles' needs?

"We held a round-table discussion with single adults in California's Silicon Valley to discuss the singles' relationship to the church. Each participant volunteered his/her own perspective of how the church is responding to the needs of singles."

Jerry Jones
Stephanie Kirtland

THE PARTICIPANTS

Interviewer—never married, 20s, free-lance writer in Palo Alto and member of a large evangelical church with two active singles groups. Acted as discussion facilitator.

Jane—never married, 20s, software engineer, attends a nondenominational church in San Jose with two large singles groups.

Rudy—never married, 30s, manufacturing production head, involved in "Careers" group at a large nondenominational church in Cupertino.

Ellen—divorced, 30s, technical writer, active in "Young Adults" at her church.

Hank—divorced, 30s, air traffic controller, attends a mainline denominational church and lives across the Bay.

Kay—single parent, 40s, personnel trainer, involved in a singles group through a Catholic church in Los Altos.

Mary—married, 60s, self-employed image consultant, involved with husband as support couple in a church singles group in Palo Alto.

How Do You See the Church's Attitudes Concerning Singleness?

Rudy: The church doesn't seem to know what to do with singles. Singles seem lonely, lost, and unaccepted. But there is so much potential to get singles going in the right direction.

Interviewer: I think it depends on the church. I've been to many singles groups in the area and find them very different. Some spend a good deal of time discussing how to find a mate; others on becoming the best person by focusing on the Lord and letting Him take care of the rest. The pastor holds a big responsibility for the group's orientation.

Kay: There has been a gradual change in the attitude of churches in the past 10 to 15 years. When we were married we felt a part of the church community. But when my husband and I separated and the girls remained with me, there was a long transition period when we felt we were no longer a part of the community—we felt a real ostracism.

Ellen: I used to go to a fundamental, family oriented church. When I was married I fit in just fine; then this divorce struck and I felt I made people uncomfortable—and that's not a time when you want to feel that way. So I stopped going until I moved and found a church which has a thriving group of single people. I felt their attitude was that you're not just a person waiting to be married—you are a person in your own right, which was crucial to me adjusting to being single again.

Kay: After a divorce you feel like half of a whole person and empty for a long time. I had to apologize to various groups because I felt like I didn't belong there anymore. I needed the support of people who were going through the same hurt and pain and alienation from church to be able to go on, to feel part of the church, and not feel like I had to marry again to be whole. It took me a long time to realize that God does not create half people; He creates whole people.

Why Are Many Singles Not Involved in Church?
Hank: Discipline has a lot to do with it. It's a lot easier to do something else on Sundays.

Rudy: As singles, we can do whatever we want to, so it comes down to where God is in our lives. It's a responsibility we need to take personally. Our media push entertainment; if you don't bring in the entertainer, it's no fun. But as Christians it's a personal issue between you and God, and not a dynamic speaker. We need to be responsible to God and get involved in the church body.

Ellen: I think that's right. Singles seem to be getting into the rut of needing to be entertained and feel good to go to church. But the key is involvement. If you create responsibilities for yourself, that will draw you in. You feel like they need you and you should go.

Interviewer: It's difficult for a singles group because they're dealing with non-Christians as well as Christians. Singles groups are mainly for fellowship. You need to have fellowship with those who understand the same problems and issues you face. Church singles groups provide that aspect for the Christian. But many non-Christians come just to be social or *don't* come because they don't understand or feel comfortable with Christian fellowship. It takes a lot to break down the barriers. We need to understand that.

Kay: Initially, you may come with the expectation of meeting a member of the opposite sex, but you'll grow to see people in the group as your brothers or sisters in Christ. You're not just in the group to be social, but a family.

Jane: And it should be different. If you go to a singles event outside of the church, like a singles bar, you expect people to be looking to find someone else of the opposite sex. I have friends who are Christians who don't go to a church singles group *because* they don't like the potential implication of being viewed as looking for someone. They actually shy away from a group for that reason.

How Can the Church Become More Effective at Reaching Christian Singles?

Hank: By not shutting them out or making them a splinter group. I went to a church where the singles meeting room was the farthest away and the group was the least supported, financially and spiritually. So we felt, more or less cast out, like we weren't worth it.

Ellen: Singles need to go to church to worship God as well as to have their needs met. I know that in order to worship God completely and freely, I need to feel comfortable in the church. It's not just a matter of what this church can do for me, it's that I want to worship God in a sanctuary where I feel like I'm normal.

This is through sermons which don't have a total family orientation, or where divorced people are in positions of leadership, or through references the leaders make which show they are aware that there are people on their own out there.

Rudy: Leaders ought to be trained to work with singles, wherever they are in their walk with Christ. Discipleship, pouring your life into another person like Jesus did, is one of the key elements of growth. I think that's lacking in singles ministry. We try to fill a social need and the real need never gets filled.

Jane: Christ is attractive. If we live as a body, people will be attracted to that.

What about Non-Christians? What Is the Most Effective Way to Reach Them?

Rudy: It depends on where they are. I work with some who are very work-oriented with no desire to be involved in any group; their goal is to get up the corporate ladder. They don't feel lonely or have any other "needs." And in singles groups, there are always singles who are looking for something, but when they see the cost of commitment to Christ is everything, they don't want to pay the price. So we need to find out what singles are looking for.

Ellen: One often sees non-Christians going to social events rather than worship services—and I think it's great when they come for social purposes. I know two people who started going to church for the potluck dinners and the basketball team. They are now both strong Christians. I think people need to be sensitive to the fact that some are not committed initially.

Mary: That's the advantage to having our singles group meeting in a restaurant. It's nonthreatening and nonchurchy. We have discussion tables with leaders who pick up on where people are coming from and can talk to them. Quite often God will use us to direct them. That's the exciting part.

Jane: Yes, it's up to the singles themselves to reach out and bring their friends.

Rudy: As with anyone, they just want to be listened to. They want someone to say, "I understand you." That is what draws them. Christ in us is attractive to them.

Kay: Sometimes a singles conference can be a place to invite a friend. They can come to the conference—which need not be in the church building—and meet people, pick up the information they're interested in, ask their own questions. They might not come on their own, but would if you asked them.

Hank: I think opportunities happen to us all the time but we don't seize them. With a film series on relationships, we could say to someone, "Let's listen to this, we can both learn."

Interviewer: There is a pastor in a local church who goes out to singles clubs to give talks, like seminars, on "How to have meaningful relationships," or "Is there more to life?" He is going out where the singles are. That's important because, even through a relationship, it is hard to initially feel comfortable in a Christian group.

Rudy: Let's face it, even Christians coming into a singles group feel uncomfortable. It's very frightening for me to go to another church and not know anybody. It's threatening. I don't know if I'm accepted, or who's who. That's always scary.

If we're committed to the unbelievers we work with, we need to personally get involved with them, pray for them, meet their needs, spend time with them.

How Can the Church Be More Effective with Single Parents?

Kay: Single parents face very special problems. For example, mom or dad are going to a church singles group, but where does that leave the child? The church needs to reach out to the children who need special help during this time. We were the first family that got divorced in our church and my children felt really segregated and different from the rest of the kids. It took a long time to deal with the children's feelings that we weren't a "family." But we were—families are families even if they don't have two parents. Children of single parents need to feel like they fit into the family structure of the church.

Hank: It could help take some of the emotional stress off the parents too.

Kay: Definitely. We are also starting a program in our church school called "Rainbows for All God's Children." It's a national program which takes children of divorced families aside in small groups during school hours. It focuses on the special problems faced by these children. We try to show them, for example, that just because they are the children of divorced parents doesn't mean that God loves them any less. I think this can work in other organizations too.

Rudy: There needs to be a support group where parents can share their struggles and encourage each other. If one parent has a struggle with his child, he can call up a friend with the same struggle and they can encourage each other. That's a part of edifying the body. Sometimes it's hard to get people to take those kinds of roles, so there needs to be a shepherd, whether a full-time pastor or elder, in each group. Someone guiding with the ambition, purpose, and goals of the group in mind, but keeping them in relation to the larger body.

What Are the Special Needs of Singles?

Hank: It's hard to define just one need for the single. There are spiritual, emotional, even physical needs. People are different. Some may only want physical needs met, but there are so many different needs.

Rudy: The most important thing is being accepted. The longing of belonging, of knowing you're needed. We're all at different avenues in life, but for the most part, we want to be accepted, cared for, and a part of a group. God didn't want us to be alone or up on the mountain by ourselves.

Ellen: Christian singles need to be loved, but you do need the person to start getting involved and make some solid relationships so that he'll get that feeling of belonging and closeness. I think the church can only do so much—the individual has to take some initiative too.

Mary: The comments we get are that it's neat to talk to married people about what we did or didn't do to make it work, as well as some of the problems. Often singles have the wrong concept of marriage with unrealistically high expectations. Single people want an older couple they can go to.

Jane: Another thing is that all younger groups have older leaders, but in a singles group, we're adults and there is a real potential to be leading ourselves. I find that we need more training of singles who can lead singles. I don't see much of that. I also see a need to be discipled by older women and for us to disciple younger women.

Rudy: We have a core group of singles that leads the group. Anyone can be involved if they want to get committed and are proven to be godly. Single people need people to look at, to set an example.

What Would You Like to Say to Singles Pastors across the Nation?

Jane: I don't want to be entertained. I'm serious about my relationship with the Lord and I want to dive right into it. As single people we have a unique position for God to really use us.

Kay: Accept single people where they are. Don't try to bring them to your level of thinking immediately. Don't try to change us; rather, meet us at our level.

Ellen: I would like to have it emphasized that you can be whole being single. The relationship between you and God is so important. When you look at eternity you can't be depending on a husband or on anyone else, which can be easy for women to do. You feel a strength in the Lord when it is just you and the Lord. He is always there and that's really positive.

How Do You Feel about the Term "Single"?

Interviewer: The term "single" can be negative. Often we have *more* relationships as singles because we're not married to one person demanding our time. Yet we're seen as "single"—as isolated. So we may need to think about how we term ourselves or how we are termed by others. Careers or young adults is good. "Single" doesn't bother me, but it bothers some.

Kay: I don't feel the word "single" is as derogatory in this particular area as elsewhere. I personally have had more problems with a label I thought was posted right across my forehead that said "Divorced." And it's easier for me now to say I'm a single parent than it was to even say divorced. So it's getting to a point where it is more comfortable to be single.

Hank: This brings up a funny twist to that whole concept. On me, I feel like the sign says "Single and employed, opportunity here." It's like I'm single, I'm a dying breed and an endangered species. It makes me wonder what the motivation of women is.

Anything Else?
Rudy: Pastors need to look at the potential they have to raise godly men and godly women. Teaching needs to be brought down to practical truth. Get down to the personal relationship with the Lord Jesus Christ. Teach us to be obedient to the Word of God and to stand true to our convictions.

Jane: It takes time, perhaps, to adjust to being single, but there's a real joy and intimacy that comes with sharing that closeness to Christ.

Kay: It took my divorce to bring me closer to God. It seems unreal; it seems as a married couple it would be so much easier. But in the horrible, agonizing part of being divorced, I had to reach out to someone, I had to. And He was there.

Jerry Jones
Editor and publisher of *Single Adult Ministries Journal*
Colorado Springs, Colorado

Stephanie Kirtland
Free-lance writer
San Jose, California

APPENDIX B

NETWORKING THROUGH NSL
A COMPREHENSIVE RESOURCE AND
SUPPORT ORGANIZATION FOR SINGLES

NSL is the National Association of Single Adult Leaders. In fact, all of the chapters in this volume are written by NSL members.

NSL is designed to encourage and be a resource for equipping lay and professional leaders for ministry. The network connects the lives and ministries of single adult leaders across our nation. This networking alone provides a great resource to single adult leaders. However, the wealth and volume of ministry materials and ideas provide invaluable ministry tools and opportunities. NSL is available to all churches and singles ministries. The following is their story as reported by former Executive Director Timm Jackson.

It was sure to be a great day in Vail, Colorado. Of course, every day is beautiful there, whether it is snowing, raining, or perfectly sunshiny. The terrain just seems to openly invite the lucky human to drink in the freshness and be inspired! But who could guess what would actually be born that spring day in 1980? Just what was going through the minds of those men and women who met there? They were singles leaders—some of them single themselves. Was there one present in that small group who happened to be discouraged? Or overworked? Or lonely? Or neglected? Perhaps all of the above! Whatever affected those special people then, we are the beneficiaries now!

Networking . . . individuals who interconnect . . . an interesting concept when used by people who share a like mind, heart, and commitment for Christ's work. The simple act of encouraging, equipping, and inspiring each other tends to make each of our tasks more fulfilling. When singles leaders, whether professional or lay, are brought together to learn and grow, the challenge of our ministry only deepens. Several denominations across the country understand the importance of such encouragement and training among singles leaders, but unfortunately the learning is often limited to denominational ties. There are many singles pastors still left in the cold, having no one with whom they can share the unique needs of single adult leadership.

The National Association of Single Adult Leaders was formed from those days in Vail and has grown to encompass a wide spectrum of single adult leaders. Designed to encourage and be a resource for equipping both lay and professional leaders for ministry, NSL has begun to fulfill those goals in an interdenominational arena.

A focus on a variety of educational avenues has produced broader ministry skills in the lives of those involved with NSL. Conferences held around the United States in eight different geographic locations offer educational opportunities within driving distance. Here leaders learn the basics of divorce recovery, grief recovery ministries, counseling singles, and single ministry programs, and they discover how to incorporate this type of programming into the local church. Studying the needs of the single adult and learning how the church and Christian community can relate and respond to those needs is another learning experience provided by NSL.

The encouragement of leaders is a constant need. Inspiring them to be creative and innovative in their programming is also something that "networking" can do. Inspiration to live in the areas of cutting-edge ministry—constantly searching for new needs and new need-meeting tools—is offered to those who need to excel in their world for the cause of Christ. Another focus of the networking experience is to help participants set and attain personal, as well as ministry, goals. Allowing the members of NSL to informally hold each other accountable for excellence and growth in ministry tasks creates a unique, profitable forum for sharing gifts and experiences in practical fellowship opportunities.

NSL, Mobilized to Serve, and some denominational ministries provide many opportunities each year for single adult leaders to connect. Annual conferences are held by each of these groups. Many regional and local leadership training workshops are also available. Some groups sponsor retreats and others offer membership opportunities to tie the leaders more closely together so they may communicate on a regular basis. A variety of ministry aids being produced and marketed through these networks supplies a continuing educational experience. Books, tapes, and videos have all become useful tools in enabling single adult leaders to have a more lasting ministry.

With God's help, let us work with and encourage each other. Instead of facing discouragement, overwork, lonely moments, or feelings of being neglected, let's learn to conserve our energies by using that strength for the necessary tasks to which we have been called by God.

The organizations listed below were also created for a very special reason—you. We are happy to help make this and other resources available, and we would like to do still more. Each of these groups is only a phone call or letter away if you need a quick prayer of encouragement or a tough question answered. If more input is desired, we want to be available to you, whether it be consulting ideas for ministry, weekend leadership seminars, or ministry retreats. We are all determined to build friendships that will enhance your ministry and help you, the single adult leader, pastor, and friend to personally grow in Christ and reach singles for Christ.

National Association of Single Adult Leaders
P.O. Box 25482
Tempe, Arizona 85282
Bill Flanagan, Executive Board Chairman

Mobilized to Serve
Elim Fellowship
7245 College Street
Lima, NY 14485
Mike Cavanaugh, Executive Director

United Methodist Single Adult Ministry Dept.
P.O. Box 840
Nashville, Tennessee 37202-0480
Karen Greenwaldt, Chairperson

Church of the Nazarene
6401 The Paseo
Kansas City, Missouri 64131
Dennis Apple, General Director

Assembly of God Adult Ministry Dept.
1445 Boonville Avenue
Springfield, Missouri 65802
Bill Campbell, Consultant

Southern Baptist Sunday School Board
127 9th Avenue N.
Nashville, Tennessee 37234
Ann Gardner & Tim Cleary, Consultants

Timm Jackson
Minister to Single Adults
Tempe, Arizona

Timm has served as Executive Director of NSL and is currently on the support staff team. His experiences include successful singles pastorates, and he was a pioneer in the formation of the national organization, NSL.

SUGGESTED READING

SINGLE ADULTS

Never Married
Celebrating the Single Life, Muto, Susan Annette, New York: Doubleday & Company, 1985.
Creative Loneliness, Hulme, William E., Minneapolis: Augsburg, 1977.
For Singles Only, Fix, Janet, and Levitt, Zola, Old Tappan, N.J.: Revell, 1978.
Getting the Most Out of Being Single, Karssen, Gien, Colorado Springs: Navpress, 1983.
God's Call to the Single Adult, Cavanaugh, Michael, Springdale, Pa: Whitaker House, 1986.
Great Leaps in a Single Bound, Witte, Kaaren, Minneapolis: Bethany, 1982.
Leaving Home, Bence, Evelyn, Wheaton, Ill: Tyndale House, 1986.
Letters to Karen, Shedd, Charlie, Nashville: Abingdon, 1977.
Living Alone and Liking It, Shahan, Lynn, New York: Warner Books, 1982.
Making the Most of Single Life, Reed, Bobbie, St. Louis: Concordia, 1980.
One Is More Than UN, Goodwin, Debbie Salter, Kansas City, Mo.: Beacon Hill, 1978.
Overcoming Loneliness, Jeremiah, David, San Bernardino, Calif.: Here's Life, 1983.
Positively Single, Smith, Harold Ivan, Wheaton, Ill.: Victor Books, 1986.
Single after Fifty, McConnell, Adeline, and Anderson, Beverly, New York: McGraw-Hill, 1980.
Single and Complete, Douglass, Judy, and Long, Kathryn, San Bernardino, Calif.: Here's Life, 1986.
Single Life, Unmarried Adults in Social Context, "Singles' Bars as Examples of Urban Courting Patterns," pp. 115-120, Allon, Natalie, and Fishel, Diane, Edited by Peter J. Stein, New York: St. Martin's Press, 1981.
Single Life, Unmarried Adults in Social Context, "Where are the Men for the Women at the Top?" pp. 21-33, Doudna, Christine with McBride, Fern, Edited by Peter J. Stein, New York: St. Martin's Press, 1981.
Single Voices, Yoder, Bruce, and Yoder, Imo Jeanne, Scottdale, Pa: Herald Press, 1982.
Singleness, Payne, Dorothy, Philadelphia: Westminster, 1983.
Singleness, Swindoll, Charles, Portland, Ore.: Multnomah, 1981.
Singleness of Purpose, Jeffries, Tula, Nashville: Broadman, 1986.
Singles Alive, Towns, Jim, Gretna, La.: Pelican, 1984.
Singles—The New Americans, Simenauer, Jacqueline, and Carroll, David, New York: NAL, 1983.
Spiritually Single, Mitchell, Marcia, Minneapolis: Bethany House, 1984.
Successfully Single, Baker, Yvonne G., Denver: Accent Books, 1985.

Wide My World, Narrow My Bed, Swindoll, Luci, Portland, Ore.: Multnomah, 1982.

Divorce
An Answer to Divorce, Wright, Norman, Eugene, Ore: Harvest House, 1977.
Beginning Again: Life after a Relationship Ends, Hershey, Terry, Laguna Hills, Calif.: Nelson, 1984.
Beyond the Broken Marriage, Correu, Larry M., Philadelphia: Westminster, 1982.
But I Didn't Want a Divorce, Bustanoby, Andre, Grand Rapids: Zondervan, 1978.
Catholics and Broken Marriage, Catoir, Father John, Notre Dame, Ind.: Ave Maria Press, 1979.
A Christian Considers Divorce and Remarriage, Joiner, E. Earl, Nashville: Broadman, 1983.
The Compassionate Side of Divorce, Lovett, C.S., Baldwin Park, Calif.: Personal Christianity, 1975.
Divorce, Swindoll, Charles R., Portland, Ore.: Multnomah, 1981.
Divorce and Remarriage, Duty, Guy, Minneapolis: Bethany, 1967.
Divorce and Remarriage, Martin, John R., Scottdale, Pa.: Herald Press, 1974.
Divorce and Remarriage in the Church, Ellisen, Stanley A., Grand Rapids: Zondervan, 1977.
Divorce and the Christian, Plekker, Robert J., Wheaton, Ill.: Tyndale House, 1980.
The Divorce Book, McKay, Matthew, Rogers, Peter, Blades, Joan, and Gosse, Richard, Oakland, Calif: New Harbinger Publications, 1984.
The Divorce Handbook, (Updated Edition), Friedman, James T., New York: Random House, 1984.
Divorce Is a Family Affair, Johnson, Margaret, Grand Rapids: Zondervan, 1983.
Divorce Is a Grown-Up Problem, Sinberg, Janet, New York: Avon, 1978.
Divorce: Is It the Unpardonable Sin? Scott, Thomas W., Forest, Va.: Published by Author, 1982.
The Divorce Myth: A Biblical Examination of Divorce and Remarriage, Laney, J. Carl, Minneapolis: Bethany, 1981.
Divorce: The Pain and the Healing: Personal Meditations when Marriage Ends, Mattison, Judith, Minneapolis: Augsburg, 1985.
Divorce without Victims, Berger, Dr. Stuart, New York: NAL, 1983.
Divorced, Smith, B.J. with Harrell, Irene Burk, Wheaton, Ill.: Tyndale, 1983.
Divorced and Christian, Peppler, Alice Stolper, St. Louis: Concordia, 1974.
The Divorced Christian, Cerling, Charles E., Grand Rapids: Baker, 1984.
The Divorcing Christian, Rambo, Lewis R., Nashville: Abingdon, 1983.
Finding Your Place after Divorce, Streeter, Carole Sanderson, Grand Rapids: Zondervan, 1986.

Forgiveness Is for Giving, Towner, Jason, Grand Rapids: Zondervan, n.d.

Growing through Divorce, Smoke, Jim, Irvine, Calif.: Harvest House, 1976.

Help for Parents of a Divorced Son or Daughter, Smith, Harold Ivan, St. Louis: Concordia, 1981.

How to Forgive Your Ex-Husband, Hootman, Marcia, and Perkins, Patt, New York: Doubleday, 1982.

The Hurt and Healing of Divorce—One Woman's Story, Petri, Darlene, Elgin, Ill.: Cook, 1976.

I Wish Someone Understood My Divorce, Smith, Harold Ivan, Minneapolis: Augsburg, n.d.

I'm Divorced—Are You Listening, Lord? Buck, Peggy S., Valley Forge, Pa.: Judson, 1976.

Is There Life after Divorce in the Church? Morgan, Richard Lyon, Atlanta: John Knox Press, 1985.

Is This Divorce Really Necessary? Hudson, R. Lofton, Nashville: Broadman, 1983.

Jesus & Divorce, Heth, William A., and Wenham, Gordon J. Nashville: Thomas Nelson, 1987.

Letting Go with Love: The Grieving Process, O'Connor, Nancy, Tucson: LaMariposa, 1984.

Living beyond Divorce—The Possibilities of Remarriage, Smoke, Jim, Eugene, Ore.: Harvest House, 1984.

Marriage and Divorce: What the Bible Says, Efird, James M., Nashville: Abingdon, 1985.

Marriage, Divorce and Remarriage in the Bible, Adams, Jay E., Grand Rapids: Baker, 1981.

May I Divorce & Remarry? Zodhiates, Spiros, Chattanooga: AMG Publishers, 1984.

Mom's House/Dad's House: Making Shared Custody Work, Ricci, Isolina, New York: Macmillan, 1980.

Now that You Are Single Again, Chapman, Gary, San Bernardino, Calif.: Here's Life, 1985.

On Divorce, Stein, Sara Bonnet and Stone, Erika, New York: Walker & Co., 1984.

An Open Book to the Christian Divorcee, Crook, Roger H., Nashville: Broadman Press, 1973.

The Parents Book about Divorce, Gardner, Richard A., New York: Bantam, 1979.

Picking up the Pieces, Besson, Clyde Colvin, New York: Ballantine, 1984.

Recovery from Divorce, Thompson, David A., Minneapolis: Bethany, 1982.

Remarriage—A Healing Gift from God, Richards, Larry, Waco, Texas: Word Books, 1981.

Remarriage and God's Renewing Grace: A Positive Biblical Ethic for Divorced Christians, Small, Dwight Hervey, Grand Rapids:, Baker Book House, 1986.

Scenes from a Divorce, Paylor, Neil, and Head, Barry, Minneapolis: Winston, 1983.

The Single Experience, Miller, Keith and Miller, Andrea Wells, Waco, Tex.: Word, 1981.

Surviving the Breakup: How Children and Parents Cope with Divorce, Wallerstein, Judith S., and Kelly, Joan B., New York: Basic, 1982.

What about Divorce, Zodhiates, Spiros, Chattanooga: AMG Pub., n.d.

When All Else Fails, Supancic, Ronald, and Baker, Dennis, Old Tappan, N.J.: Revell, 1986.

When Divorce Ends Your Marriage . . . It Hurts, Mumford, Amy Ross, Denver: Accent, 1982.

Widowed

After the Flowers Have Gone, Decker, Bea, and Kooiman, Gladys, Grand Rapids: Zondervan, 1987.

Alone Again, Krebs, Dr. Richard, Minneapolis: Augsburg, 1978.

Beyond Ourselves, Marshall, Catherine, Lincoln, Va.: Chosen, 1984.

But I Never Thought He'd Die, Nye, Miriam Baker, Philadelphia: Westminster, 1978.

By Death or Divorce . . . It Hurts to Lose, Mumford, Amy Ross, Denver: Accent, 1981.

Coping with Being Single Again, Hensley, J. Clark, Nashville: Broadman, 1978.

Don't Take My Grief Away, Manning, Doug, San Francisco: Harper and Row, 1984.

Good Grief, Westberg, Granger E., Philadelphia: Fortress, 1979.

A Grief Observed, Lewis, C.S., New York: Bantam Books, 1976.

Growing through Grief, Towns, Jim, Anderson, Ind.: Warner Press, 1984.

The Last Thing We Talk About, Bayly, Joseph, Elgin, Ill.: David C. Cook, 1973.

Living when a Loved One Has Died, Grollman, Earl A., Boston: Beacon Press, 1979.

Mourning Song, Landorf, Joyce, Old Tappan, N.J.: Revell, 1974.

On Death and Dying, Kubler-Ross, Elizabeth, New York: Macmillan, 1969.

Perspectives on Bereavement, Gerber, Irwin, New York: Irvington Press, 1978.

Questions and Answers on Death and Dying, Kubler-Ross, Elizabeth, New York: Macmillian, 1974.

The Survival Guide for Widows, Wylie, Betty Jane, New York: Ballantine, 1986.

To Live Again, Marshall, Catherine, Lincoln, Va.: Chosen, 1981.

When You Lose a Loved One, Allen, Charles L., Old Tappan, N.J.: Revell, 1959.

When Your Friend Is Dying, Burnham, Betsy, Lincoln, Va.: Chosen, 1983.

A Widow's Pilgrimage, Hersey, Jean, New York: Continuum, 1979.

You and Your Grief, Jackson, Edgar Newman, New York: Dutton, 1961.
Your Particular Grief, Oates, Wayne, E., Philadelphia: Westminster, 1981.

Single Parenting

Being a Single Parent, Bustanoby, Andre, Grand Rapids: Zondervan, 1987.
Christian Family Activities for One-Parent Families, Reed, Bobbie, Cincinnati: Standard, 1982.
Do I Have a Daddy? A Story about a Single Parent Child with a Special Section for Single Mothers and Fathers, Lindsay, Jeanne Warren, Buena Park, Calif.: Morning Glory, 1982.
Father and Son, Sifford, Darrell, South Plainfield, N.J.: Bridge Books, 1982.
Fathers without Partners, Rosenthal, Kristine M., and Keshet, Harry F., Totowa, N.J.: Rowman & Littlefield, 1981.
Going It Alone, Weiss, Robert, Basic Books, New York: Harper and Row, 1981.
How to Live with a Single Parent, Gilbert, Sara, New York: Lothrop, Lee & Shepard Books, 1982.
How to Really Love Your Child, Campbell, Dr. Ross, Wheaton, Ill.: Victor Books, 1977.
I Didn't Plan to Be a Single Parent, Reed, Bobbie, St. Louis: Concordia, 1981.
Making Up the Difference: Help for Single Parents with Teenagers, Rekers, George Alan, and Swihart, Judson J., Grand Rapids: Baker, 1984.
One-Parent Families: Healing the Hurts, Smith, Harold Ivan, Kansas City, Mo.: Beacon Hill, 1981.
The One-Parent Family in the 1980's: Perspectives and Annotated Bibliography, 5th ed., Schlesinger, Benjamin, Toronto: University of Toronto Press, 1984.
Parent's Guide to Sex Education, Mayo, Mary Ann, Grand Rapids: Zondervan, 1986.
Parents in Pain, White, John, and Smith, Donald C., Downers Grove, Ill.: InterVarsity Press, 1979.
Parents without Partners Handbook, Atlas, Stephen L., Philadelphia: Running Press, 1984.
Pastoral Care for Single Parents, Smith, Harold Ivan, Kansas City, Mo.: Beacon Hill, 1982.
Readymade Family: How to Be a Stepparent and Survive, Bustanoby, Andre, Grand Rapids: Zondervan, 1982.
Real Men Enjoy Their Kids, Singer, Wanda Goodhart; Shechtman, Stephen, and Singer, Mark, Nashville: Abingdon, 1983.
Sharing Parenthood after Divorce, Ware, Ciji, New York: Viking, 1982.
Single Again—This Time with Children: A Christian Guide for the Single Parent, Peppler, Alice Stolper, Minneapolis: Augsburg, 1982.
The Single Parent, Smith, Virginia Watts, Old Tappan, N.J.: Revell, 1983.

Single Parenting: A Wilderness Journey, Barnes, Robert G., Jr., Wheaton, Ill.: Tyndale, 1984.

The Spiritual Needs of Children, Shelly, Judith Allen, Downers Grove, Ill.: InterVarsity Press, 1982.

Children of Divorce

The Boys and Girls Book about Divorce, Gardner, Dr. Richard A., New York: Bantam, 1971.

Children and Divorce—What to Expect, How to Help, Hart, Archibal D., Ph.D., Waco, Tex.: Word, 1982.

Daddy's New Baby, Vigna, Judith, New York: Concept Books, 1982.

Divorce & the Children, Vigeveno, H.S., and Claire, Anne, Ventura, Calif.: Regal, 1987.

Do I Have a Daddy? A Story about a Single Parent Child with a Special Section for Single Mothers and Fathers, Lindsay, Jeanne Warren, Buena Park, Calif.: Morning Glory, 1982.

Emily and the Klunky Baby and the Next-Door Dog, Lexau, J.M., New York: Dial, 1972.

A Girl Called Al, Greene, C., New York: Viking, 1969.

Grandma without Me, Vigna, Judith, Niles, Ill.: Whitman, 1984.

Healing the Hurt: For Teenagers Whose Parents Are Divorced, Tickfer, Mildred, Grand Rapids: Baker, 1985.

Help Me Understand—A Child's Book about Divorce, Mumford, Amy Ross, Denver: Accent, 1984.

Helping Children Cope with Separation and Loss, Jewett, Claudia, Boston: Harvard Common Press, 1984.

Helping Children of Divorce, Buchanan, Neal C., and Chamberlain, Eugene, Nashville: Broadman, 1982.

I Wish I Had My Father, Simon, Norma, Niles, Ill.: Whitman, 1983.

I Won't Go without a Father, Stanek, Muriel, Niles, Ill.: Whitman, 1972.

It's Not the End of the World, Blume, J.S., New York: Dell, 1982.

Kick a Stone Home, Smith, D.B., New York: Harper & Row, 1974.

The Kids' Book of Divorce, Rofes, Eric E. (Ed.), Brattleboro, Vt.: Greene, 1981.

Lady Ellen Grae, Cleaver, Vera and Bill, New York: J.B. Lippincott, 1968.

Mike's Lonely Summer: A Child's Guide through Divorce, Nystrom, Carolyn, Scarsdale, N.Y.: Lion Publishing, 1986.

Mommy and Daddy Are Divorced, Perry, Patricia, and Lynch, Marietta, New York: Dial Books Young, 1978.

My Dad Lives in a Downtown Hotel, Mann, Peggy, New York: Avon, 1974.

Now I Have a Stepparent and It's Kind of Confusing, Stenson, Janet, New York: Avon, 1979.

Our Family Got a Divorce, Phillips, Carolyn E., Ventura, Calif.: Regal, 1979.

Our Family Got a Stepparent, Phillips, Carolyn E., Ventura, Calif.: Regal, 1981.

Private Matter, Ewing, K., New York: Harcourt, Brace, Jovanovich, 1975.
Surviving the Breakup: How Children and Parents Cope with Divorce, Wallerstein, Judith S., New York: Basic, 1982.
Taking Sides, Klein, N., New York: Pantheon, 1974.
Talking About Divorce: A Dialogue Between Parent and Child, Grollman, Earl A., Boston: Beacon Press, 1976.
Two Homes to Live In: A Child's-Eye View of Divorce, Hazen, Barbara, New York: Human Sciences Press, 1978.
Two Places to Sleep, Schuchman, Joan, Minneapolis: Carolrhoda Books, 1979.
What Children Need to Know when Parents Get Divorced, Coleman, William L., Minneapolis: Bethany, 1983.
When Your Parents Divorce, Arnold, William V., Philadelphia: Westminster, 1980.
Where Is Daddy? Goff, Beth, Boston: Beacon Press, 1969.

SINGLE ADULT LIFESTYLE

Dating
Beating the Break-up Habit, Purnell, Dick, San Bernardino, Calif.: Here's Life, 1983.
Before and after the Wedding Night, Ketterman, Grace H., M.D., Old Tappan, N.J.: Revell, 1984.
Choices: Finding God's Way in Dating, Sex, Singleness and Marriage, Rinehart, Stacy, and Rinehart, Paula, Colorado Springs: Navpress, 1983.
Dating and Relating, Scalf, Cherie, and Waters, Kenneth, Waco, Tex.: Word, 1982.
Dating and Waiting for Marriage, Brock, Raymond T., Springfield, Mo.: Gospel Publishing House, 1982.
Getting Ready for Marriage, Mace, David, R., Nashville: Abingdon Press, 1972.
Growing into Love, Huggett, J., Downers Grove, Ill.: InterVarsity, 1982.
A Guidebook for Dating, Waiting, and Choosing a Mate, Wright, Norman, and Inmon, Marvin, Eugene, Ore.: Harvest House, 1979.
How Can I Be Sure, Phillips, Bob, Eugene, Ore.: Harvest House, 1978.
How to Choose the Wrong Marriage Partner and Live Unhappily Ever After, Mason, Robert L., Jr., and Jacobs, Carrie, Atlanta: John Knox Press, 1979.
How to Get Married: And Stay That Way, Allbritton, Cliff, Nashville: Broadman, 1983.
Learning to Love Again, Krantzler, Mel, New York: Bantam Books, 1979.
Looking for Love in All the Wrong Places, White, Joe, Wheaton, Ill.: Living Books, Tyndale, 1983.
Marrying Again: A Guide for Christians, Hocking, David, Old Tappan,

N.J.: Revell, 1983.

More Than "I Do," an Engaged Couple's Premarital Handbook, Smith, Harold Ivan, Kansas City, Mo.: Beacon Hill, 1983.

Picking a Partner, Deal, Dr. William S., El Monte, Calif.: Crusade Publications, 1972.

Preparing for Christian Marriage, Hunt, Joan, and Hunt, Richard, Nashville: Abingdon, 1982.

The Romance Factor, McGinnis, Alan Loy, New York: Harper & Row, 1983.

The Secret of Loving, McDowell, Josh, Wheaton, Ill.: Tyndale, 1986.

The Secret of Staying in Love, Powell, John, Allen, Tex.: Argus Communications, 1974.

To Understand Each Other, Tournier, Paul, Atlanta: John Knox, 1962.

Too Close/Too Soon, Talley, Jim, and Reed, Bobbie, Nashville: Nelson, 1982.

When Your Relationship Ends, Fisher, Bruce, Boulder, Colo.: Family Relations Learning Center, 1981.

Who Says Get Married? Meredith, Don, Nashville: Nelson, 1981.

Whom Shall I Marry? Voshell, Dorothy, Oklahoma City: Presbyterian and Reformed Publishing Co., 1979.

Why Am I Afraid to Love? Powell, John, Allen, Tex.: Argus Communications, 1972.

Why Am I Afraid to Tell You Who I Am? Powell, John, Allen Tex.: Argus Communications, 1969.

Why Am I Shy? Roher, Norman, and Sutherland, S. Philip, Minneapolis: Augsburg, 1978.

Sexuality

Dating, Sex and Friendship, Huggett, J., Downers Grove, Ill.: InterVarsity, 1985.

The Effective Minister: Psychological and Social Considerations, Cavanagh, Michael E., Minneapolis: Seabury, 1986.

Eros Defiled, White, John, Downers Grove, Ill.: InterVarsity Press, 1977.

Givers, Takers, and Other Kinds of Lovers, McDowell, Josh, and Lewis, Paul, Wheaton, Ill.: Tyndale, 1981.

Living With Your Passions, Lutzer, Erwin, Wheaton, Ill.: Victor, 1983.

A Love Story, Stafford, Tim, Wheaton, Ill.: Tyndale, 1986.

The New Celibacy: Why More Men and Women Are Abstaining from Sex and Enjoying It, Brown, Gabrielle, New York: McGraw-Hill, 1980.

Running the Red Lights, Mylander, Charles, Ventura, Calif.: Regal, 1986.

Sex and the Single Christian, Colman, Barry (Ed.), Ventura, Calif.: Regal, 1985.

Sex, Dating & Love, Short, Ray E. Minneapolis: Augsburg, 1984.

Sex, Love or Infatuation, Short, Ray E., Minneapolis: Augsburg, 1978.

Sexual Counseling: A Practical Guide for Non-Professional Counselors,

Kennedy, Eugene, New York: Continuum, 1980.

Sexual Sanity, Wilson, Earl D., Downers Grove, Ill.: InterVarsity Press, 1984.

Sexual Understanding before Marriage, Miles, Herbert, Grand Rapids: Zondervan, 1972.

Homosexuality

The Broken Image, Payne, Leanne, Westchester, Ill.: Crossway Books, 1981.

Crisis in Masculinity, Payne, Leanne, Westchester, Ill.: Crossway Books, 1985.

The Effective Minister: Psychological and Social Considerations, Cavanagh, Michael E., Minneapolis: Seabury, 1986.

Money Management

Living On Less and Liking It More, Hancock, Maxine, Eugene, Ore.: Harvest House, n.d.

What Husbands Wish Their Wives Knew about Money, Burkett, Larry, Wheaton, Ill.: Victor, 1977.

Relationships/Friendships

Forgive and Be Free, Walters, Richard P., Grand Rapids: Zondervan, 1983.

Friends & Friendship, White, Jerry and Mary, Colorado Springs: Navpress, 1982.

The Friendship Factor, McGinnis, Alan Loy, Minneapolis: Augsburg, 1979.

Hold Me While You Let Me Go, Wilkerson, Rich, Eugene, Ore.: Harvest House, 1983.

I Love My Mother, Zindel, Paul, New York: Harper & Row, 1975.

INTIMACY: Where Do I Go to Find Love? Hershey, Terry, Laguna Hills, Calif.: Merit Books, 1984.

The Intimate Man, Kilgore, James E., Nashville: Abingdon, 1984.

Just Friends? Bustanoby, Andre S., Grand Rapids: Zondervan, 1984.

Saying Goodbye to Loneliness and Finding Intimacy, Ellison, Craig W., New York: Harper & Row, 1983.

Why Be Lonely? Carter/Meier/Minirth, Drs., Grand Rapids: Baker, 1982.

Why Can't Men Open Up? Naifeh, Steven, and Smith, Gregory, New York: Crown, 1984.

SINGLE ADULT MINISTRY

Leadership

The Art of Recruiting Volunteers, Senter, Mark, III, Wheaton, Ill.: Victor, 1983.

Be a Leader People Follow, Hocking, David, Ventura, Calif.: Regal, 1979.
Biblical Concepts for Christian Counseling, Kirwan, William, Grand Rapids: Baker, 1984.
Caring Enough to Confront, Augsburger, David, Ventura, Calif.: Regal, 1980.
Caring Enough to Hear and Be Heard, Augsburger, David, Ventura, Calif.: Regal, 1982.
Counseling with Single Adults, Potts, Nancy D., Nashville: Broadman, 1978.
Divorce Mediation—A Practical Guide for Therapists and Counselors, Haynes, John, New York: Springer Publishing Co., 1981.
The Effective Minister: Psychological and Social Considerations, Cavanagh, Michael E., Minneapolis: Seabury, 1986.
How to Communicate with Single Adults, Craig, Floyd A., Nashville: Broadman, 1978.
Irregular People, Landorf, Joyce, Houston: Walker & Co., 1986.
Love Must Be Tough, Dobson, Dr. James C., Waco, Tex.: Word, 1983.
The Making of a Christian Leader, Engstrom, Ted W., Grand Rapids: Zondervan, 1976.
Paths of Leadership, LePeau, Andrew, Downers Grove, Ill.: InterVarsity Press, 1983.
Single . . . But Not Alone: Leadership Study Guide, Towns, Jim, and Strebeck, Mary, Brentwood, Tenn.: JM Publications, 1982.

Ideas for Ministry
Alternative Life-Styles Confront the Church, Ferm, Dean William, Minneapolis: Seabury Press, 1983.
The Challenge of Single Adult Ministry, Johnson, Douglas W., Valley Forge, Pa.: Judson, 1982.
Getting Together, Griffin, Em, Downers Grove, Ill.: InterVarsity, 1982.
Good Things Come in Small Groups, Nichols, Ron, et. al., Downers Grove, Ill.: InterVarsity Press, 1984.
Liberating the Laity, Stevens, R. Paul, Downers Grove, Ill.: InterVarsity, 1985.
Ministering to Single Adults, Van Note, Gene, Kansas City, Mo.: Beacon Hill, 1978.
Ministry to the Divorced: Guidance, Structure and Organization that Promote Healing in the Church, Richards, Sue Poorman, and Hagemeyer, Stanley, Grand Rapids: Zondervan, 1986.
Ministry with Single Adults, Dow, Robert, Valley Forge, Pa.: Judson Press, 1979.
Reach Out to Singles—A Challenge to Ministry, Brown, Raymond, Philadelphia: Westminster, 1979.
Saturday Night, Sunday Morning: Singles and the Church, Christoff, Nick, New York: Harper & Row, 1980.

Single Adults Want to Be the Church, Too, Wood, Britton, Nashville: Broadman Press, 1977.
Single on Sunday, Reed, Bobbie, St. Louis: Concordia, 1979.
Suddenly Single, Smoke, Jim, Old Tappan, N.J.: Revell, 1982.
Young Adult Ministry, Hershey, Terry, Loveland, Colo.: Group Books, 1986.

Discipleship
The Cycle of Victorious Living, Lee, Earl G., Kansas City, Mo.: Beacon Hill, 1971.
Decision Making and the Will of God, Friesen, Gary, and Maxson, J. Robin, Portland, Ore.: Multnomah, 1981.
Freedom of Simplicity, Foster, Richard J., New York: Harper & Row, 1981.
Fully Human, Fully Alive, Powell, John, Allen, Tex.: Argus Communications, 1976.
God Can Make It Happen, Johnston, Russ, Wheaton, Ill.: Victor, 1976.
Growing in Faith, Smith, Joyce Marie, Wheaton, Ill.: Tyndale, 1982.
I Am One/Prayers for Singles, Greene, Carol, Minneapolis: Augsburg, 1985.
I Gave God Time, Anderson, Ann Kiemel, Wheaton, Ill.: Tyndale, 1982.
I'm Out to Change My World, Anderson, Ann Kiemel, Grand Rapids: Zondervan, 1983.
JONI, Eareckson, Joni, Grand Rapids: Zondervan, 1980.
The Normal Christian Life, Nee, Watchman, Wheaton, Ill.: Tyndale, 1977.
On Our Way Rejoicing, Trobisch, Ingrid, Wheaton, Ill.: Tyndale, 1986.
The Pain and the Possibility, Ripple, Paula, F.S.P.S., Notre Dame, Ind.: Ave Maria Press, 1978.
The Power Delusion, Campolo, Anthony, Wheaton, Ill.: Victor, 1983.
The Power of Your Attitudes, Parrott, Leslie, Kansas City, Mo.: Beacon Hill, 1967.
The Pursuit of Excellence, Engstrom, Ted, Grand Rapids: Zondervan, 1982.
Putting Away Childish Things, Seamands, David A., Wheaton, Ill.: Victor, 1982.
A Step Further, Eareckson, Joni, and Estes, Steve, Grand Rapids: Zondervan, 1980.
The Success Fantasy, Campolo, Anthony, Wheaton, Ill.: Victor, 1980.

Evangelism
Small Group Evangelism, Peace, Richard, Downers Grove, Ill.: InterVarsity, 1985.

299

Bible Studies

Bible Readings for Singles, Stenerson, Ruth, Minneapolis: Augsburg, 1980.

Devotions for the Divorcing, Thompson, William E., Atlanta: John Knox Press, 1985.

Every Single Day, Smoke, Jim, Old Tappan, N.J.: Revell, 1983.

Famous Singles of the Bible, Harbour, Brian L., Nashville: Broadman, 1980.

How to Read the Bible for All Its Worth, Fee, Gordon D., and Stuart, Douglas, Grand Rapids, Zondervan, 1982.

Let God Love You, Ogilvie, Lloyd John, Waco, Tex.: Word, 1978.

More Graffiti: Devotions for Girls, Schimidt, J. David, Old Tappan, N.J.: Revell, 1984.

More Graffiti: Devotions for Guys, Schmidt, J.David, Old Tappan, N.J.: Revell, 1984.

Helpful Reading for Single Adults

Anger Is a Choice, LaHaye, Tim, and Phillips, Bob, Grand Rapids: Zondervan, 1982.

Anger—Yours and Mine and What to Do about It, Walters, Richard P., Grand Rapids: Zondervan, 1981.

The Bereaved Parent, Schiff, Harriet Sarnoff, New York: Penguin, 1978.

Blow Away the Black Clouds (revised), Littauer, Florence, Eugene, Ore.: Harvest House, 1986.

Bonding, Joy, Dr. Donald, Waco, Tex.: Word, 1985.

Born to Win, James, Muriel, and Jongeward, Dorothy, New York: Signet, 1978.

The Boys and Girls Book about Stepfamilies, Gardner, Richard, New York: Bantam, 1985.

Building Self-Esteem, Van Note, Gene, Kansas City, Mo.: Beacon Hill, 1982.

Can You Love Yourself? Berry, Jo, Ventura, Calif.: Regal, 1978.

Christian Counseling: A Comprehensive Guide, Collins, Gary R., Waco, Tex.: Word, 1980.

A Christian's Secret of a Happy Life, Smith, Hannah Whitall, Old Tappan, N.J.: Revell, 1968.

Confessions of a Closet Eater, Barrile, Jackie, Wheaton, Ill.: Tyndale, 1983.

Creative Conflict, Huggett, Joyce, Downers Grove, Ill.: InterVarsity, 1985.

Cry Out, Quinn, Phil, Nashville: Abingdon Press, 1984.

Destined for the Throne, Billheimer, Paul E., Minneapolis: Bethany, 1983.

Does Anybody Care How I Feel? Tengbom, Mildred, Minneapolis: Bethany, 1981.

Dropping Your Guard, Swindoll, Charles, Waco, Tex.: Word, 1983.

The Emotional Side of Man, Schmidt, Jerry, and Brock, Raymond, Eugene, Ore.: Harvest House, 1986.

Emotions: Can You Trust Them? Dobson, Dr. James, Ventura, Calif.: Regal, 1980.

Failure, the Back Door to Success, Lutzer, Erwin, and Gould, Dana, Chicago: Moody Press, 1984.

Feeling Free, Hart, Archibal D., Old Tappan, N.J.: Revell, 1984.

Forgive and Forget, Smedes, Lewis B., San Francisco: Harper and Row, 1984.

Formerly Married, Learning to Live with Yourself, Jensen, Marilyn, Philadelphia: Westminster, 1983.

The Fragrance of Beauty, Landorf, Joyce, New York: Jove Publications, n.d.

Freedom from Guilt, Narramore, S. Bruce, and Counts, Bill, Eugene, Ore.: Harvest House, 1979.

A Fresh Look at Loneliness, Stevens, Velma Darbo, Nashville: Broadman, 1981.

The Friendless American Male, Smith, David W., Ventura, Calif: Regal, 1983.

Getting through the Night, Price, Eugenia, New York: Doubleday, 1984.

Growing through Rejection, Skoglund, Elizabeth, Wheaton, Ill.: Tyndale, 1983.

Guilt and Forgiveness, Justice, William G., Jr., Grand Rapids: Baker, 1981.

Hand Me Another Brick, Swindoll, Charles R., New York: Bantam, 1981.

A Handbook for Engaged Couples, Fryling, Robert and Alice, Downers Grove, Ill.: InterVarsity Press, 1978.

Healing for Damaged Emotions, Seamands, David, Wheaton, Ill.: Victor, 1981.

Healing of Memories, Seamands, David, Wheaton, Ill.: Victor, 1985.

Healing the Dying, Linn, Mary Jane, Linn, Dennis, Linn, Matthew, Ramsey, N.J.: Paulist Press, 1979.

Healing the Pain of Everyday Life, Tanner, Ira, Minneapolis: Winston Press/Seabury, 1980.

Help for Remarried Couples and Families, Olson, Richard, and Pia-Terry, Carole Della, Valley Forge, Pa.: Judson, 1984.

Help! I'm a Parent, Narramore, S. Bruce, Grand Rapids: Zondervan, 1979.

His Stubborn Love, Landorf, Joyce, Grand Rapids: Zondervan, 1979.

Hope for the Separated, Chapman, Gary D., Chicago: Moody Press, 1982.

How to Be a Friend People Want to Be Friends With, Walters, Richard P., Ventura, Calif.: Regal Books, 1981.

How to Be Happy in No Man's Land, Tompkins, Iverna, Plainfield, N.J.: Logos, 1975.

How to Have a Good Marriage: Before and After the Wedding, Lee, Dr.

Mark W., Camp Hill, Pa.: Christian Publications, 1981.

How to Win as a Stepfamily, Visher, Emily and John, New York: Dembner Books, 1982.

How to Win Over Worry, Haggai, John Edmund, Grand Rapids: Zondervan, 1967.

The Hurting Parent, Lewis, Margie M. and Gregg, Grand Rapids: Zondervan, 1980.

I Married You, Trobisch, Walter, New York: Harper and Row, 1975.

Improving Your Serve, Swindoll, Charles, Waco, Tex.: Word, 1981.

The Intimate Marriage, Clinebell, Howard J. and Charlotte H., New York: Harper & Row, 1970.

It's Friday but Sunday's Coming, Campolo, Anthony, Waco, Tex.: Word, 1983.

Journey into Fullness, Mahoney, James, Nashville: Broadman Press, 1974.

Journey into Wholeness, Manley, Stephen, Kansas City, Mo.: Beacon Hill, 1983.

The Kink and I, Mallory, James D., Jr., and Baldwin, Stanley C., Wheaton, Ill.: Victor, 1973.

Living in Step, Roosevelt, Ruth, New York: McGraw-Hill, 1977.

Loneliness, Weiss, Robert, Cambridge, Mass.: M.I.T. Press, 1974.

Loneliness Is Not a Disease, Timmons, Tim, New York: Ballantine, 1983.

Making It as a Stepparent: New Roles/New Rules, Berman, Claire, New York: Harper & Row, 1986.

Marital Separation, Weiss, Robert S., New York: Basic Books, 1977.

Marriage Readiness, Wood, Britton and Bobbye, Nashville: Broadman, 1984.

Meant to Last, Steele, Paul E., and Ryrie, Charles C., Wheaton, Ill.: Victor, 1983.

The Measure of a Woman, Getz, Gene A., Ventura, Calif.: Regal, 1984.

Megan's Book of Divorce, Jong, Erica, New York: NAL, 1984.

Men in Mid-Life Crisis, Conway, Jim, Elgin, Ill.: Cook, 1978.

Mending, Hsu, Dorothy, Fort Washington, Pa.: Christian Literature, 1982.

The Misunderstood Man, Trobisch, Walter, Downers Grove, Ill.: InterVarsity, 1983.

The Mystery of Marriage, Mason, Mike, Portland, Ore.: Multnomah Press, 1985.

On Caring, Mayeroff, Milton, New York: Harper and Row, 1972.

One of a Kind, Smith, M. Blaine, Downers Grove, Ill.: InterVarsity, 1984.

Open Heart, Open Home, Mains, Karen Burton, Elgin, Ill.: Cook, 1980.

Overcoming Depression, Hauck, Paul A., Philadelphia: Westminster, 1973.

Overcoming Hurts and Anger, Carlson, Dwight L., M.D., Eugene, Ore.: Harvest House, 1981.

Passages: The Predictable Crisis of Adult Life, Sheehy, Gail, New York: Bantam, 1979.

Prescriptions for a Broken Heart, Reed, Bobbie, Ventura, Calif.: Regal, 1982.

Quality Friendship, Inrig, Gary, Chicago: Moody, 1981.

A Reason to Live! A Reason to Die! Powell, John, Allen, Tex.: Argus, 1972.

A Reasonable Faith, Campolo, Anthony, Waco, Tex.: Word, 1983.

Rebonding, Joy, Dr. Donald, Waco, Tex.: Word, 1986.

Rebuild Your Life, Galloway, Dale E., Wheaton, Ill.: Tyndale, 1981.

Rebuilding, Fisher, Bruce, San Luis Obispo, Calif.: Impact Publishers, 1981.

Reconciliation, Jones, John Edward, Minneapolis: Bethany, 1984.

The Richest Lady in Town, Landorf, Joyce, Grand Rapids: Zondervan, 1979.

The Road Less Traveled, Peck, M. Scott, M.D., New York: Touchstone, 1980.

Say Yes to Your Potential, Ross, Skip, and Carlson, Carole, Waco, Tex.: Word, 1983.

Seasons of a Marriage, Wright, H. Norman, Ventura, Calif.: Regal, 1982.

Second Marriage, McRoberts, Darlene, Minneapolis: Augsburg, 1978.

The Secret Kingdom, Robertson, Pat, and Slosser, Bob, Nashville: Thomas Nelson, 1983.

A Severe Mercy, Vanauken, Sheldon, New York: Bantam, 1979.

Sex Roles and the Christian Family, Blitchington, W. Peter, Wheaton, Ill.: Tyndale, 1983.

Steering Clear, Cretcher, Dorothy, Minneapolis: Winston/Seabury, 1982.

Stepfamilies: A Guide to Working with Stepparents and Stepchildren, Visher, E.B., and Visher, J.S., New York: Brunner-Mazel, 1979.

Stepfamilies: Living in Christian Harmony, Reed, Bobbie, St. Louis: Concordia, 1980.

Stress/Unstress, Sehnert, Keith W., M.D., Minneapolis: Augsburg, 1981.

Strike the Original Match, Swindoll, Charles, Portland, Ore.: Multnomah, 1980.

Successful Stepparenting, Juroe, David J., and Juroe, Bonnie B., Old Tappan, N.J.: Revell, 1983.

Tearful Celebration, Means, James E., Portland, Ore.: Multnomah, 1984.

Telling Yourself the Truth, Backus, William, and Chapian, Marie, Minneapolis: Bethany, 1980.

Temptation: Help for Struggling Christians, Durham, Charles, Downers Grove, Ill.: InterVarsity Press, 1982.

Three to Get Ready: A Christian Premarital Counselor's Manual, Eyrich, Howard A., Oklahoma City: Presbyterian and Reformed Publishing Co., 1978.

Today I Feel Loved, Coleman, William L., Minneapolis: Bethany, 1982.

Today I Feel Shy, Coleman, William L., Minneapolis: Bethany, 1983.

The Total Man, Benson, Dan, Wheaton, Ill.: Tyndale, 1980.

Tough and Tender, Landorf, Joyce, Old Tappan, N.J.: Revell, 1981.
Toward a Growing Marriage, Chapman, Gary, Chicago: Moody, 1979.
Tracks of a Fellow Struggler, Claypool, John, Waco, Tex.: Word, 1976.
The Trauma of Transparency, Howard, J. Grant, Portland, Ore.: Multnomah Press, 1979.
Try Marriage before Divorce, Kilgore, Dr. James, Waco, Tex.: Word, 1978.
Unconditional Love, Powell, John, Allen, Tex.: Argus Communications, 1978.
Understanding the Male Ego, Blitchington, Peter, and Blitchington, Evelyn, Nashville: Nelson, 1984.
Unequally Yoked Wives, Lovett, C.S., Baldwin Park, Calif.: Personal Christianity, 1968.
What Color Is Your Parachute? Bolles, Richard Nelson, Berkeley: Ten Speed Press, 1984.
What Kids Need Most in a Dad, Hansel, Tim, Old Tappan, N.J.: Revell, 1984.
What the Bible Says about Child Training, Fugate, J. Richard, Tempe, Ariz.: Aletheia Publications, Inc., 1980.
When I Relax I Feel Guilty, Hansel, Tim, Elgin, Ill.: David C. Cook, 1979.
When the Hurt Won't Go Away, Powell, Paul, Wheaton, Ill.: Victor, 1986.
Where Is God When It Hurts? Yancey, Philip, Grand Rapids: Zondervan, 1984.
Why Me, Lord? Powell, Paul, Wheaton, Ill.: Victor, 1981.
Without a Man in the House, Burton, Wilma, Westchester, Ill.: Good News Publishers, 1978.
You and Your Husband's Mid-Life Crisis, Conway, Sally, Elgin, Ill.: David C. Cook, 1980.
You Can Become Whole Again, Miller, Jolanda, Atlanta: John Knox, 1981.
You Try Being a Teenager, Wilson, Earl D., Portland, Ore.: Multnomah Press, 1982.
You're Someone Special, Narramore, Bruce, Grand Rapids: Zondervan, 1980.

Dennis Apple
Minister to Single Adults
College Church, Olathe, Kansas

Dennis has had a wide range of single adult ministry experience as a writer, singles pastor, and denominational director of singles ministries for the Church of the Nazarene.